Dancing Texts

Dancing Texts

Intertextuality in Interpretation

Edited by
Janet Adshead-Lansdale

DANCE BOOKS

Cecil Court   London

Photographs on pp. 87, 90, 96:
Dance Collection, New York Public
Library for the Performing Arts,
Astor, Lennox, and Tilden Foundation

Published in 1999 by
Dance Books Ltd
15 Cecil Court
London WC2N 4EZ

ISBN 1 85273 064 1

A CIP catalogue record for this book is
available from the British Library

Cover design: Jane Joyce
Page design: Sanjoy Roy

Printed in Great Britain by
H. Charlesworth & Co. Ltd, Huddersfield

Contents

Illustrations

Contributors

Janet Adshead-Lansdale is Head of the School of Performing Arts at the University of Surrey, England. She was appointed Professor and Head of the Department of Dance Studies in 1992, succeeding the first European full Professor of Dance, June Layson. She has written and edited three books, *The Study of Dance* (1981), *Dance History: An Introduction* (1983, revised 1994), and *Dance Analysis: Theory and Practice* (1988), which has been translated into Korean (1997) and Spanish (1998).

Litza Bixler is founder and Artistic Director of the Litzabixler Performance Company, which she formed in 1995. She trained in contemporary and modern dance, as well as acting, ballet and Pilates. She received an MA (distinction) in Dance Studies from the University of Surrey, in addition to completing a year of training in theatre at Lancaster University. She has created several works as a freelance choreographer and lecturer in higher education.

Sally Bowden is a theatre historian who has worked professionally in theatre and television and has taught and choreographed in London. She trained in drama at the Rose Bruford College, and in dance at the Laban Centre, subsequently completing her PhD on *Petrouchka* at the University of Surrey in 1993. Her interest is in dance as a theatre art and its relatiship to drama within dramatic performance. She is now and independent lecturer and the course director at Monferrier.

Sherril Dodds is a lecturer at the University of Surrey. In 1993 she gained an MA (distinction) in Dance Studies from the University of Surrey and then went on to become a Lecturer in Dance at the City of Liverpool Community College. In 1997 she successfully completed her doctoral research at the University of Surrey on videodance. She is a regular contributor to *Dance Theatre Journal* and has published in Helen Thomas's collection *Dance in the City* (1997).

Deveril Garraghan is a drama graduate from Royal Holloway University of London. He has an MA in Dance Studies (distinction) from the University of Surrey, and is now pursuing doctoral studies. He has worked as an administrative assistant and researcher for Forced Entertainment Theatre Company in Sheffield, and has taught in youth groups and in schools. His approach to devising movement draws on many disciplines, from Japanese Noh and Butoh to contact improvisation. He is also a musician and composer, having created soundtracks for a range of works from rock video-dance to performance installations.

Jennifer Jackson danced with the Royal and Sadler's Wells Royal Ballet for 15 years in a wide range of soloist and principal roles. She left SWRB in 1988 to co-found Dance Advance, and later directed its successor VOLTaire, both small-scale companies committed to making new dance from a classical base. She gained her MA in Dance Studies (distinction) from the University of Surrey in 1995. She works as a freelance choreographer, dance teacher and also lecturer.

Naomi Jackson is an Assistant Professor in the Department of Dance at Arizona State University, who completed her PhD in performance studies at New York University in 1997. She has presented at numerous conferences since 1990 and published in *Dance Research Journal*, *Dance Connection* and *Dance Research*. She is currently writing a book on the history of dance at the 92nd Street Y in New York. Her specialisations include dance history, theory, notation, and dance and technology.

Carol Martin is Director of Academic Studies at Doreen Bird College of Performing Arts. Trained at Elmhurst Ballet School and the Royal Academy of Danceing, she spent ten years teaching ballet in London and abroad, before completing undergraduate and postgraduate studies at the University of Surrey. She has written on early British ballet, particularly Ashton's career, from a postmodern perspective, and has published in *Dancing Times*, *Dance Now*, and in *Preservation Politics* (forthcoming, 1999).

Sophia Preston is a lecturer in dance at the University of Surrey. Her first degree was in music, and she was for a number of years a professional musician, becoming a regular player for London Contemporary Dance Theatre and Rambert Dance Company. Following an MA in Dance Studies (with distinction) from the University of Surrey, she went on to gain a PhD investigating dance/music relationships, taking the work of Siobhan Davies as an example. She now lectures on dance analysis and history.

Libby Worth is a freelance lecturer and movement teacher who works at present in drama at Royal Holloway College, University of London, and in the Performing Arts Department of Uxbridge College. She trained initially in dance with Anna Halprin. She completed her MA in Dance Studies at Surrey University in 1995, and is pursuing doctoral research at Royal Holloway. She has performed professionally throughout the UK, specialising in environmental dance.

Acknowledgements

Given that the authorship of academic texts has become highly contentious in recent years and that the ideas in this book cannot be attributed to a single source, I have a number of acknowledgements to make. I have been stimulated by work in literature and in post-structuralist thinking that expounds and applies the concept of 'intertextuality' in a variety of contexts and I am grateful to live at a time when the critical literature is so extensive. Vivid examples in other fields serve to inspire the critical application of this idea to the relatively new field of dance analysis.

I am grateful to several generations of MA Dance Studies students at the University of Surrey, particularly from 1994 onwards, with whom I developed ideas about intertextuality and its applicability to dance. The consequence is evident in that several of the chapters developed directly from our explorations in this context. Editing multiply-authored collections can be fraught with complications and I approached it somewhat reluctantly, but these authors were paragons of virtue.

I am happy to acknowledge Christine Jones and Sheila Ghelani's assistance with the production of the text in various ways, and Alexandra Carter's reading of part of an early draft.

At a time when 'dance' might seem to disappear into 'performance' and when the competitive pressures of publishing increase, it is of great value to the world of dance scholarship that Dance Books continues to keep its faith with this small field of study. I am grateful to David Leonard and Sanjoy Roy for their support in publishing this text.

I am warmly appreciative of the part played by John Duke, who kept me company on this journey.

Janet Adshead-Lansdale
November 1998

Foreword

One of the most important developments in critical theory over the past thirty years has been the shift in attention from belief in the autonomy of the text and scrutiny of its formal features to a focus on the reader and his or her activity. The theory of intertextuality in its diverse manifestations has, crucially, alerted us to the fact that every text is bound up with a host of other texts, some known and intended by the author, others known only by the reader and evoked as reference points by him or her as he or she engages in the process that is reading.

The reader is now no longer viewed as a perpetual latecomer who is passively, even parasitically, dependent on the artistic text. Rather, we now recognise that in the act of reading and interpreting, the reader not only co-creates the text but engages in an act of self-creation or, more precisely, of self-definition. Interpretation is, of course, a function of identity and no two readers will 'read' exactly the same text. In this sense, reading is a personal transaction, a transaction operated between text and reader by the reader – in order to recreate him/herself.

As we think (through) our identities in ever more interesting ways, it is surely crucial that we allow our reading practices to become more than mere decodings of texts (no matter how dazzling), more than responses to texts in which the text is always-already established as the fixed point in a dialectic relationship. We need to take the risk of interpreting, of challenging the boundaries between what we define as the textual and what we define as the real or non-textual.

Of course, in its personal dimension, reading is always narcissistic to a certain degree, but we should remember that there are several forms of narcissism and that an alternative to retracted narcissism is *expansive* narcissism, which permits and enables a movement towards the other, and offers the individual possibility of transforming his or her extreme subjectivity into an openness to – and acceptance of – difference.

The essays in this volume are all personal in this sense: they articulate strongly held positions, but also reach out to us and show how dance is, of course, not only text, but that it is *also* text and can be better understood by being viewed through the prisms of intertextual gazes and speculations. Interpretation itself is not a process of reconstruction or rehabilitation –

and it is certainly not explanation (although it is all too often presumed to have explanation as its main purpose and function). Rather, interpretation is a performative act, a speculative response to a text and, crucially, a response both to the contexts in which the text was created and the contexts in which one is reading it. Furthermore, whereas an explanation can occur and have validity only within an accepted, pre-established frame of reference and expectation, a performative interpretation must bring about its own criteria and persuade the unknown reader of their worth.

In this volume, there are many such creative impositions of new criteria, as the history of dance, ethnicity or gender positions, for example, are re-textualised and 'choreographed' into historical and theoretical speculations that contribute not only to a reconfiguring of dance studies but also to a repositioning of the theory of intertextuality.

These readings, these 'dancing texts' are themselves truly performances; each of them is the staging of an act, of a process of seeing and thinking in a space between cultures and between discourses. Seeing and reading dance from new and different points of view and, constructing their own narratives of interpretation, they move between discourses in order to liberate us and the works they consider from the tyranny of *singular* concepts of telling, showing, explaining.

Michael Worton
University College London

Preface

The choice of *Dancing Texts*, or 'texts that dance', as the title for this book, emphasises the fluidity of the two central concepts underlying this exploration, namely 'dance' and 'text'. From the maze of possible theoretical insights that might inform dance analysis I look here at the concept of 'intertextuality'. While many good reasons might be given, the primary one is that this notion of 'intertextuality' allows me to keep in view the idea that a dance exists as a 'work' or 'text' while also remaining open to a range of discrete, overlapping, or quite distinct, interpretations. This approach chimes with my own view of dances and of the processes of understanding and appreciating them, and is an extension of earlier explorations (Adshead, 1988).

Transience and impermanence have always been associated with dance, so there is nothing unusual in the view that dances might be unstable. However, where previously this ephemerality might have been regarded as a weakness, and posited in explanation of both the lack of serious scholarship, and the lack of funding for its practices, *here it is seen as a strength*. Danc*ing* is the clue. Just as the activity of dancing implies constant change of position, so, too, does the act of interpretation. This is only a dilemma, or a reason for dismissing dance as an art unworthy of the same depth of appreciation and analysis as theatre and music, if one takes the view that 'making sense' of a dance is a search for an agreed 'truth'; for a single and objectively demonstrable clarity of meaning based on the existence of a stable, physical object. Following that argument through to its logical conclusion, such agreement is only *desirable* where a scientific notion of objectivity is the validating principle.

The limitations of a scientific rationality are evident in the recent post-structuralist attack on all discipline boundaries, although David Best, for example, had already argued for a different construction for interpretation in the arts based on interpretative rationality (1992). The rationale that underpins my position is that there exists a vast range of possible and valid reference points to, and within, *any* dance. It is unlikely that a universal 'truth' of interpretation – a meaning to which all observers would subscribe – could ever be reached. Moreover, such a view reveals some confusion about the nature of artistic appreciation both in earlier times and in the late twentieth century.

Interpretation, as understood here, is not an attempt to establish a one-to-one correspondence between movement and meanings (in the strictest semiotic sense). I regard it as an imaginative and intellectual process that associates movements with events and people, both within the movement/dance system and within wider artistic practices and cultural issues. Interpretation is located in a conceptual framework more akin to aspects of post-structuralist theory than to traditional epistemology. The diversity of this rich and complex field offers a treasure chest of explanations, and allows for interventions from the maker (choreographer), the performer and the audience, in coming to grips with dance.

The fluidity, I argue, resides in both 'dance' and 'text'. It has been argued that the concept of 'text' is particularly difficult and even inappropriate to apply to those performing arts which rely predominantly on movement and sound, rather than words, and those which, historically, have few written or notated records. In its older versions, which carried assumptions about a fixed identity, dance scholars might have shied away from the idea of dance as text. They might also, conversely, have had difficulty demonstrating that such a thing existed in dance. This new version of the concept, however, redolent of post-structuralist approaches to the analysis of literature, emphasises the role of the reader (normally 'spectator' in the performing arts) in the construction of an essentially unstable 'text'. Talk of 'reading' dances has become fashionable in recent years, as a term to describe the process of 'making sense' of a dance that we once simply called 'interpretation'. Although I chose not to adopt that language in an earlier book (Adshead, 1988) some of the theoretical perspectives that it encapsulates were clearly signposted. Here there is the opportunity to develop these perspectives more fully, and to rework them where appropriate to fit the particularities of dancing and dances.

On the other side of this linguistic coin lies a vital corrective. With the obviously valid insight that dance operates largely through movement and other 'non-verbal' systems, goes the possibility of overemphasis on movement *per se* and, in consequence, a denial of the importance of language. What may be obscured is the equally valid perspective that the very construction of these dance and movement systems relies upon codifications in *both* non-verbal and verbal languages. Movement, on these terms, has to be understood through everyday behavioural codes as well as through elaborated dance-specific codes. In this sense, dances are not figments of individual subjectivity and imagination but are part of a social experience; an experience that is, by definition, shared and which is shared in language as well as in movement.

The idea of 'instability' of texts is used quite deliberately in this book as a means of exploring the more recent extension of the concept to ideas or to images or to written fragments, or to movements. It is conscious play on the idea that all these can become 'texts' to which the choreographer and reader refer. Far from being fixed, these texts become a collection, or 'mosaic', of quotations which, in the framework of intertextuality, can go on multiplying indefinitely until they begin 'to speak among themselves'.

It is vitally important, I would argue, that dance theory should reflect the form upon which it comments. It should respect the balance established within each distinctive dance genre, for example, between expressivity and formal concerns, and between types of materials employed. Melrose (1994) asks the same question for theatre that I have asked for dance over many years (e.g. Adshead 1980, 1988): is dance/theatre to be regarded as a practice in its own right? If so, does it not need specific theoretical discourses which reflect its own practices? Should it not use with caution theories developed for other activities? One of the reasons for my reluctance to apply wholesale the insights from modern linguistics and from literary analysis, and to use their language, lies in the dangers this brings. In the history of dance studies such theories have been pounced upon, often uncritically, and used simply to replace another set, in this case of traditional constructs from music and theatre.

It is not a straightforward matter, since there are difficulties in knowing which of these new discourses to apply. Culler's analysis of recent critical theory (1983) has already emphasised the problematic nature of such labels as 'structuralist' and 'post-structuralist'. With deafening irony he names many theorists who have been hailed first as structuralists and later as post-structuralists. Such delineation of the critical ground, often entailing denial of previous theory, is far from helpful. It is more likely that some valid insight can be gained from each and that subsequent versions of the same theory, or claims to new theory, fill certain gaps, or approach common problems from a new perspective. Setting them up in opposition is not a choice I make here. In this sense I am more interested in the meta-theoretical framework now evident across a multitude of forms of dance analysis than in promoting a particular version of it.

An open-minded view of the potential relevance of theories from a number of different sources (including non-dance sources) has to be matched by a critical awareness of *their capacity to respond to dance, and to illuminate it.* It is significant that we do not seek the obverse, namely the capacity of *dance* to illustrate pre-existent theory – a subtle but highly significant difference for dance scholars. In the past it has often been *dance* which is judged for its adequacy to meet new theory, thus assuming, arrogantly, that 'theory' (usually derived from another art, or from literary criticism or the social sciences) precedes dance 'practice'. In my account of dance theory the *dance precedes the theory – theory is validated by the practice.* While this might be regarded as equally arrogant, or in danger of detaching dance from its cultural location, it at least has the virtue of starting from the dance and its practitioners (including its critics and theorists as well as its performers and creators). Thus, within strands of theory I do not opt for extreme positions – of authorial intention, of text analysis or of reader-response processes – but rather seek to explore their relationship in the construction of dances by both makers and spectators.

Nonetheless, it is apparent that the insights of literary theory, and of both semiotic and post-structuralist debates about the relationship between art and language, have begun to change (for the better, in my view) the terms of interpretation of dances. In particular the ideas that have recently been developing around the notion of 'intertextuality' appear to have powerful potential for application in dance analysis. The view that in interpretation we tell many stories, not one; or that juxtaposing ideas without linear linking can be meaningful; and that 'texts' signify in many ways, is no longer at issue. What remains still largely unexplored, though, are the means by which this happens in dance, the critical methodologies that might support explanations of interpretations and how recent theory might inform the further development of *dance* analysis without distorting it. In this respect dance is in a similar position to all the other arts, sharing their reliance upon verbal and written languages while establishing their own distinctive modes of communication, whether in sound, paint, light or words.

In *Dancing Texts: Intertextuality in Interpretation* we seek to elaborate some of the possibilities for analysis which arise from the concept of intertextuality and to test them against a varied collection of dances of the present time. The works have been selected for their relevance to an exploration of this kind, and include choreographers with a particular interest in 'text' in some of its many manifestations. The authors share an enjoyment of the challenge of critical thinking and a commitment to ex-

ploring its relevance to dance – not forcing relationships where none exist,
but opening up the possibilities of affinities and parallels.

Janet Adshead-Lansdale
Department of Dance Studies
University of Surrey
November 1998

References

Adshead, J. (1980), *The Study of Dance*, London, Dance Books.
———— (ed.) (1988), *Dance Analysis: Theory and Practice*, London, Dance Books.
Best, D. (1992), *The Rationality of Feeling*, Brighton, Falmer.
Culler, J. (1983), *On Deconstruction: Theory and Criticism after Structuralism*, London, Routledge & Kegan Paul.
Melrose, S. (1994), *A Semiotics of the Dramatic Text*, Hants, Macmillan.

1

Creative Ambiguity: Dancing Intertexts

Janet Adshead-Lansdale

This introductory chapter deals firstly with the development of ideas from literary theory in the interpretation of dances and secondly with the notion of dance as 'text' and its relationship to truths of different kinds. It moves on to consider the validity of such concepts for the analysis of dance performance as well as the written texts to which performance gives rise, and to illustrate the use of methodologies derived from both semiotics and post-structuralism for the construction of meaning in dance.

We expose the role of the 'reader' and seek to explain how s/he might interact with the dance. In the shadowy interface between the dance and the spectator, 'texts' of many kinds may be relevant. Notions of the 'intertext' and, therefore, of 'intertextuality' are elaborated as a potentially useful theoretical basis for exploring this relationship. It is difficult to embark upon such a project without also introducing the concept of 'discourse'. Discourse, as used in the 1990s, has taken on the character of an interdisciplinary meeting ground. It operates across fields which include language, but is not limited to it, emphasising the communicative character of many kinds of texts. Foucault's perspective alerts the reader to the historically grounded nature of 'discourse'[1] and emphasises the actively constructed nature of discursive *practices*.[2] To understand theory, as well as practice, from this viewpoint requires a significant shift of focus from internal coherence to the play of cultural forces.

Subsequent chapters illustrate the relevance of these ideas to interpreting dances from a range of styles, and address works as diverse as Fokine's early twentieth-century ballet *Petrouchka* (Chapter 2), Forsythe's deconstructionist approach to ballet (Chapter 5), and dance/theatre/spoken text relationships in Spink and Marin's work (Chapter 7). Although it spans Russia via North America to France and England of the 1980s and 1990s, this selection is not random, or even simply convenient. The range serves to remind the reader how cultural intertexts operate within and across works in different genres and at different times since a new intertextual layer is created by this means. The exploration of modern dance intertexts meeting American Jewish intertexts in the post-war years is an example of this (Chapter 4).

Elsewhere, Siobhan Davies's work *Bridge the Distance* (Chapter 3) is shown to demonstrate a rich range of intertexts across the modern novel, opera, and string quartet; while Mark Morris's *Dido and Aeneas* (Chapter 6) recalls within a single work not only early Greek culture but also its reinterpretation through Purcell's music of the mid-seventeenth century, together with twentieth-century conceptions of this particular narrative. Just as *Petrouchka* in its own time drew on street behaviour, so too, does Lea Anderson's choreography for The Cholmondeleys in the 1980s (Chapter 9). Popular culture, folk traditions and video technology together produce new images, create new codes and offer new meanings typical of the end of the century. Decouflé's French work (Chapter 10) straddles borders between media, questioning the positioning of dance at the end of the twentieth century, much as Fokine did at its start.

The application of intertextuality to work generally thought of as 'abstract' or 'formalist', which on the surface seems unlikely to be fruitful, is explored through analysis of Rosemary Butcher's *3d* (Chapter 8). Just as the clear boundaries between 'form' and 'content' have been eroded in critical thinking, so those between 'representational' and 'abstract' dance have come to seem inadequate to convey the complex shifting between movements and ideas that typifies Butcher's work. The problematic nature of work which is at once consistent through time and yet ever-changing is confonted in this essay.

Underlying such illustrations of intertextuality and weaving their way through the book are theoretical questions of how far we can or should postulate completely open texts and how far interpretations can be said to be constrained (and by what factors). On a broader canvas, methodological questions of how procedures might be adapted in interpreting dances from different periods and styles, and in analysing dances which take different types of subject matter, also need to be debated at length. Some of these implications are addressed in the chapters which follow.

Dance Theory and Practice in the 1990s

The potential contribution of an interdisciplinary approach to interpretation lies in its challenges to dance theory. In the 1990s the juxtaposition of theoretical constructs with dance practices has become a sensitive issue. We proceed bearing in mind the fragility of dancing texts, attempting to keep foremost the concerns of dance. The only writer so far to deal at length and explicitly with the application of theories derived from literary criticism is Susan Foster in *Reading Dancing: Bodies and Subjects in Contemporary American Dance* (1986). In her introduction she exposes the Janus face of the constructor of meaning who looks, on the one hand, at the choice of movement and the principles for ordering that movement and, on the other, at the procedures for referring to or representing worldly events in danced form.   (Foster 1986: xvii)

She elaborates Jakobson's linguistic model to apply it to dance and highlights the *performer's* role in the construction of meaning, a facet of dance which clearly marks its difference from literary arts. In discussion of the choreographic conventions and codes which provide the links between these Janus 'faces', she also makes explicit the relevance of the socio-historical dimension of the artistic context, and charts changes in the relationship between signifier and signified in the move from semiological to post-structuralist theoretical positions.[3]

This position is not without its critics. Auslander's challenge is that Foster does not take sufficiently seriously Barthes' denial of the possibility of *any* form of interpretative reading. He contends that the text is permanently unstable (Auslander 1988, referring to Barthes 1977b). A similar criticism could be made of Sally Banes' article on Steve Paxton's *Flat*[4] which adopts a semiotic approach in describing 'its formal components, its cultural icons, and its style' (1994: 227), from which she offers a number of interpretations based on different connotations of positions and actions within the work.

This approach is taken further in *Bodies of the Text: Dance as Theory, Literature as Dance* (Goellner & Murphy 1995) which brings together a series of articles, for example on Derrida and dance (by Mark Franko), and on the dancing body as understood in Derrida's and Cixous' writing (by Ann Cooper Albright). Susan Foster's chapter in the same volume juxtaposes historical texts with living bodily texts. In sum, this book identifies both 'bodies' and 'texts' as problematic in dancing and dance writing. It is a debate worth continuing. Lepecki (1995) proposes a case for a new 'theoretical' and 'natural' body that would either bring together or 'explode creatively' the two strands of Goellner and Murphy's book, which he argues are

that dance is a trace and its writing a theatre of memory and meaning; and that the sexuality and expressivity of the body in action are fertile breeding grounds for revolutions.   (Lepecki 1995: 70)[5]

However, problems arising from the 'wholesale' borrowing of critical concepts from literature and film, a 're-hash' of theory which may only 'bury dance beneath ready-made notions purchased from the mail-order catalogues of Derrida, Foucault and company' are a timely reminder of the dangers of lack of focus on dance in such an approach (Copeland 1993: 27). Gay Morris (1996) collects together articles which emphasise the continuity of dance scholarship rather than its explosion into other realms, although the same fear is present (of dance dissolving into other disciplines) that has bedevilled dance scholarship since the mid-1970s. Nonetheless the tension today between a more open and a more closed view of interpretation in dance, and between real and metaphorical bodies used in dance and other art debates, does mirror the questions raised by structuralism, semiotics and post-structuralism in recent years – questions that we would be foolish to ignore. The strands of this book are of dances, texts, and intertexts; their exposition includes, inescapably, differing positions on the body.

Interpreting Texts

As a way into these debates it might be argued (in post-structuralist jargon) that dances, as 'texts', are cooperatively generated. An older strategy in which critics attempted to disentangle the choreographer from the dance in order to see that person as a contributor to, rather than the sole determiner of meaning, is compounded by more recent attention to distinguishing the *performer* and the *reader* from the dance. Another way of dealing with the problem is to deny their existence and in effect to dissolve them into the dance – to see it all as text. Indeed, there is a sense in which these distinctions between creator, performer and reader can be regarded as either redundant or suspiciously positivistic.[6] The idea of a stable text can similarly be challenged.

Thus the reader is in a paradoxical semiotic position, one which Eco expounds in *The Role of the Reader* (1979). On the one hand, he suggests that the spectator has agency, in opening with the subtitle *How to Produce Texts by Reading Them*, and on the other hand almost immediately takes this away, stating that 'you cannot use the text as you want, but only as the text wants you to use it' (1979: 9). It is in this sense that the reader can be said to be 'defined' by the text and yet is responsible for its construction or 'production'.

Subsequent chapters in this book explore what it is that the text presupposes, or foresees, and what it is that the reader creates. Each one takes different aspects of the debates on text, intertext and intertextuality and uses them in detailed analyses of specific works ranging from ballet to postmodern dance, from dance on film to cabaret, from 'high art' dance to dance in pop music video. Work such as that of Siobhan Davies, Ian Spink and Maguy Marin, for example, draws explicitly on *actual* texts, and quotes liberally from the themes and images to which they give rise – a common device of intertextuality, as Preston and Garraghan demonstrate (Chapters 3 and 7). At issue here is the telling of stories, that is, the creation of texts. The question is one of who creates these stories, with whose interests in mind, and how they set up and draw on particular sets of intertexts.[7] To this extent, therefore, there are many examples where our approach overlaps with theories of narrative used in theatre studies and in the analysis of literature, although less with musicological theories. Since much dance-based work also operates within the conventions of opera and theatre, boundaries between art forms become, paradoxically, simultaneously insignificant and highly important, as in the play with preconceived ideas from the Coppélia/Sandman stories (Chapter 7) or in the interrelationship between Britten's String Quartet and *Death in Venice* (Chapter 3). The consequences of this line of argument can be seen clearly in Chapter 7 where Garraghan reveals a series of Freudian intertexts which forever change the reader's perception. They are texts which it is impossible to be ignorant of in the late twentieth century, for example, of phallocentric symbols, of the idea of an 'unconscious', of a sexually vivid fantasy life in which men manipulate women, and so on.

'Reading' dances is a fruitful way to regard such issues, taking strategies from theories which see all images and representations as 'texts'. It is an approach which seeks to explain the embodiment of ideas outside the dance, as illustrated here in Dodds' analysis of Lea Anderson's choreography and Bixler's of Decouflé (Chapters 9 and 10). All the authors in this book, however, rely on a detailed analysis of elements of the dancing 'text', on close attention to the reading process and the methods used, and to the many possibilities in constructing interpretations, in the tradition of dance analysis established in Adshead (1988). For example, Jennifer Jackson's analysis of Forsythe's *Steptext* directs attention very specifically to the material of the dancing itself (Chapter 5) as yet another 'text' of the dance. Jackson relocates the debate through an analysis of Forsythe's *Steptext*, illuminating the 'play' between the extremes of existing conventions in ballet and the everyday character of human movement, blurring one set of codes with another, to create the kind of tension by which intertextuality is typified.

In my earlier attempt to set out a theory of dance analysis (Adshead 1988) I described four stages or levels of activity and argued that clarification of their relationship was important. In some senses the analysis of movement and other components of the dance (Stage 1) is presumed in any analysis of form or structure (Stage 2). Similarly, to interpret (Stage 3), it can be argued, might be seen to require both an analysis of the movement and of the form. This view has led to misconception on occasion, that there exists only *one* way of analysing dances, from Stages 1 to 4, in that order. A three-dimensional model would remove some of the problems associated with levels, particularly that of hierarchy. As in Eco's view, the term 'level' is simply a metaphor, a theoretical construct that is helpful in sorting out types of reference and the character of the source upon which interpretations might be constructed.

The Speaking Text: a Rigorous Science or an Indiscreet Art?

The attitude of dance writers in relation to theory ranges from denial to what has sometimes been called slavish adoption of fashionable methodologies.[8] At the root of these perspectives lies the attitude taken by the scholar to the relationship of method to meaning, or of text to truth. The 'scientific' ambitions of structuralism, which in some versions of these theories are revealed in strong aspirations to truth, and which aim to establish an objectively and universally agreed connection between movement and meaning, do not sit happily with an attitude to the arts that is, historically, more open. Tolerance of ambiguity and acceptance of diversity in interpretation in the arts is not necessarily the weakness that it is sometimes assumed to be – in post-structuralist thinking it is unavoidable – and in consequence these two positions are often in conflict. The concepts of structuralism and semiotics are subject themselves to a number of interpretations just as art theory of an earlier era argued among positions and tolerated debate with some equanimity. While notions of 'systems of signification' have become commonplace, there has been less attention paid to kinesics and proxemics which, it might be thought, would have more relevance to dance and would bring the non-verbal levels of communication into sharper relief.[9]

Returning for the moment to literature, where much of this work has developed, Stanley Fish, in an extended discussion of the changing fate of Blake's *The Tyger* at the hands of literary critics, reveals a strategy that is often adopted by dance critics too. Interpretation is disavowed in the interests, so it is said, of letting the text speak, of being entirely detached and objective in describing the work. But, as Fish says, this

> is actually a gesture in which one set of interpretive principles is replaced by another that happens to claim for itself the virtue of not being an interpretation at all.   (Fish 1980: 353)

Description, he argues, can occur 'only within a stipulative understanding of what there is to be described' (*ibid.*: 353). Fish makes explicit the choice of the perspective to be adopted, the terms used for description and the relation of both these to the interpretive act – a model dance scholars might do well to follow.

Despite the recognition of the postmodern world of dance studies, Morris (1996) repeats what I regard as a misunderstanding. Even while recognising that cultures differ, these theorists, in their own way, seek universals. In Morris's text it is a common mode of analysis of movement, she argues, that will provide this much-needed disciplinary strength. On the same argument that non-ethnocentric critics would now look to the culture under study to understand *its* concepts, so the movement analyst must look at the terms in which movement is made and described in *that culture or dance style*. Schechner and Appel, too, seek coherence, but rather differently and across a wider range of activities including sport, theatre, dance, music and ritual by seeing them 'as performance' (1990: 3). This becomes a methodological enquiry into whether the same tools are valid for understanding these apparently disparate forms. They draw on Victor Turner's work (Chapter 1 in Schechner & Appel 1990) in what becomes a rather desperate search for 'universals of performance' in the process of which they tabulate types of performance practice in order to classify them according to genre and use of space categories. Their answers ultimately are couched in terms of the socio-biological function of these activities.

But the impact of the work of anthropologists is not limited to understanding the so-called 'external' features of a culture which may have a bearing on the dance. It can be felt equally strongly in the detail of terminology *and therefore of conceptual frameworks* within which the dance is analysed. So, neither Jordan's nor Siegel's supposedly 'formal' analyses (in Morris 1996) can escape this criticism – that formalist critique is already a stylistic analysis and therefore, peculiar to a particular form of dance. The relationship between matters of description and of interpretation was of great concern in *Dance Analysis* (1988) where we proposed that while the link can be made quite explicit, it is always a contentious matter since these concepts are interdependent and culturally specific. As an example of intertextuality opening up previously unresearched areas and generating new understandings, Naomi Jackson's chapter on Maslow's *The Village I Knew* is a case study which illuminates just this point. The dominance of a particular view of modernism through the 1950s and 1960s, whose proponents in dance are represented by John Martin, is exactly what underpins these formalist views. As Naomi Jackson demonstrates so cogently, these universalising theories enshrined a set of values that Jews were able to use to become identified with modern America. The ironies of accepting Martha Graham's Native American 'primitive mysteries' as transcendentally 'modern dance' while classifying Lillian Shapero's work as 'Jewish dance' and Katherine Dunham's as 'Negro dance' are well exposed by this analysis.

The debate about formalism and semiotics has surfaced in dance analysis in recent years and can best be exemplified in the articles arising from Copeland's provocative statements on the absence of 'ideas' in dance criticism.[10] In summary, to the extent that critics attempt to remain on the 'surface' of the dance, and claim to describe it without interposing their own points of view, they mislead their readers (Adshead-Lansdale 1993–94). An alternative to seeing description as capable of reflecting some pre-existing reality is to see the dance text as an open construction, having the fluidity and enigmatic quality of art. A description then becomes a text; other texts can similarly be constructed and this practice sets competing views in opposition or creates complementary structures. Debate can then be focused around the plausibility and inventiveness of interpretations in particular instances.[11] The reader is subject to the play of codes – indeed both choreographer and audience become 'readers' – equally dependent upon an ability to identify the conventions within which a work is constructed and operates, and to reflect on their own use of such conventions.

Thus formalist attempts to construct a fixed text, in which properties of the work can be discerned and described, can be challenged on a number of grounds. As de Marinis argues,

even the most strictly analytical phase of the study of performance (the phase
relating to the actualization of codes, subcodes, and textual structures) will be
inevitably incomplete and biased.   (de Marinis 1993: 77)

I would, perhaps, part company with de Marinis in thinking that this is a good
thing, which leaves the interpretive position open, rather than a bad thing
(revealed in words such as 'incomplete' and 'biased'), which then drives towards semiotic closure.

The Text and the Truth

Johnson (1980) takes the view that the 'warring forces of signification' lie within
the text itself, which becomes a 'battleground' where theorist, critic, choreographer, performer and reader fight for supremacy in the articulation of meaning; a
useful, if rather militaristic, image. In contrast to this war of signification is the
idea of a text as a series of traces, which endlessly multiply and for which there
can be no consensus of interpretation. Such traces have also been described as
'intertexts', providing rich sources of imaginative play, equally available to the
choreographer, performer and reader as to the critic and theorist. In this arena
the reader's activity becomes one of unravelling threads, rather than deciphering
fixed meanings, choosing which colour in the tapestry to follow, where and
when to start, change direction and conclude.

Some characterisations of 'intertextuality' posit pastiche and 'depthlessness'
as the result, while others find gut-wrenching subversion, and yet others enjoy
the esoteric play on exotic, and often erotic, coded references. No single or
simple characterisation of the concept of 'intertextuality' exists. It generates
controversy, which is itself an indication of the openness of the concept and of
its potential for appropriation by critics and scholars in dance. It destabilises the
notion of text as part of the wider postmodernist denial of such certainties.
Seekers after texts have been accused of being modernist searchers after truth
now that the insights of sociology and anthropology have begun to direct attention to the culturally specific nature of responses to the arts.[12]

It can readily be seen that the emergent notion of a dance 'text' is complex
and has a tenuous hold on physical objecthood, a characterisation which is in
direct opposition to McFee's argument (1994) that performances are answerable
to scores, which are themselves the 'authoritative' documents'.[13] De Marinis
(1993: 15) embarks on a detailed clarification of concepts of text, both written
and performed, by contrasting the written (literary or dramatic) text with its
'transcoded' version in performance. He argues against views of the dramatic
text as a 'constant' or 'deep structure'; that is, against positions which hold that
the text is 'primary and original' and that the performance is 'secondary, and
derivative' (*ibid.*: 18–19). He challenges the tendency to privilege the written

text as the only 'present' and 'persistent' text (*ibid.*: 16), as a tendency which neglects performance itself. He denies that the performance is unapproachable from an analytic perspective, a view which we shared in *Dance Analysis*.[14]

> It will thus become clearer why the dramatic text is not the content of the performance, since the content is dissolved into the performance in a completely irreversible way through definitive changes in codes and means of expression.   (de Marinis 1993: 26)

Thus it follows logically that verbal language cannot be the 'primary modelling system', capable of translating all expressible content and instead, de Marinis adopts Eco's stance, that 'other devices exist, covering portions of a general semantic space that verbal language does not' (de Marinis 1993: 17).

This polarisation of ideas on 'text' reflects a wide theoretical ambivalence to such ideas in the twentieth century. For dance it has particular piognancy since its 'texts' have always been fragmentary, and not only in the sense of being 'performed' texts, but in its records, its documentation and its often metaphorical status, revealed in the way it is drawn in to illuminate poetry, literature and music. De Marinis's argument has implications for dance notation as text which he regards as the equivalent of the dramatic text.[15] He emphasises the impossibility of reversing the coding and returning to an 'original' text because of the non-notational character of the language of stage directions.[16] This argument escapes McFee entirely.

Performance Texts

If any element of a performance – for example an image, a movement, a sound – can be treated as a 'text', then each element can be 'read', singly or in units, through codes on which it draws. In *Dance Analysis* this was described as the construction of meaning based on single elements, and on combinations of elements and larger structures which work across sections of the discourse which the dance sets up and which become evident only in performance (1988: 84).

Other writers who have grappled with these ideas, albeit in theatre semiotics, include Elam (1980), de Marinis (1993) and Melrose (1994). De Marinis points out in his discussion of the particular problems of performance, that a *performance* text, as distinct from a *written/notated* text, can be seen, within the paradigms of semiotics, as a material object.[17] His view is that theatrical performance can be conceived

> as a complex discursive event, resulting from the interweaving of several expressive elements, organised into various codes and subcodes (which to-

gether constitute a textual structure) through which acts of communication and signification take place, while also taking into account the different pragmatic contexts of enunciation.   (de Marinis 1993: 1–2)

He argues that the notion of a 'performance text' is a theoretical model of the observable performance[18] within which two parts can be identified. The first is based on co-textual analysis, concerned with the 'internal' regularities of the performance text, with its material and formal properties and its levels of structure.[19] The second, contextual analysis, covers 'external' aspects of the performance text, which can, in turn, be broken down into the cultural context (the relations that can be discerned between the text in question and other texts, whether performances or not, belonging to the same cultural synchrony) and the context of the performance, including all practical situations in which the text occurs and the circumstances of its coming into being. Thus, for de Marinis, this analysis of the performance includes the process of production, and the cultural context as the sum of synchronous cultural texts which are both theatrical and extra-theatrical. In turn these texts become part of the general cultural text, that is, the complex system of culture.

Like Schechner, but with rather different purposes in mind, de Marinis enlarges the scope of the performance text to include trance, religious celebrations, spectator sports, military displays, poetry readings; the label 'theatre' spans several genres and requires only

physical display in public, the copresence of sender and addressee, simultaneity of production and communication, and the ephemeral and unrepeatable nature of the work of art understood as event and action.
                        (de Marinis 1993: 56)[20]

In a similar way, avant-garde theatre itself attempts to transcend genres and to mingle interdisciplinary languages of acting, dance, mime, music, singing and poetry with painting, cinema and photography but retains some boundaries and historical links through which intertextuality operates.

The performance text, it can be argued, is a mixture of the old and the new – 'an original combination within a textual structure of pre-existing codes . . . and distinctive codes that are created anew with each performance' (de Marinis 1993: 4) – which, in turn, transforms and reinvents codes of the cultural text.

Constructing Meaning

The theme of constant motion and of fluidity in the construction of interpretation is reflected in many theoretical positions. For example, Ruffini describes the text as the site of continuous centrifugal movement towards the outside . . . and . . . a continuous centripetal return, from the cultural text . . . towards the text under analysis.   (cited in de Marinis 1993: 68)

Such a view of the text fits with Eco's theory of how codes operate. He defines meaning as the construction of cultural units 'by means of continual shiftings which refer a sign back to another sign or string of signs' (1976: 71). It is the receiver who assigns 'completeness' and 'coherence' as part of the activity of distinguishing this kind of 'text' from the rest of his or her life.

What is emphasised here is the limitation of a semiotic approach to theatre which operates within a structuralist framework; that is, 'solely within the boundaries of the text' (de Marinis 1993: 3). Many theorists now argue that the text cannot be regarded as a finite statement, complete in itself and separate from its receptive-productive context. De Marinis quotes Bettetini (1975)[21] approvingly for his identification of three areas on which a pragmatic approach can focus:

(1) the relationship of text to sources, which emphasises enunciation and intentionality;
(2) the text's relationship to other texts, where the issues of context and intertextual practices are brought into play;
(3) the relationship of the text to its receiver, which includes the act of reading and interpretation.

Since the viewer is always looking from a particular stance,[22] with a particular interest in the text it rapidly becomes unnecessary (and perhaps impossible for other reasons) to embark on a comprehensively detailed description.

In *Dance Analysis* (1988) we articulated a theoretical framework which described 'concepts through which a dance might be interpreted' as distinct from an actual interpretation in which selected aspects of context might be brought to bear upon a particular work (see Chapter 4 of *Dance Analysis*). In other words, we identified a range of contexts, from the wider political and social events of the period, to the artistic frame in which the work in question was made, to the immediate dance context of the creator and receivers of the piece. We linked these contexts to the codification of typical subject matter and methods of treating it in different dance genres and styles. These are crucial factors in the 'construction' of a new dance text, by the choreographer or reader. In analysing dances these elements interact as potential intertexts from which the reader can select in a variety of ways to construct multiple interpretations.

The authors who contribute to this book address these possibilities in a variety of ways. In Chapter 3, Sophia Preston's analysis of Siobhan Davies's *Bridge the Distance* focuses on whether the construction of 'layers of meaning' inevitably leads to striving towards *one* meaning, or whether ambiguity can be held permanently open through the juxtaposition of apparently unrelated ideas. In the context of a modernist art form the concept of intertextuality draws more obviously on its historical association with 'source criticism'. Riffaterre (1990), while responsive to intertextual methods, maintains a strong hold on the idea that all the texts thus identified must be *relevant* to the work, suggesting that there are intertexts without which a reading could not proceed. Preston's analysis supports the view that some readings may derive from everyday movement behaviour and from human understanding and experience of emotional life. This movement behaviour is culturally specific in its form, as anthropologists have discovered, just as stylised dance forms are, but is in principle available to all members of a culture. At another level the texts that inform a complex inter-weaving of literary, poetic and musical quotations from the opera and the no-vella on the same theme, *Death in Venice*, can only be used to construct a reading where the reader has that background. In this sense stylised dance forms have a vocabulary just as specific as the modern opera to which *Bridge the Distance* refers. Further, the personal experience of sexual, emotional and social situations of a kind that border on those with which the opera and the novella deal, would open another set of intertexts to the reader. Experience gained through reading about other forms of sexuality than one's own, or through friends and family, television and theatre can extend the traces available to the reader in ever-multiplying ways.

However, in post-structuralist critical practice the intertext takes on a different significance from simply a linear set of references to events and people which precede the immediate performance. Such reference, where this accords a privileged position to supposed 'origins' or prior texts *from which the present text derives*[23] draws on an evolutionary model of the development of artistic practice, and relies on notions of progression and 'influence' for its authority. This is not the model of intertextuality used here.

The Text and the Reader

The evolutionary model is plainly at odds with reader-oriented forms of criticism already alluded to, in which meanings are *created* in the *spaces between dance texts and many other texts*. While it is not a strange idea that many other texts may be relevant to an interpretation of a dance, significant differences are apparent in the late twentieth-century basis of such discussion. The entry of alien and excluded voices, and the reading of the text without the desire to create a unified whole, are examples of the way such differences are manifest.

The entry of alien voices can be seen quite literally in Forsythe's *Alie/n (a)ction*. Jennifer Jackson's discussion of the problematic nature of the balletic text (Chapter 5) takes on a particular focus in her analysis of William Forsythe's work by interrogating the use of existing codes (balletic in this instance) in a shifting context. This examination of the 'steps' as 'text' brings the linguistic emphasis of these theories into view, inviting analogies with sentences, syntax, paragraphs. The play of language, and its multiple significations, is mirrored in the dance play of steps. This is what makes the activity of determining whether Forsythe is better seen as a classicist, postmodernist or modernist (the source of much critical debate) simultaneously seem both futile and productive. Jennifer Jackson's analysis of the interweaving of classical fragments from ballet with traces of modernist works reflects the criss-crossing, loud, unrepentant shouting match echoing around the intertextual world.

One of the dichotomies of this form of analysis lies in its potential to unmask simplistic characterisations of works while at the same time driving the reader on to play among these categories. Through refusing to identify the choreographer with a single style or form the reader is endlessly teased by the possibilities, the connections, the intertexts. A key distinction which much of Forsythe's work highlights is that between the author as origin of a text's meaning and the author as absent trace, with no more control over meaning than any spectator. The first is an idea appropriate to an expressionist account of art and the second to a post-structuralist notion of 'intertextuality'.

Sherril Dodds' analysis of Lea Anderson's recycling of text and images from popular culture shows how it is possible to threaten established conventions of high art through humour and pastiche (Chapter 9). The question of whether intertextuality might subvert, rather than parody in a superficial manner, relies on the stance taken to similar issues within the debates found in postmodernism about its seriousness or lack of a moral position. As Norris states so graphically, postmodernism can be seen as a 'culpable retreat from the problems of modern society, a kind of textual fiddling while Rome burns' (1982: 131).

Conventions of high art, such as the movement of the highly trained dance body, are challenged by Philippe Decouflé, whose own background was in circus and acrobatic skills, as Litza Bixler shows (Chapter 10). Disruption, through illogical interplay crossing not only the arts but also historic movements and aspects of contemporary culture, gives the reader the chance to see how history is plundered in ironic commentary, not in nostalgic recall. The pop video versus the theatre, the cabaret versus the three-act ballet – these binarisms are pointed up both by Anderson and by Decouflé, although set in differing English and French contexts and employing distinctive techniques.

The appropriateness of a method of analysis based on intertextuality can be seen in the way it opens up the discourse of 'art' to cultural practices more widely. By its very openness to any and all threads and traces of experience and coded reference it invites the interaction of sometimes separate worlds. The exclusiveness associated with the art world can be comprehensively challenged by this means, as both Sherril Dodds and Litza Bixler demonstrate. Replete with images from modernist visual art and theatre (from Bauhaus to surrealism) and from popular culture, the medium of television and the circus, Bixler's analysis of Philippe Decouflé's work resonates with 'bizarre misfits' (p. 232), with 'dreams, nightmares and myths', a patchwork of 'swimming zebras, grotesque cyborgs and demented clowns' (p. 251).

Debates on the problematic nature of the text and new insights into the role of the reader can be usefully rooted in the view of interpretation espoused by Stanley Fish. His account falls somewhere along a continuum from a stable (rigorously scientific?) text, which carries unchanging meaning, to a position of endless proliferation of meanings (indiscreet art?) created by the reader. Something at least is common, if not immutable, in so far that readers produce interpretations based on texts, which then become 'texts' in their own right, articulated through strategies fostered and shared by specific communities (Fish 1980). This characterisation recognises changes in perspective, in and between communities, but does not accept the complete splintering and fragmenting of meaning of some champions of deconstruction.[24] Culler's criticism of this position as ultimately incoherent rests on an argument that stories of 'reading' (or narratives), or experiences of reading, require both a reader and a text. 'Interpretation is always of something' (1983b: 74) and in this sense the text and the reader cannot simply be dissolved into each other.

Barthes' later writing on the perpetual openness of texts to interpretation has to be seen against Eco's emphasis on the conventions operating in art, which in current contemporary work include the conventions of video/dance/theatre. Just as early twentieth-century theoretical frameworks had their limitations in being rooted in their own context, so too do late twentieth-century theories. The weakness, or more strongly, the colonising tendency, that results from imposing theoretical frameworks without due regard to the cultural and artistic position of the work in question becomes all too evident. In this sense, the choreographers and readers of the 1990s cannot escape a world of intertexts, a postmodernist world where television advertisements, posters and everyday communication reflect this dispersal of meaning and focus.

Intertextuality

Many philosophers, particularly from the French school, have contributed to refining the concept of intertextuality in literary theory. Each of the ideas referred to in this section has its echoes throughout the book. In *The Pleasure of the Text* Barthes refers to the intertext in his own writing in this way:

> Proust is what comes to me, not what I summon up; not an 'authority', simply a circular memory. Which is what the inter-text is: the impossibility of living outside the infinite text.
> (Barthes 1976: 36)

Early twentieth-century notions of intertextuality, usually attributed to Bakhtin, were later developed by Kristeva.[26] From a notion of a text as a 'mosaic of quotations'[26] she argues that the interpretive process is the creation of a dialogue from an intersection of textual surfaces, in opposition to a more traditional view of the construction of a single point of meaning.

> It is a permutation of texts, an intertextuality: in the space of a text numerous statements taken from other texts are interwoven and neutralised.
>
> (cited in de Marinis 1993: 97)

While intertextuality takes many forms, there might be some agreement that it has to do with the

> complex and variegated play of borrowing, citation, implicit or explicit references, dialogues from afar, and substitutions, which substantiate the relationships between the texts of a given culture (and even between texts of different cultures).   (de Marinis 1993: 4)

Thus pre-existing codes are brought into play and new ones created in a conversation between the old and new, the traditional and the innovative. While we are aware of relationships between the work in question and other works, it remains the case that this new work is not quite like any other.[27] In writing on intertextuality and drama, Elam (1980) similarly contends that the text, in its genesis, not only bears traces of other texts, in the fairly obvious sense of material which relates to it dramatically (choreographically), but also of other *performances*.

In de Marinis's terms, intertextuality is an exploration of texts, both of the time and prior to it, both theatrical and non-theatrical, which may have an

> implicit or explicit presence. It is the largely deliberate positioning of a creative work at the center of a rich network of echoes and references to other works ... the text ceases to present itself as a 'closed' entity and reveals itself instead as an unending process of production.
>
> (de Marinis 1993: 81)

In this intertextual 'collage', Eco believes, references and archetypes multiply to a point where they begin to talk among themselves (1986). The result is an excess of signification. Unlike Kristeva (1980; 1984), de Marinis argues for multiple but limited interpretations and disagrees with her notion of the infinity of poetic language. But it may not necessarily be a contradiction to talk of a form of 'interpretive free play' that is also 'rigorous' and thus to sustain a Wittgensteinian line of the variety of possible fits between language, logic and reality

(Leitch 1983). Sarup, in a study of Derrida, argues that meaning is dispersed: it is 'a constant flickering of presence and absence together' (1988: 35-6) and the total – 'a complex tissue which is never exhaustible' (*ibid.*: 36). This type of deconstructionist stance would support the view that texts are inherently subversive and self-contradictory, carrying traces both of what is *not* said as well as what is said. Probing a text reveals a scattering of meanings, the existence of gaps, and of unformulated propositions which may subvert the intentions of the author or the stance of the reader.

The idea of material which can be freely interpreted can be used to link a semiotics of theatrical codes to a larger model of textual analysis of performance. Although interpretations of Derrida's concept of intertextuality emphasise there being 'nothing but' the text, Foucault's theories

> incorporate into an expanded concept of textuality the entire panoply of historically situated economic, social, intellectual, ideological, moral, institutional, and political thoughts and limitations that constitute and regulate the life of a society ... every text emerges out of, through and back into a complex cultural network. (Leitch 1983: 157)

Thus this coded network can be seen as a set of rules which link the elements in one (conveying) system to the elements in another (conveyed) system and it is this which permits the association of contents with systems of expression. But the spectator, it can be maintained, is much more than a decoder, being an interpreter requiring 'competencies of a contextual, intertextual, and encyclopaedic order, involving pragmatic as well as syntactic and semantic problems' (de Marinis 1993: 99).[28] Recognition of self-quotation, and of ironic, parodic, as well as serious transposition in relationships between the citing text and the cited text can be seen in more or less explicit paraphrase, and citation. Plagiarism or intertextual practice?

Access to these codes allows the reader to locate precise intertextual references. Eco argues strongly that the reader has already been envisaged in the making of the text, a reader whose *interpretation* is, indeed, foreseen by it.[29] The existence of codes,[30] however, does not describe the functioning of *discourse* and it is this discourse which the reader activates in order to reduce the 'semantic space' (Eco 1984: 39) to actualise the text.

Earlier in the twentieth century, the spectator might have been seen as the target of manipulation, or reader of pre-existing formulae, but s/he can now be viewed as the co-producer of the performance, the 'active creator of its meanings' and 'in short as the only producer of the semantic and communicative potential of the performance text' (de Marinis 1993: 158). Iser, and other theorists, posit the text as a structure that allows the reader to *generate* meanings, not as a vehicle through which a predetermined meaning can be discovered.

'Reading thus constitutes an actualization, fulfilment, and materialization of the text, which produces meanings' (de Marinis 1993: 164).

Nevertheless the reader is not entirely free to complete the text, since textual structures intervene to guide the process. Eco proposes a 'model reader' who is seen to have competence, in the sense of knowledge of the performance text's conventions and codes, but who also has circumstantial competence, understands the rules of inference, and so on. The text is therefore not decoded but *inferred* on the basis of co-textual and contextual information, and genre-bound in that the genre serves as 'instructions for use'. The message is empty until completed by the reader, not in a simplistic sense of 'filling in the gaps' but in the choice of codes and levels of signification. Simultaneously, however, the text then works to change perceptions of these codes, to build on existing understandings to reformulate ideas. As Margolis argues, artworks are not just 'novel expressions of some sort *in a language*' (my italics) but they 'institute new conventions' (1980: 94).

It is in this way that we can appreciate Eco's emphasis not on the author's *intentions* but on *textual strategies*. In his view there is no one point of either origin or closure. The major outcome of these debates has been to replace

> the challenged author–text relationship with one between reader and text, one that situates the locus of textual meaning within the history of discourse itself. (Hutcheon 1988: 126)

Interpreting dances using textual analysis requires a multi-disciplinary approach, one which 'risks putting together in a single framework elements belonging to very diverse universes of discourse and research fields' (de Marinis 1993: 6-7). Some of these universes are referred to below.

Dance as Discourse

The themes, myths, and histories of religions referred to by choreographers discussed in this book, such as Davies, Marin and Spink, are part of this history of discourse. These ideas cannot be said to 'belong' to these individuals, since they have been frequently reworked as part of a heritage of cultural and dance intertexts. That this is possible depends on human experience. Choreographers rely on the reader sharing these conventions and being aware of the codes and references that they contain. Concomitantly there are limits to the range of possible interpretations, limits of experience and limits of culture. As Hutcheon says:

> what representational images and language share is a reliance upon culturally determined codes . . . This is why the ideological cannot be separated

from the aesthetic . . . why representation has always had its politics.

(Hutcheon 1989: 121)

By analogy, the traditional discourses of ballet, modern or postmodern dance, for instance, constitute separate 'languages' of dance, embodying a range of dance styles, each of which enshrines a distinctive set of aesthetic qualities. These ground the aesthetic debates about newer genres which span boundaries, notably text-based theatre/dance, video-dance and performance art.[31] The conditions which operate to filter dances are crucially important. Cultural codes are made manifest in dance through such concepts as genre and style and in idiomatic expressions within dance languages, which generate formulae and cliché, and allow pastiche and parody, as well as the making of new works within a genre.[32] These are the discourses of dance.

If the emphasis in analysis consequently shifts to the text as 'intertextual construct, the product of various cultural discourses', as Culler (1983a: 85) describes it, the problems do not thereby dissolve. John Frow, in his list of ten theses on the concept of intertextuality, refers to the identification of an intertext as an act of interpretation in itself, and therefore as a discursive structure rather than a 'source'. He suggests that understanding the discursive structure is of greater significance than understanding the 'facts', just as

detailed scholarly information is less important than the ability to reconstruct the cultural codes which are realised (and contested) in texts.

(Frow 1990: 46)

The reconstruction of a series of discourses and the realisation and contestation of codes is the subject of Sally Bowden's study of *Petrouchka*. Here a multiplicity of traces is brought to bear on *Petrouchka*, ranging from *commedia* to Harlequin, pre-history and archeology to early twentieth-century nationalism and exoticism, Slavic folklore to imperial classical ballet, religious superstition to wild carnival, archaic stage conventions to Russian modernist theatre, and a profusion of citations referring to the mask. The theatrical and cultural codes juxtaposed by Bowden with pre-existing codes confront the distinctive codes created in reading the *Petrouchka* of 1911 in the late 1990s.

If every text 'is under the jurisdiction of other discourses', as Kristeva argues,[33] then the reader is both subject to these discourses and in tension with them. It makes the reader an 'aggressive participant' in the construction of meaning (Worton 1986: 16). This is a reader who regards the intertext as a liberating force, creating tension between texts of many kinds.

By selecting one contextual framework and then another the 'text' can be 'read' in a multiplicity of ways and these partial perspectives themselves treated as threads of the intertextual web. For example one such insight is found in

Bowden's ability to see *Petrouchka* as a 'pastiche of Wagnerian heroism and idealism in art' and to hold this in tension with another view, that it grotesquely imitated Edward Gordon Craig's *Hamlet* (1912).

Interpreting Dance

While a text (or a dance) may not have *a* meaning (in the sense of a guaranteed, essential meaning) neither can it be said to be meaning*less*. The fact that a text is ambiguous results from its capacity to generate *multiple* meanings, meanings which differ in particular contexts. Creative ambiguity, as described here, remains in tension with the desire for a degree of certainty. Riffaterre goes some way to satisfying this desire in a conceptualisation of the 'obligatory intertext' as those texts the reader must know in order 'to understand a work of literature in terms of its overall significance' (1990: 56).

Certainty in interpretation has to be seen as extremely limited, and in this context it was always evident to me that the concept of dance analysis we developed (Adshead 1988) was not a specification of a methodology to be followed in a predetermined order. As a structured process it might be useful in arriving at a degree of conceptual clarification of the distinct character of different stages. The reality of interpretation is that readers enter at different points, select points of interest and, most usually, enter from an interpretive or evaluative stance. The reader then selects (chooses) those 'facts' which support that perspective. In this sense the reader constructs the dance. Eco refers to this as 'the continuous coming and going' of interpretation (1979: 5).

The reader's freedom lies in deciding how to activate these textual levels and in choosing which codes to apply from the encyclopaedic, intertextual world of codes and sub-codes. The reader's competence is demonstrated in the application of coding rules, for example of genre, and style, of subject matter and treatment. The intertextual frame recognises that 'no text is read independently of the reader's experience of other texts' (Eco 1984: 21) and this is what knowledge of genre reveals; that is, the reader's familiarity with similar dances, similar structures, similar design and musical elements, similar thematic material. The knowledgeable reader is expected and invited to pick up the appropriate references when required to do so by the text.

In the broader field of theatre studies the accepted theoretical paradigm lies in textual analysis (broadly understood as the text *of performance*). But, as ever, the alarm bells ring when particular notions of 'theatrical performance' (envisaged from within drama in this case) are used generically and applied to dance performance. We should perhaps proceed with caution in using this rather rigid 'scientific' model, in part since it explicitly aligns itself with 'theatre studies'. History, aesthetics, semiotics, structural semantics, textual linguistics, discourse pragmatics and so on, underpin de Marinis's work, although he also makes

extensive reference to biological constructs. The danger in constructing an epistemology of textual analysis, I argue, lies in seeking universal explanations
through over-arching methodological principles and a 'unified apparatus of categories and terms' in the sense that de Marinis does (1993: 7).

When we conceived of methods of dance analysis (Adshead 1988, Chapter 1)
we referred to a wide but slightly different range of relevant disciplines, namely
movement analysis, aesthetics and art theory, history, sociology, anthropology,
theology, psychology, but held to a form of textual construction and analysis at
the core. Of significance is the fact that we did not limit our investigation to
theatre forms of dance but looked more broadly at dance forms – a strategy that
ran the risk of even greater danger in the construction of a meta-theory (sometimes paradoxically misunderstood as the absence of theory).

Textual analysis (of the dance in this case) lay at the heart of this model too,
but not in the expectation that all meanings would thus be revealed, but as the
basis for the *construction* of meaning. If a 'text' is a tentative and potentially
changing construct in dance, then the making of 'meaning' is equally elusive.
The multiplying intertexts offer a multiplicity of routes through the dance. While
the construction of a narrative serves to make the work intelligible, this narrative
is constructed within the constraints of 'reference to an implicit system of units
and rules' (Barthes 1977b: 81). It becomes obvious, therefore, that the networks
connecting the construction of dances links the author, the text and the spectator
in a fluidly shifting field of references. If meaning enters, or is ascribed, through
the interaction of authors and readers with the materials, the significance of
each, and the degree of emphasis on any one of them (on the *discretion of the
reader*, or on the *fixity of texts*, or on the *privileged position of the author*) has to
be established anew with each performance. Thus the power relations in this
network are perpetually contested.

Against this backdrop Worton's contention is that

> intertextuality is vital for any theory of reading in that it denies the authorita-
> tive validity of genetic readings which seek to fix the text, like a spiked
> butterfly which the entomologist will dissect scientifically. Intertextual analy-
> sis . . . must be founded on the speculative creativity of ambiguity.
>
> (Worton 1986: 21)

The following chapters seek to explore these ideas.

Summary

In Leitch's terms, we can see shifts in theoretical perspectives and in critical
practices through the twentieth century; changes in method, a movement 'between a rigorous science seeking structural rules and an indiscreet art celebrat-

ing creative readings' (1983: 10); in the nature of argument, from 'source' and 'origin' to theory of discourse; in codification, from strict relationships between signs to an explosion of signifiers; in mood, from seriousness to play.

Recognising that these issues need deeper examination, the thrust of the argument in this book is how far a text/dance/work puts signifiers into play endlessly, as the post-structuralist might contend. The implication for method in dance analysis is that it is only possible to trace these contradictions if a close analysis of the work is undertaken. In its turn this assumes the existence of a 'text', even if it is one constructed by the reader and one which remains perpetually open.

The reader is not, then, a parasite upon a fixed object, sucking its life blood, but a co-creator of a mobile text, breathing new life into *a dancing text*.

Notes

1. The term 'discourse' which originates in discussions of the constraints operating in combining phrases and sentences in the context of successful communication (Fowler 1987) has been extended and is used across many disciplines. Literature, seen as social discourse, for example, is one among many such extensions.

2. 'Discourse defines its object . . . truth is the unrecognised fiction of a successful discourse' (Fowler 1987: 64).

3. Her references are to Jakobson's essay 'Linguistics and poetics' published in Sebeok, T. (ed.) *Style in Language* (1960). In Chapter 4 of *Dance Analysis* (Adshead 1988) Pauline Hodgens describes a similar structure for interpretation as applied to dance.

4. Sally Banes' article, written in 1987, has recently been reprinted in a collection published in 1994. A further problem that I find with this article is that the complex relationship of 'description' to 'interpretation' is not recognised.

5. Lepecki (1995) argues that an ideological fear of the body undermines their project, and 'paralyses a discussion of agency'. He suggests that what is missing is a 'metapsychology of action'.

6. For these purposes I make no distinction between the choreographer, as *reader* of her/his own work, and any other reader, since it can be argued that they are essentially in the same position. This does not deny that the choreographer requires additional skills of construction in order to make a dance, nor that the intervention of the performer, sometimes co-creator with the choreographer/ director and other collaborators, is also of vital importance in understanding *who* is reading or writing the text.

7. The contentious nature of narrative-making as it affects dance scholarship has become a matter of debate in many circles in the 1990s. Two international conferences in 1995 addressed these issues, one at the University of Surrey and the second in Canada (SDHS).

8. Ralph makes this suggestion in a recent article, polarising scholarship and 'academic fashion' *Dance Chronicle* (1995). I challenge this in a response in the same journal (1997).

9. 'Kinesics' studies the visual mode of communication through facial expressions and bodily gestures while 'proxemics' focuses on interpersonal movement and touch.
10. He suggests that there must be a middle ground between the absence of theory and 'the triumph of deconstruction, reconnecting the dance event to the larger world(s) of ideas, cultural context, social meaning and theoretical reflection' (1993: 26).
11. In a recent article I update dance analysis theory to make more explicit its relationship to these ideas (Adshead-Lansdale 1994).
12. See, for example, Janet Wolff's texts on the social production of art (1981) and on the necessity to maintain a study of texts alongside a study of institutions and processes (1990).
13. McFee's discussion centres on the question of the identity of a dance and it proceeds from a tradition that finds the art work to be a rather more stable object than does post-structuralist theory (1994).
14. See Adshead-Lansdale 1994, on the performative aspects of dance analysis.
15. See de Marinis's five requirements of a notation system, drawing on Goodman and applying ideas to both dance and music notations (1993: 50).
16. However, de Marinis's concept of a 'score' may be too rigid to reflect practice in dance. Scores can be many kinds of things, more or less specific, requiring more or less interpretation of different types on the part of the dancer, and therefore on the part of the notator.
17. Elam's earlier work on theatre offers a parallel which provides a useful starting point for dance semiotics. De Marinis gives a much more extended account (1993, Chapter 2).
18. By 'performance text' de Marinis means a theatrical performance, 'considered as an unordered (though complete and coherent) ensemble of textual units (expressions), of various length, which involve different codes, dissimilar to each other and often unspecific (or at least not always specific), through which communicative strategies are played out, also depending on the context of their production and reception' (1993: 48).
19. By properties he means 'expressive heterogeneity, multiplicity of codes, ephemeral duration'; and by structure, 'codes, textual structures' (1993: 3–4).
20. Schechner has become influential for his characterisation of performance theory (1988 and 1990), but notions of 'text' (other than the obvious literal written text) play little part in his anthropological approach. However, in recognising the 'unstable slippery bases' of performance he also constructs new theoretical planks from mathematics, game analysis and model building (1988: 27).
21. An Italian theorist whose work he translates.
22. In the introduction de Marinis articulates the basis of his theory, rejecting linguistic models, metaphorical concepts of a language of theatre, and the secondary positioning of the spectator in analysis.
23. A 'source', in this account, is something from which the creator borrows and to which s/he owes a debt. The critical act in consequence attempts to get behind the actual text through the history of the work to a supposedly 'real' text (Worton & Still 1990).
24. In his commentary on Barthes' work Culler attributes the roots of the dilemma to distinctions that came to be made between semiology (or semiotics), as the study

of sign systems of any kind, and structuralism, as the analysis of underlying structures. The gaps that open up in their relation to the construction of meaning show a structuralist pursuit of literature 'not as a representation or communication but as a series of forms produced by the institution of literature and the discursive codes of a culture' (Culler 1983: 82).

25. This is a much elaborated version of the idea that meaning is constructed by the text, the context and the individual (Adshead 1988). See Worton & Still (1990) and Leitch (1983) for an introduction to the concept of intertextuality.

26. Kristeva in Moi (1986: 36).

27. Thus de Marinis recognises the importance of reception theory to his argument. He suggests that much work remains to be done to clarify the spectator's processes (1993: 6).

28. De Marinis argues that performance codes and theatrical conventions are distinct. *Performance codes*, he says, are not specific to theatre, they can be linguistic, kinesic, rhetorical and so on, and are naturalised within a culture. *Theatrical conventions* are technical, specialised codes that regularise the theatrical use of the performance codes; that is, they are systems, not codes. *General conventions* enable us to judge the appropriateness of the occurrence to the type (1993: 108), for example genre, school, movement, artist, including structural conventions such as the play within a play.

29. Scientific characterisations of structuralism deny this concern with who is being addressed and emphasise the analytic isolation of properties of a relatively fixed object.

30. The basic materials of dance are so varied that multiple citations and references are possible, for example from scenery, costumes, music, gesture and so on; the subjects of intertextual utterance are also multiple, the choreographer, the dancers, the designer the musician. Their position and significance varies historically within the specific tradition and by genre.

31. These labels are neither well-established nor comfortable to use but they are pertinent to analysis of the work described in Chapter 9.

32. Some of the relevant parameters are addressed in *Dance Analysis* (Adshead 1988).

33. This quotation is from the unabridged French publication, translated and cited in Worton (1986: 20). 'C'est dire que tout texte est d'embée sous la juridiction des autres discours qui lui imposent un univers' (1974: 339).

References

Adshead, J. (ed.) (1988), *Dance Analysis: Theory and Practice*, London, Dance Books.

Adshead-Lansdale, J. (1993–94), 'Dance and Critical Debate. Towards a Community of Dance Intellectuals', *Dance Theatre Journal* 11:1 Winter: 22–4, 33.

———— (1994), 'Dance Analysis in Performance', *Dance Research* 12:2: 15–20.

———— (1997), 'The "Congealed Residues" of Dance History. A Response to Richard Ralph's "Dance Scholarship and Academic Fashion" – One Path to a Predetermined Enlightenment', *Dance Chronicle* 20:1: 63–80.

———— & C. Jones (eds) (1995), *Border Tensions: Dance and Discourse*, conference report, Guildford, University of Surrey.

———— & J. Layson (eds) (1994), *Dance History: An Introduction*, London, Routledge.

Auslander, P. & M. Siegel. (1988), 'Two (Re)Views of Susan Leigh Foster's *Reading Dancing*', *TDR* 32:4 Winter: 7–31.

Banes, S. (1994), 'Vital Signs: Steve Paxton's *Flat* in Perspective,' in S. Banes, *Writing Dancing in the Age of Postmodernism*, New England, Wesleyan University Press: 227–39.

Barthes, R. (1976), *The Pleasure of the Text*, London, Cape.

———— (1977a), *Roland Barthes by Roland Barthes*, London, Macmillan.

———— (1977b), *Image, Music, Text*, London, Fontana.

Copeland, R. (1993), 'Dance Criticism and the Descriptive Bias', *Dance Theatre Journal* 10:3: 26–32.

Culler, J. (1983a, 1990), *Barthes*, London, Fontana.

———— (1983b), *On Deconstruction: Theory and Criticism after Structuralism*, London, Routledge & Kegan Paul.

Eco, U. (1976), *A Theory of Semiotics*, Bloomington, Indiana University Press.

———— (1984), *The Role of the Reader: Explorations in the Semiotics of Texts*, Bloomington, Indiana University Press.

———— (1986), '*Casablanca*: Cult Movies and Intertextual Collage', in D. Lodge (1988) *Faith in Fakes*.

Elam, K. (1980), *The Semiotics of Theatre and Drama*, London, Methuen.

Fish, S. (1980), *Is There a Text in this Class? The Authority of Interpretive Communities*, Cambridge, Harvard University Press.

Foster, S.L. (1986), *Reading Dancing*, Los Angeles, University of California Press.

———— (ed.) (1995), *Choreographing History*, Bloomington, Indiana University Press.

Fowler, R. (2nd edn, 1987), *Dictionary of Modern Critical Terms*, London, Routledge.

Frow, J. (1990), 'Intertextuality and Ontology' in M. Worton & J. Still (eds), *Intertextuality: Theories and Practices*, Manchester, Manchester University Press.

Goellner, E.W. & J.S. Murphy (eds) (1995), *Bodies of the Text*, New Jersey, Rutgers.

Hutcheon, L. (1988), *The Poetics of Postmodernism*, London, Routledge.

———— (1989), *The Politics of Postmodernism*, London, Routledge.

Johnson, B. (1980), *The Critical Difference: Essays in the Contemporary Rhetoric of Reading*, Baltimore, Johns Hopkins University Press.

Jordan, S. & H. Thomas (1995), 'Dance and Gender: Formalism and Semiotics Reconsidered', *Dance Research* 12:2, 1995: 3–14.

Kristeva, J. (1984), *Revolution in Poetic Language* (1974), New York, Columbia University Press.

———— (1980), *Desire in Language*, Oxford, Blackwell.

Leitch, V.B. (1983), *Deconstructive Criticism: An Advanced Introduction*, London, Hutchinson.

Lepecki, A. (1995), Review of Gay Morris (ed.) *Moving Words*, *Ballett International* no. 8: 68–70.

Lodge, D. (ed.) (1988), *Modern Criticism and Theory*, London, Longman.

Margolis, J. (1980), *Art and Philosophy: Conceptual Issues in Aesthetics*, Brighton, Harvester.

Marinis, M. de (1993), *The Semiotics of Performance*, Bloomington, Indiana University Press.

Melrose, S. (1994), *A Semiotics of the Dramatic Text*, Hants, Macmillan.

McFee, G. (1994), 'Dance-identity and Understanding', *Dance Research* 12:1 Spring: 21–40.

Moi, T. (ed.) (1986), *The Kristeva Reader*, Oxford, Blackwell.

Morris, G. (ed.) (1996), *Moving Words: Re-writing Dance*, London, Routledge.

Norris, D. (1982), *Deconstruction: Theory and Practice*, London, Methuen.

Ralph, R. (1995), 'On the Light Fantastic Toe: Dance Scholarship and Academic Fashion', *Dance Chronicle* 18:2: 249–60.

Riffaterre, M. (1990), 'Compulsory Reader Response: The Intertextual Drive' in M. Worton & J. Still (eds), *Intertextuality: Theories and Practices*, Manchester, Manchester University Press.

Sarup, M. (1988), *An Introductory Guide to Post-structuralism and Postmodernism*, Herts, Harvester.

Schechner, R. (2nd edn, 1988), *Performance Theory*, London, Routledge.

———— & W. Appel (eds) (1990), *By Means of Performance*, Cambridge, Cambridge University Press.

Society of Dance History Scholars (1995), *Border Crossings*, Conference Proceedings.

Wolff, J. (1981), *The Social Production of Art*, London, Macmillan.

———— (1990), *Feminine Sentences*, Oxford, Polity.

Worton, M. (1986), 'Intertextuality: To Inter textuality or to Resurrect It?', in D. Kelley & I. Clasera (eds), *Cross-references: Modern French Theory and Practice of Criticism*, Leeds: 14–23.

Worton, M. & J. Still (eds) (1990), *Intertextuality: Theories and Practices*, Manchester, Manchester University Press.

2

The Avant-Garde Politics of *Petrouchka*

Retrieving the Performance Text of 1911

Sally Bowden

The Enigma of the *Petrouchka* of 1911

The first performance of *Petrouchka*, 3 June 1911 at the Théâtre du Châtelet in Paris, was, as the first and greatest of modern dramatic ballets (Monahan 1963), an important event in the history of twentieth-century dance. The collaboration between Igor Stravinsky, Alexandre Benois and Michel Fokine created a work widely recognised as a masterpiece, the supreme achievement of the Ballets Russes, which as a theatrical conception was never again equalled by Diaghilev's company (Barnes 1957). Prince Peter Lieven, who witnessed the early performances of the ballet, considers the impression it made:

> I had never had the good fortune to see on a stage before such a unified, such an integrated spectacle, satisfying simultaneously eye, ear, and mind in one great artistic expression. The decor, the costumes, Stravinsky's truly magnificent score, the actual theme with its suggestion of terrifying Hoffmannesque fantasy, the brilliant choreography, and the inspired performance – in short, every single element seemed to be originally connected in a strange, rather terrifying and yet pleasing entity.   (Lieven 1936: 130–1)

The vividness of the scenes depicting Russian life had been noted in the theatre column of *Le Figaro* on 14 June 1911; moreover, in his review for *Le Figaro* of 17 June 1911, Brussel confirmed that as the narrative unfolded in glowing fairground scenes, lifelike crowds moved within the detailed construction of Benois' nineteenth-century St Petersburg.

In contrast to such evaluation of the first performances, Coton writes of the impoverishment of mid-twentieth-century revivals of *Petrouchka*:

> From its birth in 1911 it [*Petrouchka*] was recognised almost unanimously as a masterpiece; it has been revived, frequently in careless versions, often

lacking nine tenths of the simplicities and subtleties of action that can make it the greatest dance drama yet invented.   (Coton 1957: 5)

Barnes describes the revival by the Joffrey Ballet, from which Léonide Massine disassociated himself,[1] as 'a rather sketchy choreographic outline':

The scene in the Blackamoor's cell is particularly inaccurate, but throughout there are omissions and/or unauthentic additions to the choreography, while vital details have been blurred over.   (Barnes 1970: 51)

A comparison between such regretful responses to present-day versions of the ballet and those that eulogise the early performances in both Paris and London (1913) suggests that *Petrouchka* had undergone a change. In spite of Stravinsky's music, the costume and stage designs of Benois, and Fokine's acclaimed choreography, a spectator's initial perception of *Petrouchka* today, as evident in the 1995 staging of the piece by the Royal Ballet, must cause him/her to identify the stage picture with the worst sentimentality of greetings cards. The audience is confronted with seasonal festivities in which a polite crowd of merrymakers, in some quaint Eastern European setting, is dusted over with artificial snow. Here is a carnival washed clean of ritual and eroticism, *scènes burlesques* without humour, and a tragedy devoid of dramatic impact, whilst the Russianness of St Petersburg lies unrealised and undated.[2] The hedonism and licentiousness that characterised the Russian carnival spirit and was evoked in the fairground scenes of 1911 (Benois 1964) is sanitised in present-day revivals. The bustling life of the street, the bitter cold, and the animation of high-spirited Russian citizens who throng Admiralty Square intent upon recreation, now provide little contrast with the focus of the fair, the manipulated puppets, whose individualism has been worn away into caricature. It is apparent that present-day revivals of the ballet represent distorted reflections of the original. The recognition and evaluation of the first performances of the dance-drama is vital if it is not to be viewed retrospectively merely as myth. It is the enigma of the *Petrouchka* of 1911 that prompts this study.

Petrouchka (1911), as an 'absent' performance, or one where no direct viewing is possible, can be reclaimed as a textual evocation of the past or an intellectual movement from absence to presence (Postlewait 1992). De Marinis (1993) recognises that, in such a case, it is the analyst's task to reconstruct or attempt a contextual retrieval of the performance text by consulting other texts that coincide in time and culture and which appear relevant to the performance under analysis. Thus, initially, the concept of *Petrouchka* (1911) may be centred within a network of echoes and references that reflect its Russianness, its modernity, its relationship to theatre contemporary with its creation and to carnival. Moreover, within the apparent reality of its setting and scenario the tensions that are present suggest further threads which demand unravelling, notably those that amplify the pre-Lenten festival of *Maslenitsa*, nineteenth-century street theatre, and the dichotomy of puppets endowed with human feelings whose performance to on-stage spectators serves as a show-within-a-show. The concept of intertextuality in interpretation brings into focus the multiple narrative that surrounds such a work as *Petrouchka* (1911).

This analysis of the *Petrouchka* of 1911 rests upon the release of interwoven threads that make up the web of texts which encompass the work. Designs, drawings, posed photographs, newspaper reviews, published critical texts and reminiscences bear witness to the first performances of the ballet. Such starting points are valuable yet offer personal, often biased and disparate views of the work. These separate opinions can be compared to the individual components that make up the *Gesamtkunstwerk* of *Petrouchka* (music, dance, drama, the stage setting and lighting), since, in Artaud's opinion, each element has its own 'specific poetry' as well as 'a kind of ironic poetry arising from the way it combines with other means' (1970: 28).

The text of *Petrouchka* (1911), while created from multiple expressive media, is made up of compound codes. The juxtaposition of theatrical and cultural codes and their historical specificity continually challenge interpretation. The text/reading interaction depends not upon a single discourse but on 'a signifying chain where multiple discourses intersect' (Crooks 1993: 112). The analyst is confronted by numerous disparate codes that persistently collide so that they can only be read in response to one another. The theatrical text of the *Petrouchka* of 1911 is complex and unique. The web of signs that relate to the fairground setting in the ballet, and the meanings generated, create a code of the carnivalesque appropriate to urban Russia in the mid-nineteenth century. Simultaneously, these same signs can be seen to form an alternative code whereby the ritualistic drama of the show-within-the-show might be read. A further chain of reference identifies the signs with codes relevant to *Petrouchka*'s theatrical heritage, in which Diaghilev's Ballets Russes must be located. This intertextual retrieval of the *Petrouchka* of 1911, therefore, deliberately positions the piece within a play of echoes of the Russia of the first decade of the twentieth century and its obsessive reclamation of the past, so that the materials of the ballet and the ideologies that governed its composition and performance are juxtaposed with Russian modes of theatre that were contemporary with its composition. Postlewait argues, with reference to intertextual interpretation, that there are many truths to be told:

> That there are many perspectives, many centres of order, should not unnerve us, unless of course we are determined to believe that the choices for understanding are between either a single order or a threatening chaos.
>
> (Postlewait 1992: 364)

Programme from 1913 for performances by Diaghilev's Ballets Russes in London.

The Juxtaposition of Theatrical and Cultural Codes

The extent to which the *Petrouchka* of 1911 is dependent upon its Russian heritage is apparent in this act of the retrieval of the performance text of the piece which emphasises the close connection between the ballet and the experimental modes of theatre in St Petersburg and Moscow. The avant-garde nature of the ballet is reflected in the numerous references to antique theatre that are accumulated in its composition and establish its affinity with the Russian drama theatre of the first decade of the twentieth century. In Russia, at the turn of the century, an intense interest in the antique pervaded artistic circles. It was as if a need was felt by the artists to proceed through the historical to the contemporary. Benois, in a review for *Rech'* of 25 June 1909, noted 'an undoubted return to antiquity' in the arts generally:

> In painting, in music, in poetry, in the dance of Duncan, in the sculpture of Rodin – a dream of antiquity everywhere appeared to bind up loose threads of knowledge to find a new access to that now incomprehensible but formerly vivid beauty which saturated the entire ancient world, religion and everyday affairs, the humdrum life and the imperial feasts.
>
> (cited in Wiley 1980: 103)

The obsession with pre-history, mythology and Stone-Age Russia that was exemplified in the arts during the first decade of the twentieth century is mirrored in various early ballets of Diaghilev. Nationalism and exoticism were characteristic themes of Diaghilev's productions. In 1909, when the first season of the Ballet Russes was presented in Paris, the *Polovtsian Dances* was staged and choreographed by Fokine to the ballet music Borodin composed for his opera *Prince Igor*. The divertissement depicted a barbaric and ancient Russian world. The scenario for *L'Oiseau de feu* (1910) was an adaptation of several Russian folk tales on which Stravinsky and Fokine worked in close collaboration, while the neo-nationalist persistence in recreating Russia's mythic past is illustrated in the antique pagan rituals that Nijinsky choreographed for *Le Sacre du printemps* (1913). The inspiration for these ballets sprang from the passion and fashion for the antique and for Slavic folklore that embraced the visual arts, music, literature and theatre in the early twentieth century. In the same way it may be claimed that *Petrouchka* rests upon a grid of reference that binds the dramatised rituals, myths and music with the artefacts of the ancient Slavs.

Petrouchka and the Carnivalesque

The pre-Lenten festival of *Maslenitsa* proved a propitious background for *Petrouchka*. With its pagan associations, the ballet furthered the vogue for Slavic folkloristic themes. At this time literature and the visual arts reflected the ideali-

sation of primitive art and nature, while theatre productions, notably those
operas staged by Saava Mamontov, promoted Russian music and recreated historical and folk characters.[3] The incorporation of references to Slavic mythology
within the staging of *Petrouchka* was characteristic of the sensibilities of *Mir
Iskusstva* (*The World of Art*), the symbolist journal founded in 1898 by Diaghilev
which featured the Russian arts and crafts movement and the primitive past of
Russia. *Maslenitsa* retained powerful links with the ancient pagan beliefs of the
Slavs, and the conception of the ballet as an episode of this particular festival
fused the puppet magic with the superstitions of ancient Rus', pre-literate theatre and the sorcery of the *skomorokhi* (Russian minstrels).

Schechner argues that festivals and carnivals, though comic, are often tragic
in outcome. People gather in the streets *en masse* to celebrate life's fertility. They
put on masks and costumes and construct effigies 'not merely to disguise or
embellish their ordinary selves or to flaunt the outrageous but to act out the
multiplicity each human life is' (1992: 88). Ancient customs, superstitions and
masks that are peculiar to the festival of *Maslenitsa* shape the fairground scenes
in *Petrouchka*, summon such primaeval characters as gypsies, a bear, a devil and
the animal masks of the procession of mummers to appear, and enhance the
roles of Petrouchka and the Showman. The complexity of the characterisation of
the Petrouchka role relies in part on the link between the puppet and *Maslenitsa*
as the symbol of departing winter.[4] The superstitions and customs of Shrovetide
that extend throughout the ballet are concluded with the substitution of winter
by spring, when a straw dummy, symbolic of the former and personified in
Petrouchka, the puppet, is destroyed in an act of productive magic. The flaccid
form of Petrouchka corresponds to the straw doll attired in human clothes that
represented the mythic figure of *Maslenitsa*, a carnival creature of either male of
female sex, portrayed by a human being or by a dressed effigy. The likeness is
especially apparent after the 'death' of the puppet at the hands of the Moor,
when the Showman reveals to the crowd that Petrouchka is merely a lifeless doll,
an effigy of a man, without the capacity to experience pain, and drags the inert
body towards the puppet theatre in the final part of Tableau 4. Yet Petrouchka is
apparently restored to life. The death of Petrouchka in the ballet matches the
sacrificial destruction of the effigy that symbolised *Maslenitsa*, whose over-
throw, at the season of the half-light, ensured the return of the sun to replenish
the earth. The role of the Showman in *Petrouchka* becomes more complex in
response to the awareness that the origins of the Russian puppeteer stem from
the *skomorokh* priest. The proto-puppet, or forerunner of the Russian
Petrouchka, has been associated with the straw or wooden image that played an
integral part in ancient Slavic religious rituals (Zuguta 1978). Vernadsky (1959)
recognises that the puppet theatre is an outgrowth of the old sacred drama of
heathen times, whilst it is Zuguta's claim (1974) that the *skomorokhi*, who had
their origin in the popular, pagan cult of ancient Rus', were the first puppet

masters. It is from the characterisation of the Showman's role that many of the pagan overtones of the ballet radiate. Through his sinister genius the puppets and the fairground crowd are manipulated.

The emphasis on the pagan fear of chaos that underpins the carnival gives meaning to the narrative of *Petrouchka*. The vast circular movements of the ferris wheel and the carousel and their implied magical significance is restated in Fokine's choreography.[5] With numerous references to folk and circle dance that suggest the symbolic encircling of the *khorovod*,[6] Stravinsky's music for the fairground scenes, melodies borrowed from rustic folk songs that were both sacred and secular and popular urban tunes, together with the composition of the dances that Fokine made for the Coachmen, Wet Nurses and the meandering Shrove procession of mummers, manifest the necessary circular motion of sympathetic magic.

The representation of the carnival introduces images evocative of Russia's archaic past and presents an impression of a mid-nineteenth-century fairground based on the realities of urban life in St Petersburg. The ballet is a nostalgic recreation of the Butter Week fair, and it is through the relationship of the nineteenth-century crowd to the events taking place that a notion of Russia's archaic past is perceived. Petrouchka, the Showman, the mummers, gypsies and the performing bear create continuity with antiquity. Members of the crowd, as intermediary agents between these ancient characters and the theatre audience, transmit by their response perceptions of Russian pre-history. The surging mass of mummers, Benois' 'devil's diversion', merges with the fairground crowd, already drunk with excitement and alcohol, to ensure that the final scene is one of demonic abandonment which evokes the ruffianly grandeur that Benois (1964) claimed for the conclusion of the ballet in 1911.

Masking ensured anonymity and promoted amongst the mummers a sense of liberty and psychological release at the time of carnival. Moreover, the mask of the folk tradition represented a means of symbolic communication. Bakhtin compares the mask of folk tradition, in which he recognises the connection 'with the joy of change and reincarnation . . . transition, metamorphoses, the violation of natural boundaries', with the contemporary notion of the mask that 'hides something, keeps a secret, deceives' (1984: 40). The significance of the erotic animal masks and devils of the procession was not lost upon the nineteenth-century participants in the carnival of *Maslenitsa* that *Petrouchka* presents. However, the guignol mask of the puppet that is ridiculed by the spectators during the first tableau of the ballet conceals both the spirituality of the sad clown and the symbolic reference to Petrouchka as effigy of *Maslenitsa*. Within the structure of the puppet role a tension exists between traditional and modernist concepts of the mask.

In early performances of *Petrouchka* it is apparent that the demoniacal character of carnival was represented in the boisterous drunkenness and eroticism of masked revelry, transvestite and animal disguise. The movement of a multitude of people, the ensuing overwhelming noise and sounds of musical low life depicted in the charivari of Stravinsky's score and the dance and drama, epitomised the spirit of carnival. The hostility to contemporary civilisation that was typical of the avant-garde is present in street carnival, such as that of Butter Week in *Petrouchka*. The rejection of social and artistic conventions and bourgeois values, the celebration of personal liberation and individualism, characterises the otherworldliness of both carnival and the avant-garde. Innes recognises carnivalesque qualities as the defining marks of avant-garde drama, in particular,

> the emphasis on stage production as process in opposition to the fixed art-product of classical aesthetics; and the fusion of actors and audience, breaking down barriers between performance and reality to create a communion of (in theory at least) equal participants.   (Innes 1993: 8–9)

The placing of the puppet booth at the focal point of the fairground in *Petrouchka* emphasises the allusion to folk theatre and the personal contact that is maintained between performer and spectator. The puppet theatre, modelled on the portable stages of itinerant actors and the Russian *balagani* (the covered stages and chief attraction of the fairs), the mingling of puppets with the members of the crowd and the intermediary figure of the Showman, stress the improvised nature of the performance-within-the-performance.

Bakhtin's study of Rabelais (1984) is underpinned by the pervasiveness of the carnival in popular culture and in literature. Carnival, with its emphasis on the earthly, the grotesque and the ambivalent, signifies the symbolic destruction of authority and official culture. The ugly, the half-formed or incomplete, the unity of opposites and multiple viewpoints confirm the carnivalesque, which, born of folk humour,

> discloses the potentiality of an entirely different world, of another order, another way of life. It leads men out of the confines of the apparent (false) unity of the indisputable and stable.   (Bakhtin 1984: 48)

The other-worldliness of carnival is the world of the fairground that is depicted in *Petrouchka*, where drunken bawdiness, disguise and masked mumming, underpinned by ritualistic connotations, threaten the light-hearted fun of the fair.

Petrouchka and the Russian Avant-Garde Theatre

It must be acknowledged that the borrowing of archaic models and pagan rite was not the prerogative of the avant-garde in Russia. However, the manner in

which these references to antiquity were incorporated in Russian modernist
theatre exposed the illusionary nature of theatrical art. The complexity of Russian theatre at the beginning of the twentieth century is manifested largely in the
tension that existed between realistic and anti-illusionistic methods of staging
and acting techniques. The Moscow Art Theatre, through its founders and co-
directors, Stanislavsky and Nemirovich-Danchenko, brought about a revolution
in the art of the stage. Stanislavsky (1924) records their protest against

> the customary manner of acting, against theatricality, against bathos, against
> declamation, against over-acting, against the bad manner of production,
> against the habitual scenery, against the star system which spoiled the en-
> semble, against the light and farcical repertoire which was being cultivated
> on the Russian stage at that time.   (Stanislavsky 1948: 330)

With the rejection of archaic stage conventions and clichéd devices, the
company realised 'concrete changes' in theatrical art, which Rudnitsky recognises as the 'insistence on the most exact reflection of everyday life; on verity of
"mood" and atmosphere and naturalness of communication' (1981: 9). With the
first production of the Art Theatre in 1898, *Tsar Fyodor Ivanovich*, the director
became the creator of the performance, in which he integrated the work of the
dramatist, designer, composer and actor. Braun describes the corporate style of
the company as a rejection of theatrical stereotypes and naturalistic approxima-
tions in favour of

> a corporate search for the inner psychological truth of the character's behav-
> iour, directed towards the revelation of that truth through all the available
> means of the production.   (Braun 1982: 65)

During the first decade of the twentieth century, theatre realism, as exemplified by the productions at the Moscow Art Theatre, was challenged by a further
current in Russian theatre. The new, or anti-representational drama was directed
towards the exposure of the illusionary nature of theatrical art. This common
goal united antithetical forms of drama, notably symbolist, neo-romantic and
theatricalist modes. The opponents of theatre realism rejected the proscenium
framing and 'fourth wall' conventions, and authenticity of setting, costume and
manners, in the belief that theatre, as art, probed 'universal mysteries and the
reassertion of eternal verities through new configurations of image and idea'
(Segal 1970: 56). The exponents of the new drama revived the mask and mime of
ancient theatre. Directors challenged the illusion of theatre realism by promoting
theatrical performance as the subject of plays. The direct address of the audience
by characters and/or actors was favoured, besides the use of the stage-within-a-
stage device and the revelation of those aspects of staging that by the convention

of theatre realism were concealed from the spectators by the front curtain. It was the conviction of avant-garde directors that modern theatre should encourage the spectator to remember at all times that he/she was witnessing a performance. Theatre must emphasise the 'unadulterated and intensified expression of theatricality' (Slonim 1961: 213).

In 1902, Velery Bryusov's article 'The Unnecessary Truth', questioned for the first time the naturalistic presentation of drama, and postulated that the achievements of the Moscow Art Theatre conflicted with the nature of the stage. In Bryusov's opinion, art and convention co-exist:

> The stage is conventional by its very nature . . . I summon you away from the unnecessary truth of the modern stage to the deliberate conventionalisation of the ancient theatre.   (cited in Green 1986: 26–30)

In the forefront of the movement that attacked realism was Diaghilev's journal *Mir iskusstva*. With the publication of Bryusov's article 'The Unnecessary Truth' in *Mir iskusstva* (1902), Diaghilev aligned his sympathies with those of the avant-garde.

The influx of the 'lost golden age' of the late eighteenth century, when Carlo Gozzi brought about a rebirth of the *commedia dell'arte* in Venice, permeated the theatre of the Russian anti-realists. In their attempts to dispel theatrical illusion the avant-garde theatricalists seized upon the masked acting style and staging conventions of the Italian comedies. The success of these plays, which centred on urban life, was dependent upon the balance maintained between character relationships, intrigue and farcical incidents.[7] The appeal of the *commedia dell'arte* for theatricalists such as Evreinov, Meyerhold, Tairov and Vakhtangov lay in the implicit assertion that the comedies did not imitate life.

The traditions of acting and staging of the *commedia dell'arte* infuse the composition of *Petrouchka*. The design Benois created for the fairground scenes incorporates a false proscenium arch decorated in the style of the town houses of the comic settings of the Italian Renaissance as described by Serlio in his *Regole generali di achitettura* of 1545, whilst his three depths of stage reflect the simultaneous staging of the Italian comedies demanded by the intrigues of the scenarios of Flaminio Scala, published in 1611, in which the characters of the *commedia dell'arte* first entered the stuctures of printed plays (Salerno 1992). The puppet booth in *Petrouchka* is presented as a stage-within-a-stage and, by its impermanent structure, is reminiscent of the stages erected by the troupes of itinerant actors and mountebanks of the seventeenth century. The role of the Showman in the ballet continues the link between *Petrouchka* and the theatre of the mountebanks. As an arch manipulator of the puppet performance and the spectators, the Showman reflects the authoritative charlatan doctor of the travelling Italian actors.

Pencil sketches by Valentine Gross of Nijinsky in *Petroushka*.   V&A Picture Library

The itinerant actors of the *commedia dell'arte* troupes performed in colourful costumes as dancers, masqueraders, clowns and jugglers. The style of their performance is restated in *Petrouchka*, where the masks of Pierrot, Harlequin and Columbine inspire the characterisations of the Petrouchka, Moor and Ballerina roles. Images of visual art have perpetuated the archetype that is recognised throughout European culture as Pierrot. However, there is little dispute amongst historians that although the mask of Pierrot developed initially from Pedrolino of the *zanni* (valet-buffoons) of the *commedia dell'arte*, it was the French theatre rather than the Italian that was responsible for maintaining the role, although in altered appearance and character. The masks of the ancient French Pierrots diffuse within the role of Petrouchka. The puppet's mask makes reference to Giratone's lovesick simpleton that established Pierrot as a character and a comedian (Theatre Italian, 1673), when the delicacy and sensitivity of Giratone's white-faced created isolated Pierrot from his fellow masks. Pierrot as the sensitive non-participant is suggested by Antoine Watteau's paintings of Gilles and the Italian comedians, whilst the infinite nuances of the role were exemplified by Deburau's portrayal in the harlequinades of the Théâtre des Funambules in Paris. It was during the 1820s and 1830s that Deburau played the role of Pierrot and became the idol of the fashionable avant-garde in Paris. The innovations that Deburau brought to the role, in their placidity, contrasted with the exuberance of gesture and leaps of his immediate predecessors, whose Pierrots derived from the pantomime masks of the *foires*.[8] In the early twentieth century, the appeal of this modern Pierrot was widespread. In Russia, the confused depth of images ascribed to the mask was characteristic of the social and political situations at the beginning of the century. The misfortune of Petrouchka as sad clown might be read in modernist terms as the general plight of suffering mankind, humanity persecuted by the oppressions of war or threatened for its religious beliefs. Alternatively, the mask may be recognised as the embodiment of the misunderstood and voiceless individual. Deburau's mask epitomises the personal suffering of Petrouchka, yet the puppet is not simply a reincarnation of *l'homme spirituel* of the Théâtre des Funambules. Petrouchka's identity remains locked within the guignol of the St Petersburg fairgrounds and within the clown of Russian circuses, whose painted face masks all social identity.

The role of the Moor is in the tradition of theatrical blackamoors, but is shaped by the mask of Harlequin. The posture, black face, colourful costume, baton and *lazzi* (stage tricks of business) of the Italian mask infiltrate the Moor's characterisation. The absurd, earthbound Moor reflects the mask of Harlequin in such a way as to parody the agile rogue, and to satirise the *commedia dell'arte* relationship between Harlequin and Columbine. The soulless, thoughtless doll, the Ballerina, whom Benois (1941) claimed as Columbine, is apparently the antithesis of the *servetta birichina* (artful serving maid) of the Italian *commedia*. The contrast between the roles is so apparent that it must be read as intentional. Whilst Fokine's choreography for the Ballerina suggests parody of the formulae of academic ballet in the Imperial Russian ballet theatres, it may also be read as the puppet's programmed response to the Showman's manipulation. It is the humour inherent in the roles that links the Moor and the Ballerina with the parody of the harlequinade. In the harlequinades of Russian cabaret, *commedia dell'arte* masks and living-doll routines[9] served as vehicles of theatrical parody (Segal 1987).

The influence of the Italian masks on the conception and realisation of *Petrouchka* is extensive. The scenario, staging, the puppet masks and choreography are rich in references to the *commedia dell'arte* and to the vogue for harlequinade that permeated Russian avant-garde theatre. Between the genres, as they co-exist in the ballet, a tension is created. Moreover, a further suspense occurs with the juxtaposition of theatre realism with theatricalist devices of staging. The false proscenium arch and the stage-within-a-stage locate *Petrouchka* within a modernist conception of theatre, while the detailed, realistic setting for the fairground implies that the production of the ballet was sympathetic to the concept of theatre realism. In the staging of *Petrouchka*, theatre realism merges with devices that bring into question the nature of illusion in theatre art. This tension echoes the first that relates the traditional masks of the Italian

comedies to modernist interpretations in the harlequinade. The interaction between tradition and innovation in the ballet transforms and reinvents cultural
and historical elements. Old, pre-existing codes, which refer to the conventions
of antique theatres, confront distinctive codes, such as those that emerged when
modernist directors made reference to antiquity in avant-garde theatre experimentation.

The theme of the harlequinade in early twentieth-century Russian theatre
interwove the spirits of the *commedia dell'arte* masks with those of the *balagan*
and the circus. The Pierrot-clown, in the role of protagonist, was elemental.
With his whitened face, he was identified as the mainspring of the make-believe.
In 1906, Aleksandr Blok wrote his short play *Balaganchik* (The Fairground
Booth). In his direction of the play, at the theatre of Vera Komissarzhevskaya, St
Petersburg (1906), Vsevolod Meyerhold introduced the devices of the *commedia*
masks, pantomime, the direct address of the audience by his characters, a
mediatory figure and a setting that focused on a stage-within-a-stage. The meta-
theatrical devices that Blok and Meyerhold conceived for *Balaganchik* attacked
the realistic presentation of drama and the norms and standards by which the
audience viewed theatre and, therefore, life itself. Hornby (1986) points out that
whenever the play-within-the-play is used, it is both reflective and expressive of
its society's deep cynicism about life. Blok was the first major symbolist writer to
criticise and parody the cult of symbolism that had influenced Russian literary
and dramatic thought since 1893.[10] Moreover, *Balaganchik* broke new ground by
becoming the first important manifestation of theatricalism in early twentieth-
century theatre.

From Meyerhold's own description of his 1906 staging of *Balaganchik* (Braun
1986), and from the design created by Nikolai Sapunov, it is apparent that the
stage-within-the-stage, the booth, was conceived as a tiny theatre in its own
right. Its performance space and stage machinery were modelled after the fashion of the covered stages of the *balagani* at the Butter Week fairs in St Petersburg. A similarity between the stage-within-a-stage that represents the booth in
Balaganchik and the puppet theatre in *Petrouchka* is conspicuous, so that the
spectator is constantly reminded that the performance-within-the-performance
in both dramas challenges theatrical illusion. The Author role in *Balaganchik*,
like that of the Showman in *Petrouchka*, functions as an intermediary character
to link the performers with the spectators. The character of Petrouchka recalls
the dejected Pierrot in *Balaganchik*. The death of the clown in the play is
resolved for the audience as merely clowning and make-believe, while the death
of Petrouchka is revealed as fantasy. In Meyerhold's staging of *Balaganchik* and
in *Petrouchka*, the mask of Pierrot slips from the stage to confront reality and to
question the nature of illusion as recognised by the theatre audience.

The symbolist obsessions with death, mysticism and myth are ridiculed in
Blok's text for *Balaganchik* and reinforced through Meyerhold's theatricalist

staging. In the ballet, Petrouchka is the symbolic representation of *Maslenitsa* even though the puppet's death is realised in a knockabout battle with the Moor. Since the tragic farce of Petrouchka's death resembles the killing of the clown in *Balaganchik* by the helmetted knight, can Blok's harlequinade, that centres upon the deliberate ridicule of symbolism, be acknowledged as a model for *Petrouchka*, and the ballet recognised as a parody of symbolist sensibilities? It would seem probable that *Petrouchka* was conceived as parody, for there is an additional argument that links the piece with the genre. The myths of ancient Russia, which give meaning to the fairground scenes, may be seen to be satirised through their ritual enactment by puppets and drunken revellers of the streets. Through the parody of myth the ballet comments on the interest in the antique that pervaded artistic circles at the beginning of the century. Since the form of *Petrouchka* can be claimed to be based on the harlequinade that represented a theatrical vogue in St Petersburg at the beginning of the twentieth century, it may be supposed that the ballet was so fashioned deliberately in order to suggest its burlesque nature and its links with the satirical comedies of the *commedia dell'arte*.

In spite of Benois' criticism of the exponents of theatricalism,[11] notably Meyerhold, the designs Benois created for *Petrouchka* must be acknowledged as reflecting the conventions of the *commedia dell'arte*, and therefore sympathetic to the principles of avant-garde theatre. Moreover, the masks of Pierrot, Columbine and Harlequin, the stage-within-the-stage where the puppets perform, and the metatheatrical role of the Showman, whose manipulation controls the dance drama, all confirm the choice of *Balaganchik* as a model for *Petrouchka*. The play and the ballet incorporate masks that play out the eternal love triangle in which Pierrot challenges Harlequin for Columbine's affections, and thus Petrouchka resembles the Pierrot role in *Balaganchik*. Meyerhold's idiosyncratic approach to the melancholic characterisation of Pierrot was realised through the medium of movement and pantomime. Meyerhold (1908) wrote of the need for some new means of expressing the ineffable, of revealing that which is concealed. This need was satisfied for him by the employment of what was termed plastic movement. Meyerhold spoke of a plasticity which does not correspond to the words of the play's text:

> There must be pattern of movement on the stage to transform the spectator into a vigilant observer, to furnish him with that material . . . which helps him grasp the true feelings of the character.   (cited in Braun 1969: 56)

The stylised and structured movement form Meyerhold adopted for the Pierrot role in *Balaganchik* is reflected in the way that Fokine's choreography for Petrouchka revealed the nature of the puppet through an individualised plastique.[12] In Blok's harlequinade, fantasy and allegorical characters are juxtaposed with naturalistic roles, and this mingling is reiterated in *Petrouchka*. The dual roles of the puppets as masks co-exist with the people of the fairground, who are confronted by the symbolic masks of the mummers. Within the contrasts formed in the ballet, notably by the realistic presentation of the fairground and its characters and the puppet masks, Meyerhold's concept of the grotesque, as exemplified in *Balaganchik*, is manifested in *Petrouchka*.

Balaganchik, as tragic farce, relies on the creation of harsh incongruity. The duality of the grotesque underpins the conception of *Petrouchka*. The duality of the mask symbolises a surface reality that disguises what lies beneath. The mask is a key concept of the grotesque that permeates the harlequinade and the ballet. Pierrot in *Balaganchik* and Petrouchka represent images of the sad clown. The role of Petrouchka combines puppet with symbolic effigy, whilst the Showman, through his progenitor, the puppet-master, can be identified with the *skomorokh* priest and regulator of ritual and the powerful forces of nature. The illusion of revelry and carnival, as exemplified in the dramatic episodes of the fairground scenes of *Petrouchka*, the procession of the mummers and the folk dances, conceal the ritualistic connotations that link the participants in the merrymaking and the form of their dances with pagan worship.

Meyerhold, writing in *O Teatre*, maintained that the element of deception is important to the dramatic grotesque (Braun 1969). In the ballet, Petrouchka's death and the revelation of the straw dummy to the fairground crowd are supreme acts of deception. At the same time, the theatre audience is misled into accepting that the dummy represents the puppet. A second layer of deception concludes the final tableau, when the illusion of the revived Petrouchka proves his immortality.

The Conflicting Codes of the Performance Text of *Petrouchka*, 1911

The overlapping of numerous trends of thought through which new relationships with reality were created, often by reference to antiquity, produces the eclecticism of *Petrouchka* that aligns it with the atavistic trend of Russian theatre at the beginning of the twentieth century. The relationship between the Russian avant-garde theatre and forms of antique theatre did not grow out of an attempt to recreate the past, as Stanislavsky and Nemirovich-Danchenko had endeavoured to do in their production of *Tsar Fyodor Ivanovich* (1898), or as Diaghilev had in the staging of Mussorgsky's *Boris Godonov* (1908). The link between the avant-garde and the past emphasised the position of the new drama as resulting from a transition from the old to the new. Modernity revolted against the prescriptive function of tradition and sought to use the past in a different way. Habermas characterises the modern, avant-garde spirit:

[It] disposes those parts which have been made available by the objectifying scholarship of historicism, but it opposes at the same time a neutralised history which is locked up in the museum of historicism.

(Habermas 1983: 5)

Petrouchka cannot be read as an attempt merely to recreate antiquity in the sense that pagan ritual was apparently recreated through the medium of dance in Nijinsky's *Le Sacre du printemps* (1913). Although Nijinsky's ballet succeeded *Petrouchka*, it was compositionally retrograde in terms of modernism, since *Le Sacre du printemps* was based upon a dream of antiquity and the reconstruction of Ancient Rus'. (It may be supposed that choreographically Nijinsky translated Khlebnikov's experiments, in which the poet attempted to revert to the earliest stages of linguistic evolution.[13]) *Petrouchka* is a modernist ballet of the avant-garde because the materials of its composition and its structure comment upon the antique by implication rather than by direct representation in the form of reconstruction. The reality that is claimed for the nineteenth-century carnival scenes in the stalls, booths and fairground amusements of the setting, its character types and Fokine's dances, signifies the religious overtones of *Maslenitsa*. Through the repetition of circular forms, the appearance of gypsy and animal masks and the 'devil's diversion', the supernatural and ritual are affirmed.

In his study of avant-garde theatre, Innes (1993) states that, paradoxically, what defines the avant-garde movement is not overtly modern qualities, such as the 1920's romance with technology, but primitivism. Creative artists freely reinterpreted 'primitive' models to serve aims that were alien to the original culture, so that

primitivism goes hand in hand with aesthetic experimentation designed to advance the technical progress of the art itself by exploring fundamental questions.

(Innes 1993: 3)

The paradox of the antique as a constituent of the modern is reproduced in Fokine's choreography for *Petrouchka*. Fokine (1914) stated that it was his intention to create with each piece of choreography a new form corresponding to the subject of the piece that expressed the period and character of the nation represented. While his dances for the fairground scenes denote the reality of Russian street life with characters apparently strolling naturally to the fair, the *khorovod* forms of the folk dances, which Fokine based on traditional steps, signify their ancient origin. Although Fokine reverted to antique forms of Russian dance, his representation of these ancient dances was modernist in its approach. The manner in which dance and dramatic episode were blended, as if one arose spontaneously from the other, can be interpreted as an innovation in ballet that succeeded the traditional divertissement which incorporated national dance as the prerequisite of the final acts of academic ballets.

In his attempts to create new forms of choreography, Fokine rejected the steps of academic ballet and reverted in his early works to movements that were inspired by images of antiquity, notably from Greece and Egypt. In *Petrouchka* the plastique Fokine created for the male puppets restated the *cheironomia* of Athenian acting of the fifth century BC, since the mask-like expressions on the puppet's faces demanded that the dancers used their entire bodies to define the characterisations and portray emotion. However, Fokine's psychological system of signs reflected the modernism of Maeterlinck's ideal of a motionless theatre to express the nuances of internal states in plastic form.[14] Fokine created movement *en dedans*, or with an inward focus, for Petrouchka, and a consistent body shape throughout solo dances. Within the puppet's plastique a tension is maintained between the contracted body and gestures with outward intention so that the choreography mirrors that which is central to the role – the inner life of Petrouchka and the contradiction of the puppet exterior. The spirituality and lonely suffering that is fundamental to the characterisation of the puppet as the sad clown appears diametrically opposed to the outward manifestation of the role. By tradition, the Russian guignol represented the bullying braggart of the puppet show, yet Petrouchka is analogous to the mask of Pierrot. The composition of the role juxtaposes the mask with psychological suffering. Petrouchka, through his private tragedy of alienation, appears the equivalent of the modernist tragic hero of contemporary life as promoted in the plays of Chekhov, Hauptmann, Ibsen, Maeterlinck and Strindberg. It was in their experimental staging of such plays that Russian avant-garde directors attempted to present symbolist drama.

For Meyerhold, it was the symbolist aesthetic that yielded the fundamental concepts as well as concrete ideas concerning the function and form of theatre, from which he could proceed to invent the Russian form of theatrical symbolism (Deak 1982). If *Petrouchka* is considered as a statement of the faith of *Mir iskusstva*, the relationship of the ballet to the trends of the new drama is manifested in ideologies shared with Russian symbolist drama. The early plays of the Belgian dramatist, Maurice Maeterlinck, were instrumental in the reform of Russian theatre. Maeterlinck, whose theory of 'static theatre' evoked a mystical experience and a subconscious mood in dramatic form, influenced Meyerhold's direction of *La Mort de Tintagiles* (1905) and *Soeur Beatrice* (1906) that epitomised Russian symbolist theatre.[15] Meyerhold's main principle of staging was that of motionless theatre. The plastic forms of motionless theatre, exemplified by groupings in the style of bas-reliefs and movement in slow motion, were characteristic of the aesthetics of symbolist theatre in general (Rudnitsky 1981).[16] Reverberations of Maeterlinck's essay *Le Tragique quotidien* infuse the private tragedy of Petrouchka, and elevate the role to that of the tragic hero of modernist drama. As a 'play for marionettes'[17] the ballet reflects the everyday tragedies of Maeterlinck, in which the personal suffering of the puppet-like protagonist is controlled by mysterious fatalistic forces. Petrouchka's idiosyncratic tragedy stems from his half-human existence. The puppet exterior contrasts vividly with the spiritual fears and longings of his inner life. This paradox is central to the meaning of the ballet, and within these conflicting principles lies the drama of Petrouchka.

The duality that typifies the role of Petrouchka juxtaposes the realism of the crowd with the fantasy world of the puppets, and conceals the noble suffering of a hero within the ugly and ill-formed exterior of Petrouchka. At the core of the dualism lies the concept of the grotesque that was central to Meyerhold's perception of cabotinage, mask and fairground shows. In *O Teatre* (1913) Meyerhold cites Wolzogen's manifesto of 1902:

> Grotesque usually implies something hideous and strange, a humorous work which with no apparent logic combines the most dissimilar elements by ignoring their details and relying on its own originality, borrowing from every source anything which satisfies its *joie de vivre* and its capricious, mocking attitude to life.   (cited in Braun 1969: 137)

The multiplicity of texts, viewpoints and perspectives to which a network of primary and secondary meanings are ascribed in the analysis of *Petrouchka* confirms the grotesque nature of the piece. The combination of opposites, the creation of conscious incongruity, and the unresolved tension between realism and theatricalism that the ballet shares with Blok's *Balaganchik* attest to the grotesque in *Petrouchka*. The cult of symbolism was parodied in Meyerhold's staging of *Balaganchik* through the grotesque and facetious elements of the *commedia dell'arte* and the Russian puppet theatre. The carnivalesque staging that broke new ground with its theatricalist interrogation of the conventions and artificiality of theatre was repeated in *Petrouchka*. The state of unease created by the multiple messages of the performance text destabilises the perception of the spectators in the theatre audience. In the use of techniques such as the mask, the mediatory figure of the Showman, a setting that incorporates a stage-within-a-stage and a false proscenium arch with the apparent realism of the crowd as on stage spectators, the reception of the audience is dislocated by multiple viewpoints so that the carnivalesque is doubly stated.

It becomes clear through the exploration of connections between the performance text of the ballet and other synchronous texts which evolved from the analysis of Russian modernist theatre prior to 1911 that numerous separate versions of *Petrouchka* are available to the analyst. A selective analysis of the text, or one that concentrates on each contextual aspect of *Petrouchka*, in turn enables the ballet to be read from such viewpoints as Russian neo-nationalism, neo-romanticism, symbolist theatre, the *commedia dell'arte*, the Russian harlequinade or the tradition of tragedy. In each case the selective analysis of the ballet offers an alternative version of the text. Analyses of *Petrouchka* from separate viewpoints convey partial perspectives in which a network of primary and secondary meanings are determined. An intertextual analysis of *Petrouchka* must address the synthetic nature of the piece. The synthesis of the performance text is revealed when one viewpoint is set against another. Additional correspondences and contrasts are disclosed that highlight the complexities within the composition of the ballet, and throw light on the agencies that acted upon the performance and the distinctive manner of its execution in 1911. *Petrouchka*, as a theatrical event, transmitted multiple messages in which various channels of signification were used simultaneously. The spectator was confronted by a mesh of tensions that emerged through the conflicting messages of the performance. The focus of the contradictions lies within the constitution of the Petrouchka role.

Scènes Burlesques en Quatre Tableaux

If the staging and performance of *Petrouchka* in 1911 met the requirements of its original programme description as *scènes burlesques*, it can be assumed that it was intended to be comical, ludicrous, ridiculous or absurd. In Beaumont's classification (1949) *Petrouchka* is a 'burlesque ballet', which suggests a performance that mocks by grotesque exaggeration, or by combining the dignified with the familiar or popular forms of entertainment. While the ballet transcends the mere comical, its affinity with *Balaganchik* suggests that claims for its satirical imitation of other theatre pieces might be justified. Parody involves imitation or mimicry of other styles, seizing upon their idiosyncrasies and eccentricities to produce an imitation which mocks the original. The grotesquery of *Petrouchka* borrows and combines dissimilar elements and integrates disparates into a unified whole. The multimedia style of the ballet, in the manner of Wagner's *Gesamtkunstwerk*,[1] created a *mise-en-scène* from the transformation and fusion of expressive media to form a homogeneous avant-garde work of parody.

Since Fokine's choreography for the Ballerina, the Moor and the street dancers is generally acknowledged as a parody of academic ballet, the supposition follows that the dances he composed for Petrouchka were created in a similar humorous mode. The puppet's plastique was influenced by Fokine's concept of dance expression based on movements that were true to life. The outward manifestation of the Petrouchka role supports the theory that the expressive quality of Nijinsky's dance depended on the unity between outward physical actions defined by the plastique and an inner psychological action. If the *Gesamtkunstwerk* of *Petrouchka* centres on the projection of parody, Nijinsky's success in convincing critics and the audience that within the puppet's body lay a tormented human soul may be read as a playful or satirical comment directed

Alexandre Benois' costume design for Petroushka.   V&A Picture Library

towards Stanislavsky's demands for psychological truth as the prerequisite of the
actor's performance.

The view held by both Stanislavsky and Nemirovich-Danchenko, the founders of the Moscow Art Theatre, was that the main task for the actor on the stage
was the representation of the external manifestations of his role that recreated
the inner life of his assumed character. The interaction between the inner psy-

chological and the outer physical action, they were convinced, informs the actor's role with the truthfulness of a living being in all the complexity of his or her character and behaviour. The acting technique devised by Stanislavsky was based upon a conception of truth that was realised in the actor's feelings and sensations and in the inner creative impulse and its expression. Stanislavsky recognised that in every psychological interaction there was always a physical action that expressed its psychological nature, so that the correct state of being on the stage depended upon a unity between psychological and physical actions. Nijinsky's performances in the role of Petrouchka, as described by contemporary spectators,[18] indicate that his concentration centred on the inner life of the character, whose spirituality epitomised the tragedy of the modern Everyman. It can be argued that Nijinsky's state of being as he danced the Petrouchka role was influenced by Stanislavsky's feeling for truth. However, the duality of his dancing suggested a soulful sad clown and, at the same time, the clumsy uncoordinated guignol of the Russian fairs. Fokine's choreography used movement as an expression of dramatic action that delineated character, to which the scenes in the puppet cells bear witness. The movement that Fokine devised for the intricacy of the puppet role was realised in the juxtaposition of contracted dance motifs *en dedans* and gestures with outward intention. The interaction between the outer physical actions, as exemplified in Fokine's plastique, and the inner psychological truth of the role, which Stanislavsky advocated in his theatre of authentic emotion, contributed to the complexity of the Petrouchka role on the stage.

Petrouchka has been recognised as a dance-drama of tragic dimensions, 'the Hamlet of ballet' (Hall 1958: 5). The underlying structure that supports the composition of *Petrouchka* is tragic. The conventions of Athenian drama of the fifth century BC, by which three masked actors and a chorus are engaged in a series of narrative episodes and formalised choric interludes, are reflected in the form of the ballet. In the plays and in *Petrouchka* the narrative sections and the dances of the chorus and crowd are motivated and maintained by the rhythmic pulse of the verse metre and the balletic score. The corporate voice of the chorus may be recognised in that of the crowd. Both symbolise the norm of ordinary behaviour at times of heightened dramatic tension. The form of *Petrouchka* reveals the structure of the Athenian dramas that Aristotle recognised in the conventions that govern the *muthos* of tragedy (*Poetics* 1980). However, in *Petrouchka* the tragic hero is a puppet, who by tradition insults and batters his fellows, while the chorus is made up of intoxicated carnival revellers. The similarity and disparity between the ballet and the Athenian drama may be interpreted as balletic imitation that mocks the dignity of tragedy and satirises the contemporary vogue for ancient Greece that infiltrated Russian theatre at the beginning of the century.[19]

Wagner (1914) stated that it was only from the Greek vision of life that true, dramatic art could blossom, when myth provided the subject matter. Wagner's music dramas, which had created a sensation in St Petersburg from 1889, presented the world of myth in theatrical terms and exemplified his vision of purity and idealism in art. Notions of myth and archetype permeate *Petrouchka*. The puppet, as the effigy of *Maslenitsa* and the mystical sad clown, represents a role akin to symbolist sympathies. If Petrouchka, the theatrical archetype of Pierrot, is aligned with the mythical hero of Wagner's conception, the inequality based on the high art form of operatic drama and the low life of popular street entertainment renders the characterisation of Petrouchka a pastiche of Wagnerian heroism and idealism in art.

The tension between theatre realism and anti-representational drama is inherent in the juxtaposition of the puppet booth and the false proscenium arch with the apparent realism of the fairground setting and the combination of the masks with the carefully delineated characters of St Petersburg. If the performance style of *Petrouchka* in 1911 was intended as a parody of contemporary theatre, the realism of the *mise-en-scène* must be explained in a corresponding manner. Benois' attitude to avant-garde theatre evolved from outspoken criticism that attacked Meyerhold's stylised production methods to a hypocritical recognition of the new drama. Benois' irreconcilable opposition and outspoken criticism raged for some ten years. It was apparent that Benois' sympathies lay far from contemporary theatre practices. The introduction of theatricalist devices of masked acting and staging in *Petrouchka* might be explained if Benois' intention was to parody contemporary theatre.

Benois was noted for his attention to historical accuracy and the detailed reconstruction of reality, aligning his work with the scenic realism of Stanislavsky and Nemirovich-Danchenko. In 1909 Benois was appointed the artistic director of the Moscow Art Theatre at a time when Stanislavsky and the theatre company were involved with preparations for Edward Gordon Craig's celebrated production of *Hamlet*. From 1909 to the first performance in 1912, Craig visited the theatre to discuss, prepare and stage his Moscow *Hamlet*. Craig's attitude to direction was based on the belief that art should reveal the invisible and would be reborn when architecture, music and movement were united in an ideal harmony. The realism of Stanislavsky's production style confronted Craig's abstraction and his theories concerning performance, in which he advocated the replacement of the actor by the *Übermarionette*. Craig's concept of the *Übermarionette* was precipitated by his long-standing passion for the mask, which he recognised as a safeguard against realism. For Craig, the masked actor, as symbol, became the *Übermarionette*. Craig's interpretation of *Hamlet* opposed that of Stanislavsky. Craig saw *Hamlet* as a mystery play, a monodrama concerning the conflict between spirit and matter that took place in Hamlet's soul (Senelick 1982). Means other than characterisation, therefore, were necessary to present this inner world. The setting that Craig conceived for *Hamlet*, an abstract world of shapes and lines, bore no relationship to external or material existence. To translate Petrouchka's suffering, Fokine sought a new vocabulary based upon symbolic movement to enhance the tension inherent in the puppet-Pierrot role. The confrontation between Stanislavsky and Craig that represented the challenge by the mask to the concept of *perezhivanye*, Stanislavsky's theatre of authentic emotion, is reproduced in *Petrouchka*. Benois, writing in *Rech'* of 6 April 1912, blamed the Art Theatre for the pretentiousness and tastelessness of the production, in repudiating its usual goal of truth to life. It is conceivable that Craig's Moscow *Hamlet* was grotesquely imitated in *Petrouchka*, which was itself a compromise between realism and theatricality.

Stanislavsky's influence on ballet modernism was noted in the reforms that Gorsky made to the arrangement of the crowd scenes in *Don Quixote* (1900).[20] Gorsky's example of dispersing the fixed lines of the *corps de ballet* into an animated choreographic drama revolutionised ensemble dancing. Repercussions of Stanislavsky's psychological realism, as exemplified by his crowd scenes, can also be traced in the fairground scenes of *Petrouchka*. In the same way that the Russian crowd in *Tsar Fyodor Ivanovich* (1898) was central to Stanislavsky's direction, the fairground crowd in *Petrouchka* was vital to the composition of the ballet, and attracted the attention of critics and historians. The reaction to the Russianness of *Petrouchka* in its early performances was that of French and English spectators, whose notions of authenticity were largely romanticised. A retrospective evaluation of the Russian character types who made up the crowd suggest that the characterisations of dancers in the roles of the coachman and wet nurses or the merchant and the gypsies were exaggerated and closer to pastiche than reality. The carnivalesque dance drama that Benois and Fokine devised in the fairground scenes of *Petrouchka* suggests a larger-than-life approach, or a satirical imitation of Stanislavsky's celebrated crowds.

The illusion of reality that is created in *Petrouchka* in the depiction of the fairground scenes is perpetually challenged by the avant-garde nature of the ballet, which is determined by the numerous references to theatricality. Although it can be acknowledged that *Petrouchka*, as a depiction of a theatrical event of the past, has much in common with Evreinov's reconstruction of medieval dramas at the Starinny teatr, St Petersburg (1907–08),[21] the ballet, after the manner of *Balaganchik*, is predominantly anti-realist and indicative of the convoluted irony, confusion of identity and carnivalesque nature of the avant-garde.

The multimedia style of *Petrouchka* and the unity of presentation that blended disparate cultural elements was a unique achievement in the ballet theatre of 1911. As an avant-garde theatrical event, *Petrouchka* extended the boundaries of ballet modernism. The theme of the carnivalesque which permeates *Petrouchka* determines the humour of the piece that is reflected in satirical imitation of contemporary theatrical styles. The conflicting tensions of the ballet that emerge from the multiple meanings of its materials and form confirm the capricious, mocking attitude to life and theatre art that *Petrouchka* as '*scènes burlesques*' indicates. The outstanding difficulty in restaging the *Petrouchka* of 1911 in the ballet theatre of today lies not in recapturing its Russianness, nor in the realisation of its dramatic *mise-en-scène*, but in the conceptualisation that the nature of the ballet is parody. The creation of the tantalising humour of the piece rests on the identification and understanding of the complexity of theatrical references that are echoed in *Petrouchka* and the compound nature of Pierrot, who ceased to represent the theatrical archetype of contemporary Everyman. Without such initiation, neither ballet-masters nor dancers nor theatre audiences can reflect upon the exaggeration, imitation and therefore humour implicit in the piece. The omission of the carnivalesque from present-day revivals of *Petrouchka* has left the ballet bereft of its life force. The negation of the grotesque has robbed the ballet of its facetiousness, leaving a pale, sentimental and misunderstood reflection of the original.

The *Petrouchka* of 1911 emphasised the transitional position of the new drama and the new dance in the modernist theatre. As a tool of comment, the ballet implied the redundancy of the balletic vocabulary of academic ballet and advocated choreography that was essentially a means by which movement was utilised as an expression of dramatic action to delineate character. The solo and ensemble dances and the dramatic action of the crowd form a unified whole. The unity of *Petrouchka* that was manifested in the fusion of the music, dance and drama and setting is underpinned by the capricious nature of carnival and parody that unite the multiple codes of the performance text.

Notes

1. Léonide Massine was the first Petrouchka in the United States, when Diaghilev's Ballets Russes appeared at the Century Theatre in New York in 1916. The first US performance of *Petrouchka* took place on 25 January 1916, when Massine danced the role of Petrouchka with Lydia Lopokova as the Ballerina and Adolph Bolm as the Moor. Massine, with the assistance of Yurey Lazowski, was engaged by the Joffrey Ballet to revise Fokine's choreography for a revival of *Petrouchka* in 1970. Massine disassociated himself from the production apparently because changes had been made in the revival during his absence (Barnes 1970).
2. For reviews of some revived stagings of *Petrouchka*, see 'The Sitter Out' (1950), Clarke (1957), Lawson (1957), Sheridan (1958), Sokolova (1963), Williams (1972), Percival (1992), and Sorley Walker (1995). Such evaluative descriptions reflect by comparison the nature of the *Petrouchka* of 1911 and provide, therefore, additional relevant texts that bear witness to the original staging of the piece.
3. Five of Rimsky-Korsakov's works were presented by Mamontov's Moscow Private Opera between 1896 and 1899: *Ivan the Terrible* (*The Maid of Pskov*), *Sadko*, *Snegurochka*, *May Night* and *Mozart and Salieri*.
4. Hubbs (1988) describes *Maslenitsa* as a festival to reawaken the earth. Shrovetide ceremonies were connected with charms to call out the warmth of the

returning sun in springtime. The Shrove procession, resembling a Slavonic Bacchanalia, enlivened by a liberal supply of vodka, was headed by *Maslenitsa*. Sokolov (1966) and Varneke (1951) both state that the ceremonial custom of the burning of Shrovetide in the form of a straw dummy is related to the magic linked with the springtime sun.

5. In later stagings of *Petrouchka*, when the ferris wheel and carousel have been omitted, or merely indicated on a painted backdrop, their magical significance has been lost.

6. In Russian folk history *khorovodnyia* (roundelays) are the most primitive forms of dramatic expression, being both religious and magical. Their circular pattern is linked with the cult of the sun and the symbol of the succession of life and death. The continuous cycle of rites and ceremonies of the agrarian year found expression in the *khorovod*, with each season impressing its own character through song and movement

7. The *commedia dell'arte* tradition represented a return to theatre in which masked actors displayed a balance between discipline and the freedom of personal initiative. Each player was identified by his mask and costume and retained his name, costume and basic features or peculiarities in a succession of plays. Each play offered a new circumstance and relationships, yet, since the mask's personality remained constant, the character created the illusion of a living being.

8. During the eighteenth century, the Pierrot who appeared at the Foires Saint Germain and Saint-Laurent, the two great Parisian fairs, inherited the immaculate white costume worn by Giratone, together with his playfulness, naïve candour, laziness and the ancient traditions of performance of itinerant actors – dancing, singing, and acrobatics. The mask of Pierrot fragmented, and the cohesion created by Giratone, by the strength of his own personality, was eroded.

9. From 1912, the Moscow cabaret theatre, the 'new' Bat, featured the so-called living-doll entertainments. Actresses assumed the roles of puppets, marionettes or dolls in silent or music-accompanied scenes or tableaux which sprang to life. Segal, in his discussion of the phenomenon (1987) recognises the source of these entertainments as the contemporary interest in both the puppet and the marionette. The costume of the traditional masks of the *commedia dell'arte* provided the inspiration for several productions, as did the rococo style of eighteenth-century France.

10. The beginning of symbolism in Russia dates from the publication of Dmitry Sergeevich Merezhkovsky's lectures concerning the decline of Russian literature, as he perceived it in 1893. In these lectures he praised Ibsen, Poe and the French symbolists for their mysticism, symbolism and impressionism. The verse of the French symbolist poets, Mallarmé, Rimbaud and Verlaine, became a decisive influence on later Russian symbolist thought.

11. Benois, as a theatre critic, was sympathetic to theatre realism, and known for his opposition to the Russian avant-garde. The artist/poet, David Burliuk's pamphlet of 1913, *Galdya shchie 'benua' i Novoe Russkoe Natsionalnoe Iskusstvo* (The noisy 'benois' and the new Russian national art) commented upon Benois' criticism of the Russian avant-garde over a period of several years. Burliuk had deliberately printed 'Benois' with a lower case 'b' to show his contempt for him as a leading artist, critic and art historian.

12. In February 1910, Meyerhold danced the role of Pierrot in the first production of

Fokine's ballet, *Carnaval*, at a ball organised by the St Petersburg journal, *Satiricon*.

13. Khlebnikov's narrative verse *I and Ye* (1911, 1912) reveals his interest in primaeval times, in the gods of pagan Russia, in Shamanism and folk cults. His linguistic experiments resulted primarily from his attempts to get back to the earliest stage of linguistic evolution.

14. The plastic forms of motionless theatre, whereby Maeterlinck's interior monologue was expressed on stage in Meyerhold's productions, was exemplified by stylised groupings in the manner of bas-reliefs, and movement in slow motion.

15. Meyerhold directed Maeterlinck's play, *La Mort de Tintagiles* at the Theatre Studio in Povarskaya Street, Moscow, and *Soeur Beatrice* at Vera Komissarzhevskaya's theatre in St Petersburg. Both stagings were based on stylised groupings and movement in slow motion reminiscent of the forms of ancient bas-reliefs.

16. The bas-relief, that came to characterise symbolist theatre, was apparent in opera and ballet stagings of the same period. As a stylistic device, it wove its way into dance theatre, notably Nijinsky's innovative *L'Après-midi d'un faune* of 1912. It has been maintained that the frieze-like design and two-dimensional choreography was in response to archaic Greece. Bakst, who designed the ballet, had previously undertaken some organisation of Vera Komissarzhevskaya's theatre with Meyerhold in 1906. *Faune* may be recognised as a translation of the 'motionless theatre' of the symbolists.

17. Maeterlinck's early cycle of dramas were designated as 'plays for marionettes': *L'Intérieur* (1890), *Les Aveugles* (1890) and *L'Intérieur* (1894). These neo-mysteries, which dramatised man's spiritual fears and longings, became models for symbolist drama.

18. For evaluations of Nijinsky's characterisation of the Petrouchka role, see Lieven (1936), Massine (1968), Krasovskaya (1979) and Nijinska (1982).

19. Greek dramas were staged at the Alexandrinsky Theatre in St Petersburg, notably Euripides' *Hippolytus* (1902) and Sophocles' *Oedipus at Colonus* (1904). Bakst and Fokine created settings, costumes and choreography that found inspiration in archaic art for *Narcisse* (1911) and *Daphnis and Chloe* (1912). Richard Strauss's opera *Elektra* was directed by Meyerhold at the Maryinsky in 1913.

20. Gorsky's reform of ballet began in 1900 with its revival of *Don Quixote* at the Bolshoi Theatre, when he treated the whole ensemble on the stage as members of a 'choreographic drama, according to the principles of the Art Theatre' (Roslavleva 1965).

21. The founders of the Starinny teatr were Nikolai Evreinov and Nikolai Vasil 'evic Driezen, who determined that the staging of the first season of plays (1907-08) should be in the manner of the Middle Ages so that each performance of the liturgical dramas and mysteries was accompanied by an on-stage audience made up of actors.

References

Aristotle (1980), *Poetics*, introduction and commentary by D. Lucas, Oxford, Clarendon Press.

Artaud, A. (1970), *The Theatre and its Double*, London, Calder.

Bakhtin, M. (1984), *Rabelais and his World*, Bloomington, Indiana University Press.

Barnes, C. (1957), 'Fokine Revival in London, *Petrouchka'*, *Dance and Dancers*, 7–11 May

Barnes, P. (1970), 'City Centre Joffrey Ballet at the New York City Centre', *Dance and Dancers*, June: 50–1.

Beaumont, C. (1949), *Complete Book of Ballets*, London, Putnam.

Benois, A. (1912), Review of Hamlet, *Rech'*, 6 April.

――――― (1941), *Reminiscences of the Russian Ballet*, London, Putnam.

――――― (1960, 1964), *Memoirs*, 1, 2, London, Chatto & Windus.

Blok, A. (1986), 'The Puppet Show', in M. Green (ed.), *The Russian Symbolist Theatre: An Anthology of Plays and Critical Texts*, Ann Arbor, Ardis: 47–57.

Braun, E. (ed.) (1969), *Meyerhold on Theatre*, London, Methuen.

――――― (1982), *The Director and the Stage: From Naturalism to Growtowski*, London, Methuen.

――――― (1986), *The Theatre of Meyerhold: Revolution on the Modern Stage*, London, Methuen.

Brussel, R. (1911), 'Théâtre du Châtelet: *Petrouchka'*, *Le Figaro*, 17 June: 6.

Bryusov, V. (1986), 'Unnecessary Truth: *Mir iskusstva'* (1902), in M. Green *The Russian Symbolist Theatre: An Anthology of Plays and Critical Texts*, Ann Arbor, Ardis: 25–30.

Clarke, M. (1957), 'The Royal Ballet in *Petrouchka'*, *Dancing Times*, May,: 355–7.

Coton, A. (1957), 'London Ballet Month', *Ballet Today*, May: 5–19.

Crooks, R. (1993), 'Double Suture: A Semiotic Approach to Film Reception', *American Journal of Semiotics*, 10, 3–4: 109–33.

De Marinis, M. (1993), *The Semiotics of Performance*, Bloomington, Indiana University Press.

Deak, F. (1982), 'Meyerhold's Staging of Sister Beatrice', *The Drama Review*, 26:1, Spring: 42–50.

Fokine, M. (1914), 'The new Russian Ballet Conventions in dancing M. Fokine's principles and aims,' to the editor of *The Times*, *The Times*, 6 July.

Green, M. (ed.) (1986), *The Russian Symbolist Theatre: An Anthology of Plays and Critical Texts*, Ann Arbor, Ardis.

Habermas, J. (1983), 'Modernity – An Incomplete Project', in H. Foster (ed.) *The Anti Aesthetic: Essays on Postmodern Culture*, Port Townsend, Washington, Bay Press: 3–15.

Hall, F. (1958), 'London Reviews Helpmann's ballets', *Ballet Today*, June: 4–5.

Hornby, R. (1986), *Drama, Metadrama and Perception*, London, Associates University Presses.

Hubbs, J. (1988), *Mother Russia: Feminine Myth in Russian Culture*, Bloomington, Indiana University Press.

Innes, C. (1993), *Avant-garde Theatre, 1892–1992*, London, Routledge.

Krasovskaya, V. (1979), *Nijinsky*, New York, Dance Horizons.

Lawson, J. (1957), 'Memories of Petrouchka', *Dancing Times*, May: 359.

Lieven, P. (1936), *The Birth of the Ballets Russes*, London, Allen & Unwin.

Maeterlinck, M. (1986), 'Le Tragique Quotidien' in *Le Trésor des humbles*, Paris, Société du mercure de France: 179–201.

Massine, L. (1968), *My Life in Ballet*, London, Macmillan.

Monahan, J. (1963), 'Firebird and Petrouchka', *Dancing Times*, April: 404–5.

Nijinska, B. (1982), *Bronislava Nijinska: Early Memoirs*, ed. and trans. I. Nijinska, I.

& J. Rawlinson, London, Faber.

Percival, J. (1992), 'Winning Tricks: Birmingham Royal Ballet Sadler's Wells in Life and Times, *The Times*, 31 March.

Postlewait, T. (1992), 'History, hermeneutics, and narrativity', in J. Reinelt & J. Roach (eds), *Critical Theory and Performance*, Ann Arbor, University of Michigan Press: 356–68.

Roslavleva, N. (1965), 'Stanislavsky and the Ballet', *Dance Perspectives*, 23.

Rudnitsky, K. (1981), *Meyerhold the Director*, Ann Arbor, Ardis.

Salerno, H. (ed.) (1992), *Scenarios of the Commedia Dell'Arte Flaminio Scalals ll Teatro delle Favole Rappresentative*, New York, Limelight.

Schechner, R. (1992), 'Invasions Friendly and Unfriendly: The Dramaturgy of Direct theatre', J. Reinelt & J. Roach (eds), *Critical Theory and Performance*, Ann Arbor, University of Michigan Press: 88–106.

Segal, H. (1970), *Twentieth-Century Russian Drama: From Corky to the Present*, New York, Columbia University Press.

——— (1987), *Turn of the Century Cabaret*, New York, Columbia University Press.

Senelick, L. (1982), *Craig's Moscow Hamlet*, London, Greenwood Press.

Serlio, S. (1545), *Regole generali di architettura*, Book 2, Paris.

Sheridan, H. (1958), 'Royal Ballet Season in New York', *Ballet Today*, February: 4.

'The Sitter Out' (1950), Review, *Dancing Times*, December: 115–6.

Slonim, M. (1961), *Russian Theatre from the Empire to the Soviets*, London, Methuen.

Sokolov, Y. (1966), *Russian Folklore*, Hatboro, Pennsylvania, Folklore Association.

Sokolova, L. (1963), 'Sokolova Speaks Out: The Sad Condition of Fokine's Ballets', *Dancing Times*, June: 519.

Sorley Walker, K. (1995), 'A Quartet of Stravinsky ballets', *Dancing Times*, May: 772–3.

Stanislavsky, C. (1924, 1948), *My Life in Art*, London, Bles.

Varneke, B. (1951), *History of the Russian Theatre*, trans. B. Brasol, New York, Macmillan.

Vernadsky, G. (1959), *The Origins of Russia*, Oxford, Clarendon Press.

Wagner, R. (1914), *Gesammelte Schriften und Dichtung*, ed. Golther, Berlin.

Wiley, R. (1980–81), 'Alexandre Benois' Commentaries on the Frst Saison Russes', *Dancing Times*, October 1980: 28–30; November 1980: 102–4; December 1980: 176–7; January 1981: 250–1; February 1981: 320; March 1981: 390–22; April 1981: 464–5; May 1981: 536–37.

Williams, P. (1972), 'London Festival Ballet at the New Victoria Theatre', *Dance and Dancers*, March: 44.

Zuguta, R. (1974), 'Origins of the Russian Puppet Theatre: An Alternative Hypothesis', *Slavic Review*, 33:4, December: 708–20

——— (1978), *Russian Minstrels: A History of the Skomorokhi*, Oxford, Clarendon Press.

3

Dance, Music and Literature

The Construction of Meanings through an Interplay
of Texts in Siobhan Davies's *Bridge the Distance*

Sophia Preston

Bridge the Distance was made in 1985 by one of Britain's leading choreographers, Siobhan Davies, for London Contemporary Dance Theatre. It is set to Benjamin Britten's String Quartet no. 3 op. 94 (1975) written just a year before he died. It is well known that the quartet contains musical quotations from Britten's last opera *Death in Venice* op. 88 (1973), with a libretto (by Myfanwy Piper) which is closely derived from the novella of the same name by Thomas Mann, written in 1912. Musicologists have frequently constructed an iconography of musical motifs, tonalities and devices in Britten's oeuvre (Matthews 1987; Palmer 1984; Whittall 1990) and a parallel attempt is made in this reading to suggest a similarly rich mosaic of associations and references in Davies's choreography. The position argued for here is that the more a reader knows of the range of possible references and associations a work carries, the greater her ability to construct appropriate readings and create interpretations of it.

The suggestion that there can be more (and less) appropriate readings of a dance immediately calls into question the possibility of an infinite range of readings of an artwork.[1] It also implies that the work itself may generate meanings that are to a certain extent determined by the choreographer. This seems not only to deny Barthes' 'death of the author' (1968) but also to engage in an intentionalist fallacy. Barthes writes that

> a text is made up of multiple writings, drawn from many cultures and entering into mutual relations of dialogue, parody, contestation but there is one place where this multiplicity is focused and that place is the reader, not, as was hitherto said, the author.
> (Barthes 1977: 148)

He was writing (thirty years ago) in reaction to 'classic criticism' which, he said, 'has never paid any attention to the reader; for it, the writer is the only person in literature' (*ibid.*). 'The author' has since suffered such a complete demise, however, that I am here simply reviving her to the status Barthes himself allowed, that of a mixer of writings 'none of them original' (*ibid.*: 146). While artists cannot control the generation of texts and intertexts in their work, since this is so much a part of the active role of the reader, the author does have a degree of control over how texts are seen in relation to each other in a reading which is not, to use Worton's phrase, a 'wilful misreading' (Worton 1994, np).

In *S/Z* Barthes sets up a distinction between those texts he considers *scriptible* ('writerly', that is, those that invite the reader to write them anew on each reading) and those he calls *lisible* ('readerly'). He asks,

> Why is the writerly our value? Because the goal of literary work (of literature as work) is to make the reader no longer a consumer, but a producer of the text ... Opposite the writerly text then is its countervalue, its negative, reactive value: what can be read but not written: the *readerly*. We call any readerly text a classic text. (Barthes 1975: 4)

In this 'close reading' of *Bridge the Distance* I might seem to be suggesting that it is a more *lisible* than *scriptible* text in that I relate the movements and apparent relationships on stage directly to the references and associations set up by the music. This is not a 'closed' reading, however, but one in which texts generated by tracing the references and associations brought by the dance, music, novella and other related artworks are juxtaposed to form intertexts which play on one another forming a complex and apparently ever-expanding web. The reader is thus the active producer of the text that Barthes calls for, while at the same time acknowledging that the intertexts are generated by a response to the *dance*.

To return to the biographical threads of this intertextual web, Davies (born in 1950) initially studied sculpture (at the Hammersmith College of Building and Design) but in 1967 took classes in Graham technique with the newly-founded Contemporary Ballet Trust in London. Davies took part in the very first performances of the company, which later became London Contemporary Dance Theatre, and went on to become a leading dancer, Associate Choreographer (in 1974), and one of a triumvirate of directors, in 1982. From 1981 onwards, however, Davies has also developed her work with her own independent companies: Siobhan Davies and Dancers in 1981; Second Stride, which she co-directed with Ian Spink from 1982–85; and, since 1988, the Siobhan Davies Dance Company.

Davies's choreography to date can be divided into three periods which reflect not only her changing company positions but also the ways in which she has worked with music (Preston 1995). Both these factors have an effect on the texts to be found within her works. The context within which Davies has made and presented her work has influenced not only her choice of subject matter and

Siobhan Davies's *Bridge the Distance.*   Photo: David Buckland

treatment (the textual matter of the dance) but also the way in which it has been viewed, and therefore the texts generated by its reception.

In the first period of Davies's choreography, from 1972 to 1980, all but two pieces were made for London Contemporary Dance Theatre, and all involved commissioned music or musical arrangements with the composer working closely alongside Davies. Davies created dance phrases before the music was added, which meant that she could work independently of musical timing. She remembers thinking

> that I'd never learn that area of my craft if I constantly adopted the dominant shape of the music itself or the dominant rhythm. I would never have learned that, with breath, dance has its own phrasing.   (Davies 1984: 16)

Whilst a viewing of these early works reveals the independence of the dance in terms of timing, the music can be seen to be devised specifically to support the dance's qualities. The music can, and does, still carry associations from other works by the same composer, other works in the same genre and any other associations sparked off in the listener's mind. The sophisticated web of specific references, allusions and even citations which might be brought by a pre-existing piece of music is, however, unlikely to be found in music written especially for the dance.

An important thread in constructing a reading of Davies's work is the aesthetic context of the making and initial viewing of the work. A study of the movement vocabulary Davies trained in, performed and saw, combined with the typical subject matter being dealt with in companies she worked with, not only provides an insight into how she developed her own choreographic material but also sets a historical context for the reception of her work. In 1976 Davies took a sabbatical in order to study and perform in New York. She remembers these months as a time when she

> started moving away from the support of LCDT . . . doing a lot of ballet classes and a lot of Cunningham classes, and simply seeing . . . two or three New York dance performances every night, and having a lot of one's preconceived ideas changed just by exposure to the different works.
>
> (Davies 1984: 37)

Davies's work, when she returned from New York, reflected an increased desire on her part to find a choreographic identity separate from London Contemporary Dance Theatre.[2] She had already extended her choreographic vocabulary from the strong Graham influence she received through the company, both by watching as many Cunningham performances as possible and through a determination 'not to use always accepted dance movements' (Davies, cited in Gow 1976: 142). Davies's works in this period are characterised by what one critic called 'an enchantingly light touch' (Williams 1974: 32), with subjects far removed from the mythic grandeur and psychological angst of much of the company work.

Davies's first work, *Relay* (1972), took 'images from running, hurdling, boxing, wrestling, tennis . . . and even boating' (Percival 1972: 46). In *Pilot* (1974) Davies can be seen to be dealing with images and feelings from her own everyday life on tour, and she reports that she was also influenced by books about railway stations and train journeys through India and Afghanistan which provided what Davies called 'the starting off points . . . somebody just quietly playing something in a corner, and waiting, and the train never coming, and the hot and dusty air' (cited in Gow 1976: 142). Davies continued to draw on her own life experience in her next work, *Diary* (1975), and she herself questioned 'why should one always deal with large-scale events? . . . One could actually deal with something small and still it would say a lot in the piece' (1984: 7).

The second period identified in Davies's work to date (Preston 1995) extends from 1981, when Davies formed her own part-time company, to 1987, when she made a second, longer trip to North America with the first Fulbright scholarship ever awarded to a choreographer. In one year (between 1986 and 1987) Davies made three final works for London Contemporary Dance Theatre in rapid succession, before leaving the company.[3] These three works stand almost as a separate group within Davies's *oeuvre* employing the minimalist music she was to favour on her return from North America. The two works she made in 1985 can thus be seen to mark the end of a move towards more literal content in Davies's choreography in this second period. The final dance Davies made for Second Stride, *The School for Lovers Danced* (1985), is the only work to date in which Davies has given her dancers the names of specific characters.[4] The extent to which two of the dancers in *Bridge the Distance*, made in the same year, can be identified with characters from associated artworks is a determining factor in the construction of one of the texts called into play in this reading.

Another aspect which makes the second period of Davies's work distinctive is that (with one exception) all the work uses pre-existing rather than commissioned music.[5] In the third period identified here, from 1988 to 1998 Davies has renewed her earlier practice of commissioning music for her works, as well as using existing scores. On a number of occasions she has combined both practices, working with the composer on the selection of parts of their earlier scores to construct the music for her work. In this case some of the interplay of texts can be seen to be controlled by the composer as well as the choreographer. In the mixed-media nature of dance the 'author' may be some combination of choreographer, composer, performer, designer, director and editor/producer. In Davies's works to date, however, she has always retained overall control of the piece.[6] To the extent that the authorial intention is acknowledged in a reading of a Davies work, therefore, that author is Davies herself.

Whilst this brief categorisation of Davies's choreography into three periods provides one framework onto which *Bridge the Distance* can be placed, identifying it as one of the last works to be made for the company with which she trained and developed, there are many other frames of reference within which the work can be seen. In the case of *Bridge the Distance* these references and associations are brought to the work by both the dance and the music. The direct musical quotations make the link between the quartet and the opera in Britten's own mind clear, but there are also indirect links, through motifs and tonalities, which suffuse the whole quartet with intimations of the opera and also other related works by Britten.

The opera libretto contains philosophical soliloquies (similar to those in Mann's novella) for the central figure Aschenbach, an eminent writer tormented by his love for a beautiful young boy. The boy, Tadzio, is (as in Mann's narrative) wordless, and is represented in the opera by a young male dancer. Both Davies and Britten also make reference more directly to life, in the dance and quartet respectively, employing associations with what Stephen Davies refers to as 'emotion characteristics in appearances' (1994: 239). Stephen Davies contends that in the relationship between music and emotion,

the analogy resides in the manner in which these things are experienced rather than being based on some inference attempting to establish a symbolic relation between particular parts of the music and particular bits of human behavior. Emotions are heard in music as belonging to it, just as appearances of emotions are present in the bearing, gait, or deportment of our fellow humans and other creatures. The range of emotions music is heard as presenting in this manner is restricted, as is also true for human appearances, to those emotions or moods having characteristic behavioral expressions: music presents the outward features of sadness or happiness in general.

(Davies 1994: 239)

This conclusion on how music can be expressive of emotion does, of course, assume that 'human movement, gait or bearing' is itself inherently expressive, an assumption which has been questioned by those working in the field of cultural differences in body-space awareness (proxemics) and gestural codes (Hall 1969; Williams 1991). It can be seen, however, that Davies employs the codes of Western (indeed, in terms of space, specifically English) late twentieth-century behaviour in her choreography.[7] Some movements in *Bridge the Distance* can be identified as gestures with a meaning apparent to all who share those codes. For example, in the fourth section of the dance, when Lauren Potter swings her right arm across her body at Darshan Singh Bhuller's head level, only missing him because he has just ducked out of the way, she looks as though she meant to strike him. In the same section Singh Bhuller lifts his shoulders momentarily in a shrug that, *given the content and context of the dance*, seems Italian. It is immediately apparent (from my emphasis) that any reading of a dance is constructed from both the viewer's own awareness of different references and the connections she chooses to make between them. In this reading I am following associations that are signalled by the music and connecting them not only back to the dance but also out to a wider network of texts. It is an intimation of the type of intertextuality being employed here that I am concerned to determine to what extent these more far-reaching strands can be appropriately woven into a reading of the dance. The first place to look for external references carried by this particular dance is in the music.

In the introduction to the final movement of the quartet, 'Recitative', there are five direct musical quotations from the opera. The first is an extended solo phrase for the 'cello that echoes the dipping rhythm and pitch contours of the music which accompanies Aschenbach's first, mysterious gondola journey (see Ex. 1).

The same music is heard in both the Venice overture (Rehearsal number 41) and in Scene 9 of the opera when Aschenbach crosses to Venice in order to remain as close as possible to Tadzio and his family (see Ex. 2). In both versions the bass line reiterates a pedal note of A, which in Scene 9 descends to G in the second bar and then, through F, to E-flat in the third. In the quartet the 'cello line

Ex. I. Bars 1–3 of the final movement of Britten's String Quartet No. 3.

twice reaches up to an E-flat (or D-sharp) and finally floats away to a high harmonic A. The original pedal A is significant in the tonal scheme of the opera as Tadzio's key, which, as Roseberry points out, is

> so strong . . . that it may well seem a more strongly affirmed tonal presence than that of Aschenbach's original E major, and therefore an alternative 'tonic' to which Aschenbach's E major functions as a kind of 'dominant' preparation. (Roseberry 1987: 90)

Thus the reiterated A in the Venice Overture music can be thought to reveal Aschenbach's subconscious awareness that he is crossing to Venice specifically to seek out Tadzio.

Christopher Palmer's essay 'Towards a genealogy of *Death in Venice*' (1984) (which provided the starting point for this reading) extends the significance of Britten's use of A as a tonal centre to other works dealing with similar subjects throughout his career, not only his first opera *Peter Grimes* (1945) and the later *Billy Budd* (1951), but also

Ex. 2. Rehearsal no. 201 (opening of scene 9) of Britten's opera *Death in Venice*.

> *Young Apollo* . . . composed in 1939 (but published only in 1982) . . . *Young Apollo* begins with . . . an empty and (because deprived of its third) indeterminate chord of A, prolonged through a total of thirty-two bars . . . This is the elemental backdrop, the 'state of nature'. Then the thunderbolt, the irruption of primordial light: sparkling rills burst from the piano, rippling wave-like major scales . . . The intermingled musical images of water and light are unmistakable . . . The Apollonian key of A major, with the Lydian sharpened fourth [D-sharp], the key in Britten not merely of light but of *light on water* [Palmer's emphasis]. So it is no surprise to discover that A major, Lydian fourth and all, is the key of the sea music that begins and ends *Grimes*.
>
> (Palmer 1984: 112)

Mann makes repeated references to Apollo in his novella, conflating his image of Tadzio running out of the sea 'with dripping locks and beautiful as a young god' (Mann 1993: 227) with Aschenbach's dawn visions in which 'with the splendour of the god irradiating him the lone watcher . . . closed his eyes and let the glory kiss his eyelids' (*ibid.*: 242). Whilst watching Tadzio, Aschenbach recalls the myth of Hyacinthus, loved not only by Thamyris 'the first man who ever wooed one of his own sex – but [also] by Apollo himself, the first God ever to do so' (Graves 1985: 36).

Peter Grimes, Billy Budd and *Death in Venice* not only have in common that they deal with sea and sunlight but also that they stand as clear examples of a recurring theme in Britten's work, that of the death of an innocent, usually a young boy.[8] Mellers suggests that aspects of Britten's own life pervaded his writing, contending that, in dealing with innocence and persecution Britten knew what he knew, both from his obsession with the presumptive Eden of his childhood and from the alienation caused by his homosexuality. The grandest, most tragic statement of this motif is in *Peter Grimes*, the opera that made him famous . . . while its most explicitly poignant revelation occurs in *Death in Venice*, in several senses his consummatory work. (Mellers 1984: 97)

In *Death in Venice* it is Aschenbach who dies, rather than the beautiful young boy. Mann makes it clear that Aschenbach is not simply in awe of the boy's beauty but in love with the boy himself, a love he knows to be shocking, if not sinful. When Aschenbach realises that Tadzio's family is calling the boy away from him Mann writes that 'although his pride writhed . . . under the appalling insult that this implied, he could not in conscience deny its justice' (Mann 1993: 252). Ronald Duncan contends that Britten was 'a man in flight from himself . . . he was a man on a rack' (Duncan 1981: 27–8). In Britten's opera of *Death in Venice* Aschenbach can be seen as the innocent victim of his infatuation just as Britten was of his sexuality.[9]

In Piper's libretto Aschenbach's moment of self-awareness, mixed with self-loathing, is conflated with two other crucial points in the book, the moment when Aschenbach realises he is quite unable to communicate naturally or easily with Tadzio, and Tadzio's fateful smile which leads to Aschenbach's undoing. The second quotation in the quartet's 'Recitative' (see Ex. 3) is taken from this point in the opera and all the other passages in which Aschenbach follows the Polish family around Venice.

The solo violin line in the quartet follows the same contours, and at one point exactly the same pitches, as when Aschenbach sings 'So longing passes back and forth between life and the mind'. Over these first two quotations referring to Aschenbach's infatuated pursuit of Tadzio/Apollo and his self-conscious awareness of the boy, Davies sets a solo which she made specifically for Patrick Harding-Irmer, a dancer she had worked closely with for some fifteen years, and whose maturity in performance she greatly admired.[10]

In the first quotation Harding-Irmer repeatedly raises both arms and arches back slightly, only to drop his elbows in a sudden movement drawing the backs of his hands towards his face as if shielding his eyes from the sun. He continuously alternates between outward-reaching, pointing or yearning movements and a pulling-inwards of the limbs accompanied by a clenching of fists and contraction of the diaphragm. A number of times his arms are lifted awkwardly behind his back with his hands again in fists as though he is constraining himself. A viewer's own experience of similar movements will very likely lead to conclusions about the character's constant vacillation between two states. A knowledge of Mann's conflation of Tadzio and Apollo and Britten's echo of this in his use of tonality heard at this point in both the opera and the quartet,

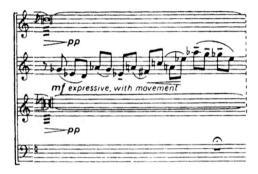

Ex. 3. Bar 7 of the final movement of Britten's String Quartet No. 3.

colours and delineates these more generalised emotional qualities with specific images and resonances.

Harding-Irmer ends the first quotation by reaching out with his right arm in the same direction he is walking, as if wanting to approach and touch someone. He comes to a standstill, however, and turns back to walk slowly in the opposite direction. Over the second quotation he half reaches out again but turns it into the classical gesture for beauty, circling his hand around his face before turning himself to point far out and, yet again, to draw his arms high up behind his back.

Harding-Irmer goes on to curve his arm out in front of him as though placing it protectively around something or someone. The reference, made through the music, to the point when Aschenbach realises that he cares for the boy, means that there is a clear suggestion of who it is the dancer wants both to reach out to and to protect, without Davies ever making it overt. Neither Aschenbach nor Tadzio is named in programmes for *Bridge the Distance*, whereas the opera characters are identified in *The School for Lovers Danced* made in the same year. Indeed, there are many ways in which the dance is *not* 'about' the book. What is presented here, however, is not merely a protective gesture and a man at odds with himself but all the emotional resonances of Mann's novella and Britten's opera in addition to the moods evoked by the movements and their reference to life.

The third quotation from the opera also refers to Aschenbach's philosophical contemplations when the first violin plays *pizzicato* semiquavers that echo the harp motifs which accompany Aschenbach's 'Phaedrus' soliloquy in the opera. The harp figures themselves are taken from the melody of the chorus that accompanies a 'formal solo dance for Tadzio' in the opera score. The chorus are recounting the image of Socrates and Phaedrus whom Aschenbach sees in his mind's eye beneath

the old plane tree not far from the walls of Athens . . . On the grass which sloped down gently so that one could hold up one's head as one lay, there reclined two men, sheltered here from the heat of the noonday: one elderly and one young, one ugly and one beautiful, the wise beside the desirable.

(Mann 1993: 238)

A younger male dancer enters to echo some of Harding-Irmer's movements over the first *pizzicato* semiquavers. He dances short phrases in time to the violin entries and, as well as circling his own face with his hand, he also ends two phrases lying on his back in a relaxed position with his arms bent above his head on the floor. Whether he is suggesting Tadzio reclining on the beach or Phaedrus under the tree in Athens, or simply a younger man, more relaxed and in some way distanced from the older figure (who stands almost fully turned away from him), is dependent on the choice, and knowledge, of the viewer.

The sickness which pervades Venice and which destroys Aschenbach is called to mind in the fourth quotation in the quartet's 'Recitative' (see Ex. 4). In bar 16 the viola begins to sound the motif which, in the opera, becomes inextricably linked both to Aschenbach's own illness and the corruption that seems to be endemic to Venice. During this quotation both dancers move in turn; the young man again echoes some of the older man's movements and Harding-Irmer repeats fragments from his extended solo which forms the whole middle section of *Bridge the Distance*. The quotation of sickness and foreboding is melded into the final quotation, played by all the quartet in unison, of the 'I love you' motif which forms the revelatory climax of Act I of the opera (see Ex. 5).

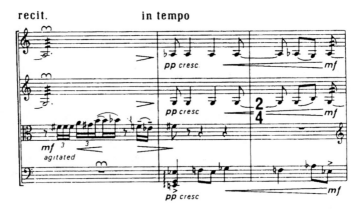

Ex. 4. Bars 16–19 of the final movement of Britten's String Quartet No. 3.

That Davies is aware of the significance of this motif is made clear by the fact that this is the only time in the dance when Harding-Irmer dances in unison with anyone else on stage. He and the younger man both perform a short three-movement phrase which starts with the left arm reaching diagonally upwards away from the body whilst they are in deep *plié* in second position, followed by a stretch across the body with the right arm, now standing upright, only to draw back, making a fist with the hand as it is pulled into the chest as the dancers turn back on themselves.

Harding-Irmer has performed individual movements from the phrase in both his long solo and in this introduction to the final section, and he performs it complete when the viola begins to move from the sickness motif to the 'I love you' motif, highlighting the similarity between the two musical quotations. He then waits in position ready for the younger man to 'catch up' and the two perform the phrase twice, the second time to the repeated falling major third 'love you' that Aschenbach sings so often at the beginning of the second act of the opera. Harding-Irmer turns back again just before the younger man so that they are facing each other for a moment at the point when other dancers begin to

Ex. 5. Bars 20–25 of the final movement of Britten's String Quartet No. 3.

enter the stage. The young man turns away, converting this final movement into a walk upstage where he subsequently lies on the floor again.

The whole passage is reminiscent of the moments in the novella when Aschenbach realises that Tadzio knows he is being followed but does not tell his mother, does not betray the older man. There are also the moments when Aschenbach thinks that perhaps Tadzio is moulding himself on Aschenbach's example, learning taste and decorum from him.[11] The young man's performance of Harding-Irmer's material, in particular the movement phrase that eventually becomes identified with the 'I love you' motif, acts as a physical metaphor for both suggestions in the novella.

In the novella the final image Aschenbach sees as he dies is of Tadzio walking into the sea, raising one arm towards the sinking sun. Mann writes that, to Aschenbach,

it was as if the pale and lovely soul-summoner out there were smiling to him,

beckoning to him; as if he loosed his hand from his hip and pointed outwards, hovering ahead and onwards, into an immensity rich with unutterable
expectation.   (Mann 1993: 267).

Intimations not only of characters but also of specific movements described by
Mann can therefore be identified in Davies's choreography.

A reading of the middle section 'Solo' reveals many more instances of Davies
apparently referring directly to Mann's text as well as reflecting the emotion of
both the music and the novella. To begin his solo which forms the whole middle
section of *Bridge the Distance*, Harding-Irmer enters the stage at the end of the
preceding 'Ostinato' section of the work, and stands motionless at the side with
his arms folded, looking on silently. This apparently causes all the others, who
have taken a 'proffered handshake' position, to withdraw, turning away from
him. Harding-Irmer walks to just beyond centre stage where he slowly folds one
arm and then the other across his diaphragm. The light that washes across the
stage to meet him is dimmer and warmer than that in the two sections either
side of the solo.

Harding-Irmer turns backwards out of this locked-in position, opening his
arms as though they are released by the turn. The music begins on the dancer's
cue as the turn begins, as though he has called it into existence, drawing it out
with his widening hands which eventually arrive at shoulder height, the palms
open to the audience. At a pivotal point in the novella, after his abortive attempt
to leave Venice, Aschenbach is described watching Tadzio from his hotel window and realising 'that it was because of Tadzio that it had been so hard for him
to leave' (Mann 1993: 233). Mann writes that Aschenbach

> sat quite still, quite unseen at his high vantage-point, and began to search his
> feelings. His features were alert, his eyebrows rose, an attentive, intelligently
> inquisitive smile parted his lips. Then he raised his head, and with his arms
> hanging limply down along the back of his chair, described with both of them
> a slowly rotating and lifting motion, the palms of his hands turning forward,
> as if to sketch an opening and outspreading of the arms. It was a gesture that
> gladly bade welcome, a gesture of calm acceptance.   (Mann 1993: 234)

There is a clear similarity between the first movement in the solo and Aschenbach's arm-opening, welcoming gesture, and a moment later Harding-Irmer
leans his upper body backward releasing a contraction and letting the lower
spine make a single straight line with his pelvis and torso. As his arms swing
back the whole of his upper body is rendered exposed, vulnerable; he is again in
a position described by Mann, both in the quotation above and at the moment
when Tadzio smiles at Aschenbach. Mann writes that Aschenbach is 'so deeply
shaken' that he seeks refuge in the darkened garden of the hotel, sinking down

on one of the seats, deliriously breathing the nocturnal fragrance of the flowers and trees. And leaning back, his arms hanging down, overwhelmed, trembling, shuddering all over, he whispered the standing formula of the heart's desire – impossible here, absurd, depraved, ludicrous and sacred nevertheless, still worthy of honour even here: 'I love you!'

(Mann 1993: 244)

Many times during the solo Harding-Irmer reaches a hand forward as if to shake hands with someone. This 'proffered handshake', which has already been seen at the end of the second section, recurs frequently both in this solo and in the final section of the dance when Harding-Irmer performs it towards other dancers. It is never reciprocated; indeed Harding-Irmer never makes any physical contact with the other dancers during the course of the piece. The gesture thus comes to symbolise the distance that is never bridged between the single (apparently older) figure and the couples in the work.

Both the lack of physical contact and the recurring positions with one hand tentatively reaching out echo Aschenbach's two failures to communicate with Tadzio in the novella. The first occurs when he considers it will be 'natural', 'irresistibly obvious' to exchange a few words with the boy on the way to the beach 'to lay his hand on his head or shoulder' (Mann 1993: 240), but in the event finds himself breathless and unable to speak. The second is when Aschenbach imagines warning the Polish family of the cholera epidemic when 'he might then lay his hand in farewell on the head of a mocking deity's instrument' (*ibid.*: 258) but senses 'an infinite distance between himself and any serious resolve to take such a step' (*ibid.*: 259).

These moments are also echoed in the dance after a faster middle section of the 'Solo' when, as the violin slows down, Harding-Irmer slowly lowers his full weight to rest on one hip on the floor. He pulls his right elbow slowly into his hip, sinking and rotating slightly away from his arm into the floor in a long anguished contraction as if in the first intimation of Aschenbach's hidden illness and imminent dissolution.

Harding-Irmer reaches out very slowly, very much as if to touch someone on the shoulder, but instead takes his arm across and out, tracing a line on the horizon. He takes his left, supporting, hand off the floor and sinks down deeper, only holding his shoulder and knees off the floor through a deep contraction. The image of Aschenbach watching Tadzio cross in front of him on the beach before collapsing back into his deck-chair comes inexorably to mind.

Throughout the solo Harding-Irmer repeatedly curves his upper body over to look down at the floor, sometimes standing tall, sometimes in a horizontal arabesque with his arms hanging down to the floor and, in the return to the slower music of this section, kneeling on the floor. Again this can be seen as a reference to an image from the novella as Mann describes Tadzio's smile as

Patrick Harding-Irmer in *Bridge the Distance*.   Photo: David Buckland

the smile of Narcissus as he bows his head over the mirroring water, that profound, fascinated, protracted smile with which he reaches out his arms towards the reflection of his own beauty.   (Mann 1993: 244)

Whittall suggests that

the Narcissus theme . . . applies not merely to Tadzio's image of himself, his self-love, but also to Aschenbach's hope that Tadzio might somehow see himself in Aschenbach.   (Whittall 1990: 260)

If Tadzio's smile towards Aschenbach is linked to the smile Narcissus gives to the reflection of his own beauty then Aschenbach can be seen as a personification of that beauty. Thus Harding-Irmer gazing at the floor with his arms reaching down is not emulating Tadzio but still echoing Aschenbach's thoughts about himself and the boy.

The extent to which the movements of the dance 'reflect' motifs of the novella and opera is still open to question. Connections such as those outlined above between the dance, the quartet, the opera and the novella may be consciously created by the choreographer, exist *in* the work, and/or be constructed by the reader. It is undeniable, however, that the connections are there, and whether Davies knowingly reflected descriptions of movement in the novella in her dance or simply alighted on similar movement images to portray related emotions does not necessarily affect the reading. Once the viewer has made such intertextual connections it is both appropriate and rewarding to pursue them. That it is appropriate is clear from the evidence that Davies is using more than the acoustic qualities of the music in *Bridge the Distance*. The reward comes from the added definition and therefore stronger identification both of, and with, the situations being portrayed.

Another network of identifiable resonances can be added to an interpretation of *Bridge the Distance* through the investigation of the movements in terms of Davies's other work. Palmer (1984) is able to build up an iconography of Britten's compositional style which gives rise to a series of references in *Death in Venice* that are both detailed and far-reaching. A similar exercise carried out on Davies's oeuvre allows another text to be constructed that can be brought into play in this reading.

While there is no direct link in *Bridge the Distance* to other specific dances (as there is in the music) there are, however, discernible references both to the movement vocabulary employed by Davies in a number of other pieces and to gestures found in everyday life. A survey of the former can lead to specific meanings when, for example, the other works carry a text or an overt 'programme'. Even when this is not the case, the recognition of movements can help to place *Bridge the Distance* very specifically in the context of Davies's own choreographic style and that of colleagues working in similar styles. An examination of the references to movements found in life outside the dance takes us into the problematic realm of non-verbal communication with all the pitfalls of ambiguity and possible assumptions of 'universality'. Having established the context within which Davies is working (and being viewed), however, there are clear associations to be made, leading to appropriate interpretations of meaning.

Harding-Irmer ends the initial movement of his solo in a cruciform position he regains at many points. This is a recurrent position in Davies's choreography and the first section of *Bridge the Distance* also contains many wide arm positions with the arms in line with the shoulder girdle. To a certain extent this can be read simply as a conventional modern dance position, influenced as much by Cunningham as Graham, and not necessarily evocative of any specific imagery. On the other hand Davies has used the position to refer to aeroplanes and flight, in *Pilot* (1974), and with religious connotations in *Plain Song* (1980). In this instance the position can be seen to carry resonances of Aschenbach's torment over his 'depraved', yet 'sacred' love (an inner conflict also identified in Britten's experience) whilst also being one of the more expansive, open positions of the solo, the culmination of Aschenbach's opening, welcoming arms, perhaps.

One position which recurs in a number of Davies's works (including *Bridge the Distance*) can serve as an example of ways in which meanings can cross-reference between works, adding extra resonances to their appearance in any one work. In *Bridge the Distance* it occurs near the end of the first section, taken up firstly by two couples as part of a shared phrase, then held by one couple towards the end of the section and then by all the other three. In this support, or counterbalance, the woman allows her weight to lean forwards away from the man whilst she still has one leg wrapped around one of his. He, correspondingly, leans his weight back slightly and has an arm across the front of her hips to stop her falling. This arm also, of course, stops her from stepping forwards in the direction of her focus, as does the awkwardly held leg. This image, in which the woman is reaching out, being at once held back by her partner, but also able to lean further out in the direction she wants to move because of his support, is both powerful and frequent in Davies's work.

There are telling examples in the three works Davies made immediately after nursing her husband through a near-fatal illness on their return from the USA in 1988. In *White Man Sleeps* (1988) there is a duet nine-and-a-half minutes into the work, which begins with the woman shooting her arms forward through space at shoulder level with the palms joined, in a long horizontal arabesque, only to be caught at the hips by the man who counterbalances her forwards momentum by pulling back with his own weight. The whole duet is a series of manoeuvres in which the woman's progress is held back by the man, who at one point pushes back against her forehead bringing her focus downwards.

In the final duet of the television version of *Wyoming* (1988) when the woman's voice has told us 'I let him in' the shared phrases, which send the two dancers skimming across the stage in a physical enjoyment of each others' movement material, come to a standstill. The man holds the woman's hips and counterbalances her weight as she slowly leans further and further forward as if trying to escape, or test his hold on her. In the stage version of *Wyoming* the couple are facing downstage with the woman focusing out into the audience, giving a compelling personal immediacy to her situation.

A similar position is crucial to *Embarque* (1988), which features a central duet for a couple who have the stage space alone for five minutes of the fifteen-minute dance. In their duet the woman is not only held back by the man as she reaches out but she is even carried back by him, a few paces at a time, up the diagonal of the stage to the far upstage right corner. Indeed, the final glimpse we have of them at the very end of the work, which has also been their opening position incorporates the same imagery with the woman reaching and focusing out, away from the man. There are clear references that can be drawn from the simple fact of being held back whilst reaching and focusing outwards away from a partner. The extent to which it might be appropriate also to read this as a suggestion that women's frustrations and inability to fulfil themselves might be bound up with their need for support is another question. Similar positions can also be found in another work with a text, made for Second Stride in 1983, just two years before *Bridge the Distance, Minor Characters*.

In *Minor Characters* positions in which one partner (usually but not always a woman) is held back, counterbalanced and supported by another, appear in a number of different forms just after a text has been spoken hinting at missed opportunities and a lack of fulfilment in a woman's life. Two women hold a conversation either side of a solo female dancer whilst she remains inactive between them.

> 'Doesn't she remind you of someone?'
> 'Yes! Whatever happened to her?'
> 'She married. Working.'
> 'Do you remember how crazy she was?'

The woman breaks out to dance a solo full of little leaps and fast, circling arm movements. The speakers continue:

> 'That laugh of hers came from way down.'
> 'I cannot imagine her settling down and being locked into a family situation for the rest of her life.'

Both the narrators and the woman are still for a moment, they go to her and appear to examine her, one pulling her head back into an exposed vulnerable position. The woman raises her arms straight in front of her with her hands hanging to the floor, then again turns away from them to leap across the front of the stage with both arms circling rapidly backwards (against the direction of her passage).

The narrators repeat the previous sentence, splitting it up between them. Then they continue:

'Maybe she got a job – that takes up a lot of her time?'
'One where she could use her imagination.'
'Her enthusiasm, curiosity.'

The woman walks to the narrators and physically pushes them into a new position ending on *demi-pointe* with a hand on each narrator's shoulder, turning as they walk around her in a circle. The narrators talk whilst walking.

'She travels a lot.'
'Didn't she want to go around the world on a boat?'
'We were all going.'

As the narrators confess 'we were all going' (that we have all failed to fulfil *all* our youthful ambitions) the woman drops her arms to turn on her own axis and raises them again with the narrators a little closer to her so that she has an arm across the collar bone of each one. They all take a few paces (the dancer backwards, the speakers forwards) until the woman appears to halt their progress and leans forward into the other two. The three women are held in a stasis, leaning their weight against each other, with a clear correlation between a lack of progression across the stage and unfulfilled potential in life.

A male dancer enters and takes the woman's hand. The other two women depart and the man and woman begin to counterbalance each other's weight sideways. There follows a duet full of counterbalances in which one member of the couple reaches and leans outwards, being held back by the other. In this duet the two dancers alternate roles in this counterbalance but this duet is followed by another, which still seems to be related to the same text in that the second pair enter paralleling the position then being taken by the first couple.[12]

The second duet, which also has many links to the duets in the first section of *Bridge the Distance*, has a number of different supports, all with the woman reaching and focusing away from the man but being both counterbalanced and held back by him. The duet comes to a stillness when the woman is apparently trapped, her arm held across her own body pulling against the man's restraining hand as he lies on the floor, and looking out as though to a far, unattainable horizon. The woman breaks out of this position to dance a solo behind the man, who remains lying on the floor, only to return to him and the same position. The couple then repeat their duet, at the end of which the man breaks out into a solo whilst the woman moves upstage into the shadows.

At the end of his solo the man lifts the woman into a duet which has a number of transitory supports of the man by the woman until they end in the same counterbalanced and constricted position as at the beginning and end of her solo. She is only freed from this stasis by the man of the first couple who runs over to lift her away from her partner on the floor, who is in turn lifted to his feet by the woman of the first couple.

What I am proposing is that it is possible to support a reading of one work with references to others in which the same issues are apparently being addressed. I want to stress that I am *not* suggesting that in Davies's work a particular position or movement 'means' a particular thing or emotion. It is easy to imagine the same movements being used to a very different end, but when a dance contains 'characteristics in appearances' of a particular emotion, a knowledge of other works by the same choreographer, in a similar area, can add shades of much more specific meaning which colour the interpretation of the work being viewed.

An example of a recurring device which carries *different* emotional qualities in different contexts also appears in the *Minor Characters* duet detailed above. When the man breaks into his solo he appears bereft of the woman's weight, repeatedly holding off-centred suspensions and even going through his half of their duet positions such as when he is raised from the floor and when he is lifting her over his back. This is a device which also appears early on in *Bridge the Distance* when the second duet phrase is repeated by both couples with one couple divided by the other three couples.

In a number of works Davies has divided a duet so that one or both partners have to try to perform the movement material without the physical support (to counterbalance, support or lift) of the other one. Perhaps the most moving, certainly the most explicit, version of this device occurs in *Different Trains* (1990). The text of Steve Reich's eponymous String Quartet has just told the story of 'one girl, and she had a beautiful voice, and when she stopped singing the guards clapped and shouted "more, more".' One dancer takes on the American Sign Language signs for 'girl' and 'beautiful voice' and dances a duet with the man who has been signing her story, skimming in a large quadrangle around the stage in long, low, sweeping lifts and balances. She is then left alone and tries to retrace the line on her own, unable to maintain the same balances or cover the distance in the air without support. She walks towards the audience repeating the sign for 'a beautiful voice' coming to a standstill as the piece ends with the horrific (but unstated) knowledge of her death.

The man's off-balance solo in *Minor Characters* also seems to demonstrate his need of the woman and he ends by running to her and lifting her around on his hip to begin their duet again. The split duet in the first section of *Bridge the*

Distance is abstract in comparison. One couple perform, as nearly as they can, the same movements as the other three couples when they all repeat a phrase (starting at bar 29). The phrase in its original duet form only has two lifts, which are turned into low hops by the woman and slow *passé* turns by the man, and is in quality so controlled, without much giving or taking of weight between the partners, that it is perfectly feasible for each to dance it on their own. Nonetheless, since they are positioned either side of the group and look across at each other, turning themselves to dance in a different direction from the others, they seem isolated and make reference to each other even though not dependent on each other.

As well as direct references to other texts (be these dance, music or literature) through similarities in pitch or movement shape or description, there are also more tangential allusions to related and interrelated works by all three artists. The musical material which opens the first section of *Bridge the Distance* is linked to the opera of *Death in Venice* in both character and pitch shape. Evans (1979) has noted a similarity to the 'Venice Overture' music which the 'cello quotes at the beginning of the 'Recitative'. The same rocking, lapping rhythm is also to be found in a work Britten wrote immediately prior to *Death in Venice*, the Third Solo 'Cello Suite in C. This is the piece that Davies chose for *Something to Tell* for London Contemporary Dance Theatre in 1980. The suite is based on three Russian folk-songs and the Kontakion (the Hymn for the Departed), and Whittall remarks that 'the presence of a 'death' theme in the work immediately preceding *Death in Venice* needs no labouring' (1990: 258). Whittall also notes that there is an 'appearance of the unusual genre-piece "Barcarola" (Movement IV) with its hints of the rhythms found in the opera's "Overture" '(*ibid.*: 258) thus bringing us back to the first reference to the opera in the Third String Quartet.

The 1980 Sadler's Wells programme note for *Something to Tell* states,

> in a room setting, two people are already 'talking'. Visitors arrive and depart and through their interplay characterisations gradually emerge.

Davies danced the part of one of the 'two people' and she made herself an anguished solo to the Allegretto movement marked in the score 'dialogo'. Her solo has the same swings down of the upper body, lifted and restricted arms and arm swings past the body as those in the woman's solo in *Minor Characters*. Thus the three pieces *Something to Tell*, *Minor Characters* and *Bridge the Distance* can be seen to have a web of interconnections through both the music and the dance.

Roseberry sums up the abidingly nostalgic mood of the Third Solo 'Cello Suite when he writes that,

> the brooding soliloquy pivoting on a monotone, the anapest march rhythms,

the extreme contrasts of mood ranging from frenzy to deep introspection . . .
the overall impression of this strange, touchingly personal work is of a
sequence of impulsively jotted down moods and reminiscences – as if one
was turning over the pages of a private diary.   (Roseberry 1987: 382)

This was bound to appeal to Davies, with her emphasis on the personal and
reflective in her work, and the same qualities are evident in the other works by
Britten to which Davies has chosen to choreograph.

The other two pieces by Britten that Davies worked with in 1980 were the
Nocturnal after John Dowland op. 70 (1964) and the *Lachrymae* op. 48 (1950),
both of which she used in one piece for the final-year students of the London
School of Contemporary Dance in 1980. Both works are based on songs by the
sixteenth-century English composer John Dowland. The *Lachrymae* is subtitled
'Reflections on a song of John Dowland', the song being 'If my complaints could
passions move', the title Davies gives to her dance. Kennedy describes the
relationship between the Dowland original and the Britten *Lachrymae*.

This poetic piece comprises ten variations on the first eight-bar strain of a
beautiful song which epitomizes Dowland's melancholy, each manifestation
of hope being followed by depression. The key is C minor, with bitonal
innuendoes; the sixth variation quotes Dowland's *Lachrymae* song 'Flow my
tears', a touching anticipation of the ending, in which the final strain of the
work's basic song, with Dowland's harmonies, is haloed by Britten's most
expressive eloquence.   (Kennedy 1993: 183)

This structure of variations on a theme not heard until the end of the work
can itself provide another text and intertext. It is one Davies has favoured
throughout her career and one which she employs, to a certain extent, in *Bridge
the Distance*. In Britten's music it is a clear set of variations on a theme which is
only heard at the end of the piece, thus setting up its own play on a pre-existing
text uncovered only after being 'hidden' through variation. Davies employed a
looser version of the structure in her earliest works such as *The Calm* (1974) in
which a central slow-moving couple remain on stage throughout with entries
and exits from duets and trios of more fast-moving 'agitated' dancers. By the end
of the piece all the dancers are drawn together into a slow unison phrase built
from positions found in the earlier movement material. Davies is thus using the
structure itself to represent a state of mind. Since Britten also employs both
structure and tonality to aid his expressive ends (Whittall 1990), the interplay
between the structures of the dance and the music can be seen as another
intertext, indeed, another text.

In the second section of *Bridge the Distance* labelled 'Ostinato' in the music
score Davies echoes the regular crotchet rhythm of the music's ostinato in

walking patterns around the stage but she does not create an ostinato phrase for the four dancers. Instead she gives them a number of phrases, sometimes performed in canon between the two couples which at the end of the section are performed in succession as though they form one long phrase running from the repeat of the canon in bar 71 to the end.

Kennedy remarks of the 'hidden variation' technique employed in *Nocturnal* that,

> the eight movements, in which harmony is elusive, make use of variants of a line of the song or its accompaniment as though it was being tentatively composed in our presence. The second strain should be repeated but is left unfinished in each variation and is not heard complete until the end. The finale is a passacaglia based on Dowland's accompaniment. At its stormy climax E major emerges to guide the music to the Dowland original.
>
> (Kennedy 1993: 231)

E-major is the tonality that the Third String Quartet seems to be aiming for and is (not coincidentally) Aschenbach's key in Britten's opera of *Death in Venice*. As Matthews points out 'one of the advantages of a tonal composer is the subtlety of expression he can achieve' (1987: 160). He writes of the first movement of the quartet that,

> the two-flat key signature of this movement would seem to imply B flat, which is at the furthest tonal remove (an augmented fourth away) from the quartet's E major goal. But the tonality is not defined; this is the least tonal movement of the quartet and consequently the least stable. The quartet is about the rediscovery of stability, and it begins at a point which corresponds to Aschenbach's psychological condition at his death. (Matthews 1987: 160)

There has been much discussion about the uncertainty of the sonata form of the first section of the String Quartet no. 3 (Evans 1979; Matthews 1987; Whittall 1990). From the very beginning of the quartet the rocking seconds between the second violin and viola also elude a definite ascription of tonality.[13] Davies's choreography does not appear to reflect the specific overtones ascribed by Matthews to the fluctuating tonality of the first movement of the quartet; indeed the dancer later identified with Aschenbach is not included in this section. Instead four couples, frequently dancing two duet phrases in pairs, share, repeat and fragment the phrases until the dance follows a more clearly identifiable sonata form than the music (Preston 1995). The uneasiness created by the uncertain musical structure and the ambiguous tonality is, however, apparent in the dance material, as is the abiding sadness. Each partner in the couples stays close to the other, apart from the split duet already identified. The movement is restrained in dynamic, and the revisiting of phrases, in one case to the slower music of the recapitulation, creates a potent feeling of nostalgia.

In the first two sections of the dance more connections and references can be made to other works by Davies than to *Death in Venice*. The movement vocabulary is evocative of relationships between couples, particularly in their 'public' personae, as they present themselves to the outside world. Davies says that she imagined the walking passages (found in both the first two sections) to be 'like couples out on the street' (Davies 1986, np) and the lighting, by Peter Mumford contributes to the suggestion of an outdoor scene with the shadows shifting as the sun moves across the sky. A frontcloth designed by David Buckland, (displayed before the dance begins) does, however, make overt references to the opera and to Venetian bridges and the costumes suggest European street clothes of the period of the novella.

The middle solo section is therefore distanced from the outer sections in a number of ways. Not only are the references to *Death in Venice* much more explicit and detailed but there is also a shift in texture on stage, with only one dancer and a much more intimate feel to the lighting as well as the movement quality. This is only one of the distances that Davies establishes in the dance and she links it to what she sees as 'the distance between the central section musically and the outward sections, the distance between Patrick [Harding-Irmer] as an individual and the group' (Davies 1986, np). Davies says that whilst she was making *Bridge the Distance* she was 'trying to think of more complicated issues, more complicated passions . . . not just the story, not just the characters' (1986, np). Thus, whatever references and allusions to *Death in Venice* (both Mann's book and Britten's opera) can be identified in *Bridge the Distance*, other issues may also be apparent, perhaps informed and elucidated by the literary and musical associations.

The title Davies gives her dance hints at what is apparently, according to her introduction to the work on video (1986), the strongest single issue for her: the distance between youthful ignorance and older experience. In the final section of the work, a 'Passacaglia', Davies does not follow the musical structure in terms of constantly repeating a single phrase but instead gives each dancer a personal phrase and then combines these in a way that itself carries possible meanings. The phrases are initially combined to form duets between the original four couples in a reverse of the 'split duet' device seen in the first section. At one point the young man who has danced with Harding-Irmer interpolates himself into another couple's duet, both physically and by taking on some of their material.

After a combination of duets in unison and canon has culminated in a series of lifts, Harding-Irmer quietly walks on stage and begins to perform the individual phrases one by one. As he finishes each dancer's phrase that dancer repeats it whilst Harding-Irmer goes on to the next. Each dancer continues to perform the others' phrases so that by the end of the section all eight are moving in unison, still one phrase behind Harding-Irmer. On one level this creates the effect that Harding-Irmer is alone in a crowd. At times they all turn their back on him and seem united, if not against him, then in a different pursuit of their own. That his greater experience serves only to distance him and that this distance is never bridged is made evident in the qualities of both the dance and the music.

The music's passacaglia bass line of oscillating crotchet seconds is at once a lengthening out in time of the opening seconds of the quartet and another reference to the opera. When the clerk warns Aschenbach of the real dangers of disease in Venice (no. 267 in the opera score) a similar whole-tone oscillation on triplet crotchets is heard in the bass line. The clerk sings 'Sir, death is at work!' suggesting that there runs throughout the final movement of the quartet a preoccupation with death. When Aschenbach begins to follow Tadzio's family, the 'pursuit' motif passacaglia has beneath it another, slower bass line climbing up (as this one does) from E to G-sharp and then dropping back down again. In the opera this is a version of the 'I love you' realisation at its original pitches; in the quartet the bass line winds down each time not to Aschenbach's E but to a D. Whittall finds this shift in the quartet particularly meaningful. He observes that,

> the Passacaglia theme, with its whole-tone rotations about E, always ends on a D natural, and when Britten composed his ending, with the final D in the bass and a non-cadence above, he provided perhaps the most perfectly economical example of his dissolving, inconclusive conclusions, in which a last page of pure diatonicism (the E major triad prolonged without actual progressions) is dramatically, determinedly 'corrupted', if not positively con-tradicted. (Whittall 1990: 282)

Davies's ending is less 'fateful' but no less poignant, with the central charac-ter left in stillness and isolation after his hopes of reaching out and bridging the gulf between youth and age, between innocence and experience, are again frustrated.

Another thread in the tapestry of associations can be found in Whittall's characterisation of the sensitive balance between formal structures and motivic references in Britten's late compositional style. He suggests that Schmidgall, in his interpretation of *Death in Venice*,

> rightly observes that 'the crux of the story is not sublimation of homosexual instincts, but more generally the sublimation of vital instincts – the instincts of life – which is a danger courted by the superior intellect'. Hence its value in any interpretation of Britten which sees him as at heart an Apollonian artist, one who understands 'the power of reticence'. And, of course this reticence is expressed through a technique, not of positive indecisiveness so

much as of functional ambiguity. *Death in Venice*, like all Britten's successful
structures, balances its formal and procedural clarity with harmonic ambivalence.   (Whittall 1990: 261)

This description of powerful reticence and understatement of Britten's work
could equally apply to Davies's choreographic style. The frequently recurring
descriptions of Davies's work as 'lyrical', 'cool' and 'understated', belie the
passion that can be identified on close reading. An investigation of the associations and references which Davies allows to play on each other reveals something of the 'functional ambiguity' that Whittall discerns in Britten's compositional technique. The references cited in this reading, from life, from other
works by Davies, other works by Britten and other associated texts are all
allusions rather than quotations.

The rich complexity of different layers and types of meaning in Davies's work
leads to the construction of intertexts which intersect with those of Britten's
music and Mann's writing. The play between these texts and intertexts creates
an ever-expanding web of connections that is typical of the sophistication of
Davies's work. *Bridge the Distance* becomes, in an intertextual reading, far more
than a formulaic restatement of Britten's String Quartet No.3 or a collection of
references to Mann's novella. In this reading the work is seen to be a rich mosaic
providing subtle nuances and resonances of meaning that typify Davies's choreography and make the works particularly rewarding in interpretation.

Notes

1. The argument being proposed here is that while there is an infinite *number* of
   readings to be made of a work there is not an infinite *range*. We might debate the
   old adage that it would be a mistake to read *Hamlet* as a comedy, but we would
   surely have to agree that it is not *Romeo and Juliet*; thus there is at least one
   reading which is, simply, wrong.
2. Davies has said, 'I tried to clear my system in New York . . . The idea was to
   break down what I'd learnt and try to start again, with the knowledge I'd gained
   of course, but clearing away all the mess one tends to gather up like surplus
   luggage' (cited in Gow 1976: 142).
3. The three works are *Run to Earth* (1986, music by Brian Eno), *and do they do*
   (1986, music by Michael Nyman), and *Red Steps* (1987, music by John Adams).
4. Their roles are taken from Mozart's opera *Così fan tutte* and the dance reflects
   aspects of the opera's plot.
5. The one exception is a piano solo by Michael Finnissy for *Rushes* (1982) and
   Finnissy had already begun the score for *Rushes*, as one of his growing sequence
   of 'Verdi transcriptions', before Davies approached him with her ideas for a new
   piece.
6. When Davies was asked in a panel discussion with the composer Kevin Volans,
   with whom she has worked repeatedly, who takes final responsibility for the

piece, she answered unhesitatingly 'Oh, I do' (Davies 1995). In my experience, playing for dance performances for London Contemporary Dance Theatre and Rambert Dance Company, I saw all questions about the piece in preparation being referred to Davies as the final arbiter.

7. *Something to Tell* (1980) provides a clear example of the detailed nuances of relationships Davies evokes through precise resemblance to both gestures and proxemics seen in social situations in middle-class English social gatherings at the time.

8. Colin Matthews reports that around *Death in Venice* time, 'Ben [Britten] read out to me an article in *Opera* magazine which said, "All Britten's operas are concerned with the loss of innocence." And he said, "this is absolute *rubbish!*" and picked the thing up and threw it to the other side of the room (cited in Carpenter 1992: 536). This will not be the first time that an artist has not recognised an aspect of her/his work that is perceived by many outside observers, however, and Matthews continues the recollection by saying 'I've regretted ever since that I didn't have the courage to say, "Well, what *are* they about then?"' (*ibid.*).

9. Whittall suggests that this renders Britten's recurring theme most explicit in *Death in Venice* 'since here youth, in all its beauty and inaccessibility, is not so much doomed as the cause of doom in those who seek to regain it' (1990: 259). Mellers suggests that 'we are obsessed with innocence because we have lost it, and for the same reason we persecute those who have not' (1984: 97).

10. Davies says of Harding-Irmer that 'he has reached a stage of experience where he can do a great deal technically, and he can do nothing and it comes over as the most remarkable moment. He has age that works for him; that fascinated me' (1986: np).

11. In the novella Aschenbach is charmed to note that the boy, like himself, is not amused by a band of comic musicians. Mann writes that 'in the general commotion and distraction he [Aschenbach] ventured to steal a glance at Tadzio, and as he did so he became aware that the boy, returning his glance, had remained no less serious than himself, just as if he were regulating his attitude and expression by those of the older man, and as if the general mood had no power over him while Aschenbach kept aloof from it' (1993: 255).

12. The link between the couples is reinforced by the fact that the second couple perform their duet in front of the first who remain in their final position, with the woman kneeling next to the recumbent man throughout, only to join and swap partners with the second couple at the end.

13. As Evans points out, 'a disembodied second, whether major or minor, is in itself tonally enigmatic, and the whole movement amplifies that phenomenon . . . so that, while local tonal attractions can be isolated, they are rarely unequivocal or protracted. Only in the coda, from bar 76, does an outcome in G minor . . . become a clear goal: even here the second pair of instruments (second violin and viola) are scarcely less intent on implying a dominant of A flat' (1979: 341–2).

References

Barthes, R. (1975), *S/Z* (1970), London, Jonathan Cape.

———— (1977), 'Death of the Author' (1968), in *Image Music Text*, London, Fontana: 142–8.

Carpenter, H. (1992), *Benjamin Britten: A Biography*, London, Faber.

Davies, Siobhan (1980), Programme note for Contemporary Dance Trust Gala performance, Sadler's Wells, 18 November, np.

———— (1984), Unpublished interview held at The Place Archive, The Place, London.

———— (1986), Introduction to *Bridge the Distance*, video produced by Colin Nears, BBC TV.

———— (1995), Panel discussion chaired by Sophia Preston, Choreographers' and Composers' Exchange, Royal Festival Hall, London.

Davies, Stephen (1994), *Musical Meaning and Expression*, Ithaca, Cornell University Press.

Duncan, R. (1981), *Working with Britten: A Personal Memoir*, Welcombe, Devon, Rebel Press.

Evans, P. (1979), *The Music of Benjamin Britten*, London, J.M. Dent.

Gow, G. (1976), 'Extremes of Energy', *Dancing Times*, LXVII, 795: 142–3.

Graves, R. (1985), *Greek Myths*, London, Cassell.

Hall, E.T. (1969), *The Hidden Dimension: Man's Use of Space in Public and Private*, New York, Doubleday.

Kennedy, M. (1981, 1993 [revised]), *Britten*, London, J.M. Dent.

Mann, T. (1993), *Selected Stories*, London, Penguin.

Matthews, D. (1987), '*Death in Venice*, and the Third String Quartet', in D. Mitchell (ed.) *Benjamin Britten, Death in Venice*, Cambridge: Cambridge University Press.

Mellers, W. (1984), 'Paul Bunyan: The American Eden', in C. Palmer (ed.), *The Britten Companion*, London, Faber.

Mitchell, D. (ed.) (1987), *Benjamin Britten, Death in Venice*, Cambridge: Cambridge University Press.

Palmer, C. (ed.) (1984), *The Britten Companion*, London, Faber.

Percival, J. (1972), 'Experimental Summer', *Dance and Dancers* 23: 11, pp.46–9.

Preston, S. (1995), 'Revealing Relationships: An Analysis of the Structural and Expressive Characteristics of Dance and Music in Siobhan Davies's *Bridge the Distance*', unpublished PhD thesis, Guildford, University of Surrey.

Roseberry, E. (1987), 'Tonal Ambiguity in *Death in Venice*, a Symphonic View' in D. Mitchell (ed.), *Benjamin Britten, Death in Venice*, Cambridge: Cambridge University Press.

Whittall, A. (2nd edn, 1990), *The Music of Britten and Tippett: Studies in Themes and Techniques*, Cambridge, Cambridge University Press.

Williams, D. (1991), *Ten Lectures on Theories of Dance*, Methuen, NJ, Scarecrow Press.

Williams, P. (1974), 'Contemporary Variety', *Dance and Dancers*, 25: 4: 29–32.

Worton, M. (1994), Seminar with PhD students at University of Surrey, Department of Dance Studies, np.

4

Jewishness and Modern Dance in Sophie Maslow's *The Village I Knew*

Naomi M. Jackson

As the atrocities of the Second World War became more evident, modern dancers who had previously stood aloof from their Jewish identity consciously began to make work based on Jewish themes. How they went about this was informed by their life in the American Jewish community as well as their position within the modern dance world. Many Jewish modern dancers were exposed to traditional Judaism, but grew up in largely non-observant, leftist households. During their teens and twenties, many became drawn to the work of Martha Graham and Doris Humphrey, as well as the more radical dance practices being developed within left-wing circles during the 1930s. How these diverse influences left their traces in choreographic practice is examined in this chapter in relation to the American Jewish choreographer Sophie Maslow and her dance *The Village I Knew* (1950).

Sophie Maslow (born c. 1912) was raised in Brooklyn by Russian Jewish parents. Her father had been a revolutionary printer in Moscow, and was an ardent socialist, belonging to the Workmen's Circle, a Yiddishist fraternal institution with close ties to the Jewish unions and Jewish labour press. Maslow, like many New York Jews of the time, was introduced to modern dance at the Neighborhood Playhouse which had been established by the German Jewish sisters, Irene and Alice Lewisohn, to help immigrants from Central and Eastern Europe improve their quality of life through training in the performing arts. At the Playhouse, Maslow studied dance with Blanche Talmud, Martha Graham and Louis Horst, among others. She joined the Graham company in 1931, and remained with it until 1942. While in the Graham company, Maslow became involved with the New Dance Group and the New Dance League, two organisations that reflected the various left-wing views important in that time. In 1942, she joined Jane Dudley and William Bales to form the Dudley–Maslow–Bales Trio, a successful company which toured the United States and Canada during the 1940s and early 1950s.

It was as part of the Dudley–Maslow–Bales Trio that Maslow presented her first major work on a Jewish theme, *The Village I Knew*. The dance received its premiere on 18 August 1950 at the Palmer Auditorium, Connecticut, New London, as part of the American Dance Festival (ADF). The piece was an expanded version of a prior dance entitled *Festival*, which had been presented by the company at ADF the previous summer.[1] *The Village I Knew* was based on the stories of Sholom Aleichem, the paintings of Marc Chagall, and events of significance in Jewish lives drawn from ritual and oppression. The seven sections were, briefly: 'Sabbath', celebrating the coming of the Jewish Sabbath; 'It's Good to Be An Orphan', showing an older woman giving some boots to a young girl; 'A Point of Doctrine', about a verbose housewife who presents the details of her domestic difficulties so vividly that a Rabbi faints; 'Festival', a collective dance of celebration; 'The Fiddler', showing a girl who is in love with a poor fiddler against her mother's wishes; 'Why Is It Thus?', concerning three studious young men; and 'Exodus', portraying Jewish villagers fleeing persecution.[2]

The Mosaic of Quotations in *The Village I Knew*

Within the history of dance, *The Village I Knew* has often been treated as a charmingly competent work in the modern style. From its original performances in the early 1950s, through several revivals, critics have frequently interpreted the dance as a warm and tender depiction of Jewish life in Czarist Russia, offering straightforward evaluations of what they consider a relatively simple piece. The work is enjoyed, but remains lightweight beside the designated masterpieces of a choreographer such as Graham. In a 1977 review, Deborah Jowitt of the *Village Voice* characteristically observed:

> Maslow's work has always been cozier than Graham's. Her epics usually fail, while some of her theatrical genre pieces like Folksay or A Village I Knew (1951) [sic] have a soundness, sturdiness, and sweet-natured wisdom. It was to see A Village I Knew that I went to Maslow's season at Riverside Church, to see again, and with pleasure, how economically she draws a society of European Hassidic Jew . . . Perhaps Village works because Maslow doesn't belabor her points, because the movement is appropriate – clumsy if need be, never glamorized, because, I suspect, the lives of these people meant a lot to her.
> (Jowitt 1977: 77)

Recent studies in dance history and theory have opened up the possibility of more complex readings of seemingly subsidiary dances like *The Village I Knew* to show how they simultaneously both reflect and contribute to social formation. Contemporary developments in critical theory, cultural studies, art history, and film studies have challenged the idea of a stable art work that carries single interpretations. Instead, these disciplines have brought to bear newly refined methodologies from feminist theory, Marxism, discourse studies, and psychoanalysis to investigate the operations of social power and the ideological underpinnings of aesthetic practices (Desmond 1997). What is suggested is that *The Village I Knew* was shaped and interpreted by diverse communities who were, and still are, actively engaged in a process of social definition, including normative constructions of gender, race, class and ethnicity.

To see *The Village I Knew* as a complex mosaic of quotations drawn from a variety of sources offers a method for unravelling its complexity. These quotations mark the presence of different interpretive communities engaged in constructing notions of self and society through distinct practices and master narratives. To this extent the strands do not always lie together in comfortable coexistence, but play off each other in sometimes conflicting and incomplete ways. By disentangling the textual strands in a choreographic work, a dance historian or critic can juxtapose narratives constructed for different purposes by different people, showing how they shape subjectivity and either challenge or support culturally dominant views about gender, race, ethnicity and the arts.

For the purposes of this chapter, looking at *The Village I Knew* from the perspective of intertextuality clarifies particular American Jewish interests and modern dance concerns of the 1940s and 1950s, and explores how they interacted with each other to create a new American Jewish identity and broaden the dominant modern dance narrative of the time.

After the Second World War, second and third generation American Jews were beginning, on a visible scale, to rediscover their Jewish 'heritage', and to reimagine and recreate their Jewish identity. This process was marked by two somewhat conflicting strands. On the one hand, there was a move to locate Jewishness in traditional Judaism and the religious community. On the other, was an interest in remaining true to contemporary American society and its support of individual expression and secular humanism. The result of the particular way people were combining these two strands was a new perspective which constructed quintessential images of Jewishness that were uplifting, timeless, and spiritual, yet largely purified of any negative associations with the old world, immigrant life or actual Orthodoxy. As the Jewish community increasingly intersected with the dance world, modern dance helped reinforce as well as shape the new perspective to work against the traditional religious narratives. It might be argued that this is because modern dance practices tended to simplify, abstract and stylise, and its theories validated female expression, individuality, creativity, and universalism of communication.

For its part, as modern dancers intersected with Jewish dancers, audiences and institutions, modern dance itself also underwent revision. During the 1940s and 1950s, modern dance in America fully matured and crystallised as a form distinct from ballet and social or revue dancing. Internally, however, debates lingered between the more art-for-art's-sake and activist dimensions of the form. Many involved in the promotion of modern dance followed John Martin in defining it as a largely apolitical, pure art characterised by universally expressive movement, best exemplified through the works of Graham and Humphrey. At the same time, the progressive orientation of some dancers led to a continuing challenge to modern dance to recognise and embrace racial and ethnic diversity. Within this debate Jewish forces in New York (in particular) played a central role in trying to reframe modern dance as an expression of social consciousness and as a hybrid style with disparate ethnic and religious influences. This re-orientation was attempted through patronage of African-American, Hispanic and Jewish artists at institutions such as the 92nd Street Young Men and Young Women's Hebrew Association (YM-YWHA), and choreographic experiments which focused on minority experiences.

The power of an intertextual reading of dance is illustrated by following the sometimes complementary and sometimes conflicting Jewish and modern dance texts in *The Village I Knew*. Little of substance initially seemed possible from analysis of the choreography, but subsequently through this type of reflection, windows now open onto overlapping communities passionately engaged in defining themselves and the worlds they live(d) in.

Redefining Jewishness[3]

Looking back over Maslow's career, it is possible to trace at least two central ways in which Jewishness was constructed in New York during this century, while recognising the constantly shifting nature of Jewish subjectivity. In the pre-Second World War period, Jews like Maslow found a comfortable way to manifest their Jewishness largely through participation in non-parochial American culture. For these largely non-observant men and women, any conscious awareness of their Jewish identity was secondary to their embracing of general American culture. Young Jews flocked to modern dance and music concerts, art exhibits, and lectures on contemporary literature and philosophy.[4] For them, there was a strong desire to participate in the shaping of modern life. As Maslow once described it, 'We could feel life changing around us and new things happening in the arts, and we wanted to be part of that future' (Horosko 1991: 51).

To the young Maslow, modern dance seemed to express beautifully the spirit of contemporary life. She was captivated by the strong, emotionally compelling dancing of Graham, whose technique and choreography she greatly admired. Maslow reminisced, 'Even though I was an adolescent, I felt that everything Martha was doing was right. All of her movements were meaningful' (*ibid.*). As Maslow began to choreograph, she remained committed to modern dance themes of a general nature, rather than working with Jewish subject matter. In many of her dances she focused on social problems of the poor and on Ameri-

Sophie Maslow's *The Village I Knew*.   Photo: Walter Owen

cana themes. In 1941 she choreographed *Dustbowl Ballads*, which concerned the plight of people struggling to survive the Great Depression and the Dust Bowl. In 1942 she created *Folksay*, a dance performed to verses from Carl Sandburg's 'The People, Yes,' interspersed with folk ballads and stories.

With the Second World War, however, a dramatic shift occurred as American Jews learned of the devastation in Eastern Europe, and became more self-conscious of their 'Jewish' identity. Jews who for many years had remained disinterested in religious and ethnic identification, soon became committed to a reappraisal of their lives. As Maslow later recalled,

> this horrible experience [Holocaust] made me realize that as much [as] I thought I was American, I was just as much Jewish . . . I then wanted very much to do something Jewish.   (Josephs 1996: 45)

The form of Jewishness which arose during this time merged new interests in traditional sources of identification (Jewish history, community, religion and custom) with existing modernist influences.[5] Specifically, Jewish artists and intellectuals increasingly located Jewishness in Eastern Europe, the bible, and the religious community in an attempt to vindicate the horrors of the war. In her introduction to Mark Zborowski and Elizabeth Herzog's *Life is with People*, the first major anthropological study of East European culture (originally published in 1952), Barbara Kirshenblatt-Gimblett observes that the book 'represents a

turning point in the relationship of American Jews to their East European past.'
She writes,

> Created in the wake of World War II, *Life is with People* encouraged its
> readers, demoralized by the annihilation of European Jewry, to take pride in
> the distinctiveness of their heritage. Attempts to minimize Jewish difference
> had failed to stem anti-Semitism. The task, now a sacred duty, was to recover
> the inner life of East European Jewry, its values and the distinctive culture
> they animated.   (Kirshenblatt-Gimblett 1995: ix)

The new identification of Jewishness, at least in part, with more traditional
narratives is clearly identifiable in *The Village I Knew*. In the dance, Maslow
attempts to capture a particular moment in the Jewish past, specifically life as it
was lived in a small Jewish village in Czarist Russia at the end of the nineteenth
century.[6] This interest in reliving a specific period in Jewish history is clear from
programme notes and from the numerous articles and reviews of the dance from
the time which clarify that the work, such as the following:

> [It] celebrates the homely little episodes of life in the improbable village of
> Vasrilevka, the ecstatic Sabbath ritual, the over proud matron who thinks her
> daughter much too good for the village fiddler, the apple cider drinking Rabbi
> who also loves to dance.   (Dzhermolinska 1951: 12)

Here, Maslow also plainly connects Jewishness to life in a religious community. In the dance, women cover their eyes and circle their arms as they perform
the blessing over the candles in 'Sabbath,' while five men pretend to *daven* (a
praying motion involving rocking back and forth) upstage. In another section,
students appear engaged in study (this is mimed) of the great books of Judaism
(the Torah and Talmud), during which they assume expressions of meditation,
questioning and insight. A Rabbi character, moreover, appears numerous times
throughout the dance, with his own spirited solo in the section titled 'Festival'.
     That these kinds of references might have been problematic in the hands of a
modern dance choreographer seems to have been briefly, but not seriously
considered. Maslow realised that saving East European culture was not an easy
task, but she presented what she considered a sensitive and accurate portrait.
An extensive article in *Jewish Life* from November 1949 supports Maslow's
intentions for *The Village I Knew* (which at the time was yet to be fully completed) within the larger context of the difficulties facing someone creating a
dance on Jewish themes. One section of the article describes the breadth of
Jewish culture, both geographically and historically, that artists could look to for
inspiration. Another, entitled 'Some Common Pitfalls', outlines the various dangers facing a choreographer in working with Jewish themes. These include

simplistic surface treatment of subject matter and character, and the reliance of
stereotypes which fail to grasp the subtleties of Jewish life:

> and worst of all: how often have we seen, hidden under the fig-leaf of the
> finest 'folksy' intentions, the hackneyed, false, so-called 'Jewish gesture.'
> Dancers who cling to a trite and outworn stereotyped style, are not correctly
> interpreting that segment of Jewish culture with which they are concerned;
> and are presenting their audiences with a counterfeit instead of a gem.
>
> (Platon 1949: 35)

The author continues, 'none of these pitfalls will threaten the dancer who will
not compromise with surface treatment,' proposing that just such a dancer is
Sophie Maslow.

With the final dance, many people, both Jewish and non-Jewish, seemed to
believe that Maslow was in fact largely successful in portraying Russian Jewry.
Walter Terry wrote in the *Herald Tribune* that, 'its glimpses (sharply focused and
knowingly selective) of Jewish community life in czarist Russia are amusing,
touching, colorful and intensely human' (Terry 1951). These sentiments were
shared by Deborah Pritzker, a reviewer writing for the 92nd Street YM-YWHA's
YMHA Bulletin, who stated that the piece 'rendered the flavor of Jewish life in
Czarist Russia with warmth and humor' (1956: 1). In 1952, a reviewer in *Theatre
Arts* asserted:

> the folksiness may become too cozy at moments, but most of it seems
> entirely genuine. It is in fact one of the happiest and liveliest works to be
> danced in years, using the simple footwork and occasional flashiness of folk-
> dance motifs as dramatic devices in painting a way of life which has disap-
> peared.   (Anon. 1952: 82)

Despite these glowing assessments, however, it can be argued persuasively,
with the aid of the intertextual lens, that the way Jewishness was constructed in
the dance was far from straightforward. Rather, in *The Village I Knew* the Jewish
past is represented in a highly stylised way typical of the post-war period. This
was due to a reworking of the traditional Jewish narratives by modern Jews who
were interested in creating positive images of Jewish identity which were emotionally compelling, yet relatively simple and untainted by religiosity. It was also
the result of the convergence of the new conception of Jewishness with the
particular conventions of the contemporary art (in this case modern dance)
world, which in many ways reinforced the new conception of Jewishness.

In his celebrated work *The Invention of Tradition*, Eric Hobsbawm has argued
that 'traditions' which appear or claim to be old are often quite recent in origin
and sometimes invented. By 'invented' Hobsbawm refers to a process of formali-

'Sabbath' from *The Village I Knew*.   Photo: Arnold Eagle

sation and ritualisation, characterised by reference to the past (Hobsbawm & Ranger 1983). In her reflections on *Life Is with People*, Kirshenblatt-Gimblett draws on this perspective in her analysis of the way Eastern European life was construed by many American Jews in the post-war period. Her argument is that the book's authors constructed or invented a particular heritage by searching for something essentially Jewish, identifying it with the *shtetl*, and then imbuing the *shtetl* with timeless, endearing qualities such as warmth, group solidarity, and affirmative joy in being Jewish.[7] This configuration of the *shtetl* did not, she argues, match the reality of the heterogeneous nature of the settlements in which Jews lived in Eastern Europe (Kirshenblatt-Gimblett 1995: ix–xlviii).

Similarly, Maslow's *The Village I Knew* is in many ways an *idealised* commemoration of Jewish life made by locating Jewishness in the world of the *shtetl*. Like Zborowski and Herzog's community, it 'narrows to the world of Sholom Aleichem, the world of our fathers . . . an exclusively Jewish world, a vanished world' (*ibid.*: xviii). The dance is based on the selective tales of Aleichem, and it portrays the Russian Jewish community as a place full of quaint, endearing men, women and children who live simple lives of worship, love, study, sorrow and celebration. The various members of the community are represented by generic character types, such as 'Housewife', 'Orphan', 'Fiddler', and their behaviour is frequently stiff, repetitive, and has a naïve, doll-like quality that suggests a charming fairy tale.[8]

For instance, the section called 'A Point of Doctrine' is based on Aleichem's story 'The Little Pot' and consists of simplistic characterisation and gesture.[9] In this part of the dance the Housewife stands stage left of the Rabbi who is seated in a high-backed chair facing upstage with his back toward the audience. She gestures boldly with arms in a mime-like manner as she 'speaks' to him of her troubles. Other more specific mime-like gestures include crying and cradling a baby. The Housewife character repeatedly lifts her arms and legs stiffly in one unit, adding dancerly movements such as leg extensions and turns to the central gestures of the hands. The piece ends with the Rabbi comically sliding to the floor beside the chair in apparent exhaustion from listening to her chatter.

Significantly, such a stylised representation of life in a Jewish community had precedents. Examination of the history of twentieth-century choreographers working with Jewish themes shows that Maslow was extending a set of conventions initially popularised in the mid-1920s by the Russian Jewish dancer Benjamin Zemach. Zemach was a performer and choreographer who had worked with the Habima theatre group in Moscow and travelled to America in the 1920s in order to find greater artistic freedom and opportunity. In America he often performed what was called 'Jewish dance,' stating that his sources were:

> the actual physical movements of the Jewish folk in their daily life and the other is their religious practices, such as those especially of the Chassidic sect.   (Martin 1929)[10]

Analysis of Zemach's work suggests that the locating of a Jewish 'essence' in the religious community was important more for its symbolism of the timeless Jewish spirit rather than for the authenticity of its representation. Zemach had witnessed the Habima's production of Ansky's *The Dybbuk*, and was aware of the power of a mythic, abstract representation of Jews being connected to supernatural forces. His performance style was highly expressionistic, using exaggerated gestures and elaborate stage make-up. He drew heavily from stories by Jewish writers and fictional life situations. One of his favourite characters was a religious Jew who gradually becomes more enraptured as he begins to pray, swaying ecstatically and lifting his arms heavenward (Prevots 1986).

When Maslow turned to Jewish subject matter it is evident that she followed closely Zemach's lead. Within *The Village I Knew* what is significant is the uplifting and generous nature of Jews, as opposed to realistic presentation of religious behaviour. The extent to which the dance as a whole departed from any actual 'heritage' is borne out by the response of members of the religious community to the dance. In 1951, William Kolodney, then the Educational Director of the 92nd Street YM-YWHA, arranged for a group of rabbis to see a performance of the dance. His intent was to show off the choreography as a wonderful example of Jewish art. According to Maslow, however, the rabbis were not very pleased. In particular, they criticised her incorrect use of certain traditional movements such as dancers kneeling on the floor for the blessing of the Sabbath candles, and men and women dancing together holding hands.[11] The kneeling or rolling on the floor was considered poor judgement not only because it went against tradition, but because it showed the women's legs, which was considered indecent. The rabbis also complained that the women danced with scarves, but not when they danced with the men, which is where the scarves were supposedly most needed to hinder the sexes from touching.

An intertextual reading of *The Village I Knew* clarifies the rabbis' perception of conflicting texts present in the dance. On the one hand is a narrative of Jewishness tied to traditional beliefs and practices as defined by the religious community. On the other lie conventions of 'contemporary American woman' and 'dance as art' which move constructions of Jewish subjectivity towards individual freedom and away from ancient tenets. In the dance, these two texts coexist in potentially disruptive form. For the progressive Jewish viewer of the 1950s, the texts lay together relatively comfortably, embodying a new form of Jewishness shaped by individuality, artistry and female consciousness. For the more observant, traditional Jew, however, the texts were glaringly exposed as opposing entities unacceptable in their implications regarding the nature of Jewish identity.

What is of special interest is that in relaying this story about the rabbis, Maslow made it clear that they were at fault for not understanding that her work was 'modern dance'. Her perspective indicates just how extensively *modern* dancers' approaches to choreography were mediating the construction of their Jewish heritage, thus reinforcing the new understanding of Jewishness in its individualised and aestheticised form.

Turning to the modern dance world, it is well established that many modern dancers of the period advocated the free adaptation of folk forms through a process of abstraction and artistic manipulation. In his writings, John Martin summed up this attitude in his distinction between dancing which has gone through a process of artistic transformation, and that which has not. In *Introduction to the Dance* (1939), Martin writes that contemporary dance is defined by its 'individuality,' and

> consists in extracting a certain essence from authenticity and employing it to give flavor to the whole, with no notion of archeological or ethnological accuracy.
> (Martin 1939: 107–8)

On the other hand 'dance arts of the East' and 'Spanish dance' (amongst many others) are said to be 'intricately interwoven with religion and social custom' (*ibid.*: 105). Such an outlook had important implications for a Jewish dancer like Maslow. If she wanted to reference her heritage, she needed to transform her source material.

As it happened, this was easy for Maslow, who had long advocated this position and been involved in adapting folk dancing to the concert stage. Maslow's approach to choreography had crystallised in the 1940s when she made *Dustbowl Ballads* and *Folksay*, the suite of dances which recreated a small-town atmosphere in America at the turn of the century. In *Folksay* couples perform carefully staged square dance sequences, men ogle as women strut by, and a community gathers for fun and festivity. As historian Joanna Harris observes, the movement is relatively uncomplicated and streamlined:

> The movement-style of this work consists primarily of big locomotor patterns characteristic of the vast American spaces and look like what every child should be able to do – run, leap, jump, turn, and swing. (Harris 1996: 273)

It is within the context of this folk-oriented 'modern dance text', that Maslow created *The Village I Knew*. The same kind of modern dance conventions for manipulating 'folk' and everyday movement that appear in her earlier Americana dances intervene to reimagine Jewishness. As Louis Horst wrote in 1949 of the antecedent version, *Festival*, it was 'almost like a Jewish Folksay, only infinitely more tender' (Horst 1949). In *The Village I Knew*, naturalistic gestures of the hands and arms are extended into the whole body and linked to basic dance-like movement. For instance, a pointing motion may lead into an attitude, or playing with a kerchief may lead to an unfolding of the leg in a *développé* to the side. In other cases, the use of unison, precise spacing and timing create a 'dancey' version of everyday activities, such as in 'Sabbath', where the five men pretending to *daven* do so in unison and in two carefully positioned lines. Other modern dance conventions include the use of bare feet, and incorporating floorwork through kneeling and sitting.

These practices and ideas, however, were not the only aspects of the modern dance world to affect Maslow's creation. One other primary tenet of modern dance played a central role. In addition to a belief in freely adapting folk forms, modern dancers upheld the rather more mystical ability of an artist to uncover the essences of existence through their process of choreographic manipulation. Modern dance was a 'point of view' in which the artist drew on his or her own experience, but abstracted from it to arrive at an underlying truth of an emotional (as opposed to cerebral, or conventionally religious) nature. Again, Martin voiced these assertions when he wrote,

> the artist must take away from his material those aspects of it which attach it

to his exclusive personal experience, and must confine himself to those aspects which are of more universal experience. (Martin 1936: 91)

Later he stated,

not representation but interpretation is his business, his duty to nature itself; abstracting into essences of those deep-rooted experiences of human living which appearances, surface truths, naturalism cover and deny.

(Martin 1936: 105)

Maslow, again, was an articulate spokesperson of this perspective from early in her career. In many instances she spoke passionately about the possibility for modern dance to grasp universal truths. A 1944 article announces 'Sophie Maslow Looks for Concept of Universal Emotion in Dancing', with an observation that, 'She has studied in a serious way for many years to make her dancing express a basic concept of universal emotions that touches the level of everyone's experiences' (Hickman 1944).

Such a perspective meant that when Maslow began working with Jewish themes from the 1950s onward she did not believe she was fabricating a fictional Jewish life. Rather, she sincerely thought she was getting to the essence of Jewish experience, which in turn had a universal message. Maslow and her admirers wanted to 'find the truth,' about village life in Czarist Russia. And they believed that carefully chosen gestures could evoke an entire epoch, mood and character:

This deep search [by Maslow] does not aim at a mechanical authenticity. On the contrary, it leads to a fuller, more inspired use of herself as an artist and of the potentialities of her art. To a dancer whose language is so potent, so magic, so special and at once so universal, to translate this truth into terms of her art, is the gist of her work. (Platon 1949: 36)

What this discussion of 'universals' implies is that while some Jews of the post-war period might not have realised that they were searching for a quintessential Jewish mode of expression that transcended a specific time and place, modern dancers were propelled in that very direction by the theory they espoused. Indeed, what is so fascinating about *The Village I Knew* is the way it illuminates the extent of the compatibility of modern dance with the project of post-war American Jewry. The intersection of the new form of Jewishness with modern dance in this piece reveals that the two complemented each other in important ways. Modern American Jews' quest for an essential, timeless Jewishness rooted in a heartwarming 'folk' community, fitted beautifully with modern dancers' search for universals and their fascination with 'the common man'. In this way, aspects of the modern dance world helped shape a new Jewish consciousness in the post-war period.

Redefining Modern Dance

If the intersection of modern dance with Jewish texts helped transform the nature of Jewishness, the reverse is also true. In participating in the practice of modern dance on a large scale, Jews like Maslow, along with Jewish producers, audiences, institutions and other choreographers, helped broaden the modernist aesthetic. Specifically, many members of the Jewish community drew on the universalistic discourse of modern dance to make a space for themselves and other minorities in the dance world. At the same time, their progressive orientation in terms of social justice led them to challenge the narrow definition of modern dance espoused by John Martin and 'The Big Four' (Martha Graham, Doris Humphrey, Charles Weidman, Hanya Holm). In this way many Jews helped reframe modern dance as a more inclusive practice to embrace greater ethnic and racial diversity.

Modern dance has long been conceived as pure, non-ethnic and generically American. Susan Manning argues in her book *Ecstasy and the Demon* that this position was closely tied to the gathering of John Martin and the Big Four at Bennington College in the mid-1930s, which 'showed the possibilities of a national experience shared by dancer and spectator' (Manning 1993: 261). Rather than admitting to foreign influences, either from Germany (especially Mary Wigman) or the Far East, choreographers working at Bennington were seen to be searching for a dance form that captured, in broadly accessible terms, the contemporary American experience. This experience was to lack overt reference to non-Western traditions and instead focus on life in the United States. The perspective was captured in the words of Doris Humphrey who passionately queried: 'We adopted ballet, we adopted Spanish dancing, we adopted Oriental dancing – are we never to have a dance that is our own?' (*ibid.*).

Within John Martin's discourse, a clear distinction was consequently established between 'modern dance' and 'ethnic dance'. As stated earlier, 'ethnic dance' was associated with those forms ('dance arts of the East' and 'Spanish dance') where the individual's concerns were said to be subsumed by those of the larger cultural group, while 'modern dance' was closely associated with the American dancer who could transcend the particular experience and create work that had universal significance.

The modernist perspective in dance implied that an individual could transcend one's ethnicity (and even gender and race) in the act of representation. If one was no longer tied to one's cultural and religious traditions one could, at least theoretically, dance about 'other's' experiences, along with one's own. And if one could transform the particular into the universal, one could present what

The three students in Maslow's *The Village I Knew.*

might otherwise be perceived as purely the concerns of a small local group as of importance to the general American population. Martha Graham, for instance, might make dances loosely based on American Indian rituals such *as Primitive Mysteries* and *Ceremonials,* and be praised for doing so.

At the same time as this dominant conception of modern dance was taking hold, another related set of values was being espoused by the radical sector of the modern dance community. Scholars Ellen Graff (1994), Mark Franko (1995) and Joanna Harris (1996), have examined recently the intense controversy that raged in the 1930s over the movement and themes suitable for a dance form that was to reflect contemporary American society. If Martin, Horst and Graham valued aesthetic issues more highly than political issues, the other group sub-sumed artistic concerns to the goal of social reform. These left-wingers believed that 'folk dance, not individual vision, was the ultimate source', and that the most suitable themes for dances were those that celebrated the common man (Harris 1996: 272).

Within this debate over the nature of modern dance, Jews intersected at varying levels. At a fundamental level, Jews such as Maslow capitalised on the rhetoric of openness basic to Martin's modern dance theory to make room for themselves in the American cultural landscape. Maslow was in effect proposing that her experience was equally valid to white, Anglo-Saxon Protestants. After all, she lived in America and could, as well as anybody, make the same claims to transcending her particular circumstance in the creation of a 'modern art' as anyone else.

The particular enthusiasm with which Maslow participated in modern dance was closely connected to the needs and values of second and third generation American Jews. These Jews directly aimed to create an American Jewish identity that depended on a synthesis of the 'general' and the 'particular'. They wanted to be able to be American and participate fully in American life, while retaining some sense of their unique history, culture, and religion. Modern dance sanctioned such Jews to synthesise these two aspects of themselves, when they so desired, by allowing them to draw on their own particular traditions and present them as meaningful to a broad-based non-Jewish audience. Audiences educated in modernist conventions largely accepted that it was possible for minority artists to present universal truths; consequently their work was widely appreciated and accepted.[12] Characteristic responses to *The Village I Knew* suggest the extent to which audiences were willing to accept that it had a transcendent message. Nik Krevitsky of the *Dance Observer*, for instance, wrote:

> it [the dance] is conceived throughout in terms of flowing movement which in dance quality makes the work universal and timeless. It might be Breughel as well as Chagall, Boccaccio or Mark Twain as well as Aleichem. One need not be an authority on Jewish life in Czarist times to appreciate its obvious good humor.   (Krevitsky 1950: 102)

However, Jewish dancers' acceptance of these basic tenets of modern dance were countered by substantial involvement in the leftist dimension of the modern dance movement. In his book, *Jews and the Left*, Arthur Liebman demonstrates that a significant 'Jewish left subculture' existed in America during the twentieth century (1979: 26). He uses the term 'Left',

> to designate a political ideology that is in some way or to some significant extent informed by Marxism. In this sense it is used to describe the politics of individuals, groups or movements.   (Liebman 1979: 2)

He then traces the roots of an American Jewish Left to the status of Jewish workers in Russia in the nineteenth century, suggesting that it was largely as a reaction to their dual status as an impoverished class and oppressed people that many turned toward radicalism.

In America, Liebman argues that Russian Jews were highly represented in national left-wing organisations such as the Socialist Party of America (SPA) and Communist Party (CP) during the first part of the century. These Jews tended to be working-class, non-religious, and intimately connected with other Jews through an elaborate network of Jewish institutions and associations. He writes:

> They were sharing common experiences and problems in the context of their shops, neighborhoods, and voluntary, self-created organizations. The channels of communication for the sharing of defined grievances was thus highly developed among them.   (Liebman 1979: 144)

This ferment of leftist activity provided the larger context in which the arts were experienced by many Russian immigrants. In the case of dance, many Jews were involved in the radical sector of the dance world. Anna Sokolow had formed her radical Dance Unit, and Nadia Chilkovsky and Miriam Blecher helped establish The New Dance Group as a collective modelled after the communist cell. The dancers discussed politics and danced about the impoverished and downtrodden workers, slum childhood and juvenile delinquency.

The extent of Jewish involvement in the radical dance movement suggests that such an approach represented, in fact, a valid way of being Jewish. The dance content may not have directly referenced Jewish experience, but a good number of the dancers concerned were Jews, grew up in predominantly Jewish communities, and largely married within the Jewish religion. In the mid-1930s, for example, the soloists of the Workers Dance League (later the New Dance League) were predominantly Jewish. The participants consisted of Sokolow, Chilkovsky, Blecher, Edith Segal, Lillian Mehlman, and Sophie Maslow.[13]

The implication here is that Jews were not involved in a simple 'assimilation' process, using the contemporary arts as a means to gain social mobility and acceptance by mainstream American society. Whatever the ideas of 'modern dance' and 'America' (as well as 'Jewish') represented, they remained in flux, and Maslow, along with others from socially conscious backgrounds, were passionately engaged in redefining these entities, even as they joined them. Theirs was an active reshaping of art and society in line with long held progressive and humanistic views. Such views were rooted in the moral tenets of the Jewish religion as well as Jewish trends since the Haskalah, a period in Jewish history known as the Jewish Enlightenment.[14]

The important role played by Jewish choreographers is evident when the potential for ethnocentrism and racism of the dominant view of modern dance is considered. The universalising discourse discussed above meant that various cultural indicators (such as ethnicity, race, gender) were not perceived as significant. The attempt to erase difference might have been successful except that in *practice* there was often a contradictory state of affairs. A double standard was commonly adhered to in which John Martin and his followers understated the ethnic/racial dimensions present in modern dance when it came to the dances of their favourites (such as, white, Anglo-Saxon, Protestant choreographers like Graham), but not necessarily when it concerned minority artists (such as Jewish, African-American, and Hispanic choreographers). When Graham choreographed *Primitive Mysteries*, for instance, it was simply considered modern dance, even though it was strongly influenced by Native American traditions. However, when Lillian Shapero created work it might be classified as 'Jewish dance', and when Katherine Dunham performed it was regularly labelled 'Negro dance'. In other words, when it came to the 'other', ethnicity and race were read as significant, and by implication subtly dismissed as less 'pure' than the modern dance of the Big Four.[15]

Sophie Maslow was one of the Jewish choreographers who challenged this double standard by fully embracing the multicultural promise, if not the reality, of the modern dance movement.[16] She not only assumed the acceptance of Jewish dancers but hired black dancers to perform in her pieces when it was far from a common occurrence. The New York premiere of *The Village I Knew*, for instance, included Ronne Aul and Donald McKayle. Aul played the Fiddler and McKayle was one of the three students in 'Why Is It Thus?', along with other roles. McKayle later recalled his enjoyment and appreciation of working with Maslow as a beginning modern dancer. He also remembered an incident that underscored the way African-American dancers, in particular, were faced with a mixed message in the modern dance world. According to McKayle, John Martin had 'said he didn't understand why there was a black boy in a Russian Jewish Village'. McKayle continued:

> I wrote to him . . . and said well if he really was interested in why there was a black boy in a Russian Jewish village he should ask the question why there wasn't a Russian Jew in that whole Russian Jewish village because there wasn't one on stage . . . because that didn't seem to bother him, only that there was one that was black.[17]   (McKayle 1993)

Martin responded, much to McKayle's disgust, that with McKayle present on stage the work lacked 'verisimilitude'. Clearly, blacks were not always allowed to represent others, despite the openness otherwise espoused by Martin.[18]

Maslow's attempt to embrace the full potential of modern dance to respect both the general and particular was not an isolated affair. As one of the central Jewish artists patronised by influential Jewish institutions, Maslow participated in a wide-scale reappraisal of the modern dance movement by the New York Jewish community. To support this claim it needs simply to be observed that *The Village I Knew* received its New York premiere at the 92nd Street YM-YWHA on 28 January 1951. The 'Y' was a major cultural venue in New York which had a long history of presenting Jewish as well as African-American and Hispanic choreographers. As a place interested in promoting contemporary forms of Jewish expression, as well as the general arts, the Y was a perfect venue for Maslow to showcase her work. The Y constantly brought together Jewish and non-Jewish patrons, dancers and audiences in a broad array of classes, lectures and performances on modern dance along with other contemporary arts. The impact of the Y's involvement in the modern dance field was immense, and it highlighted, on a visible, institutional scale, the potential of the modern dance framework for expansion to include and validate diversity.[19]

Following the creation of *The Village I Knew*, Maslow increased her participation in Jewish affairs while retaining her interest 'in the entire human experience' (Josephs 1996: 45). Along with works on non-Jewish subjects, she created the dance sequences for New York City Opera's production of *The Dybbuk*, which premiered in the fall of 1951, and *The Golem* in 1962. Beginning in 1955 she created incidental dances for the annual Hanukkah Festivals produced at Madison Square Gardens. Other dances on Jewish themes include *Anniversary* (1956), which commemorated the Jews who died in the Warsaw Ghetto, *From the Book of Ruth* (1964), and *Ladino Suite* (1969).

Nonetheless, *The Village I Knew* remains the best known of her works on Jewish themes, projecting into the future, as well as the past. The fact that it captured so completely the post-war ethos of American Jews as well as the socially conscious side of modern dance meant that it resonated with audiences through the 1960s. It is likely that such a happy union ultimately led to the popular success of Jerome Robbins's *Fiddler on the Roof*, which premiered in 1964. Robbins's musical, based on Sholom Aleichem's story 'Tevye, the Dairyman' in many ways was the culmination of the forces shaping *The Village I Knew*.

Studying a dance from the perspective of intertextuality thus brings to light the complex web of relations which exist both synchronically and diachronically. Traditionally, writers on modern dance have retained a narrow definition which focuses on the writings of John Martin and the choreographers Martha Graham, Doris Humphrey, Charles Weidman and Hanya Holm. One of the major goals of this chapter is to enlarge the conception of the genre to encompass the works of Jewish artists whose choreography often involved the grafting together of different experiences and communities. Studying these dances illustrates the inherently complex nature of cultural and artistic practices, revealing the multifaceted nature of interpretations of modern dance and Jewishness in the middle part of the twentieth century.

Notes

1. *Festival* was loosely based on Sholom Aleichem's story 'The Merrymakers' about three men (Alek the Mechanic, Kopel the Brain, and Mendel the Tinman) who sing and dance through the village on *Simchas Torah*.

2. The version described here is based on a film of a performance of the piece on stage at the Riverside Church, New York City, May 1977 (Dance Collection, New York Public Library).

3. The distinction between Jewishness and Judaism indicates the difference between Judaism the religion, and Jewishness, which may, but need not, be based on religious identification.

4. Classes and performances on contemporary subjects were offered at the 92nd Street YM-YWHA and New School for Social Research, amongst other institutions.

5. These are termed traditional sources of identification since the common ways of defining Jewishness are in terms of birth from a Jewish mother, adherence to the religion, religious observance and practice of customs passed down from generation to generation.

6. For a general history of the Jewish people see Johnson (1987).

7. A *shtetl* is a Jewish village or small-town community in Eastern Europe.

8. The one section which departs from this overall idealising treatment is the final episode called 'Exodus', showing individual figures rushing in anguish in front of a background of distorted marching figures. However, many reviewers of the time noted that, due to its sombre tone, this section stands out as an anomaly from the rest of the work.

9. It is worth noting that in Aleichem's story, the woman is not a generic character but presented as an individual – Yenta the Poultrywoman – with a detailed saga to relate. See Aleichem (1949).

10. A particular sect of Judaism which evolved in eighteenth-century Europe, the Chassidim turned the stern God into a merciful God who desired to be worshipped with singing, festivity, joy and dancing. Chassidim were well known for their ecstatic dancing in prayer and overall enthusiastic acceptance of bodily movement as a form of worship. See Gellerman (1972), Berk (1975), Lapson (1937), and Trolin (1979).

11. Interview with Sophie Maslow by Naomi Jackson 1995.

12. It is interesting to note that with postmodernism and multiculturalism there is less tolerance and greater sensitivity than occurred under modernism regarding who may represent what. For instance, white dancers are no longer considered able to represent African-Americans, and Europeans are no longer permitted to represent non-Westerners.

13. From a poster entitled 'Soloists of Workers Dance League' (Franko 1995: 31).

14. The Haskalah refers to a Jewish ideological movement initiated in the eighteenth century that aimed at modernising Jewish life and thought. Haskalah was the Hebrew term for 'enlightenment'; literally, 'rationalisation'. The ideals of the Haskalah included reason (Judaism as rational belief), tolerance and human perfectibility. See Zinberg (1978).

15. For an insightful study of the implications of the labelling of ethnic and modern for black dancers see Myers (nd).

16. There are clearly various manifestations of multiculturalism. I refer here to the

variety which believes that people can maintain their uniqueness while living together in harmony. See Kirshenblatt-Gimblett (1992), for a discussion of different forms of multiculturalism.

17. Note that other members of the initial cast, as listed on the programme for the January 1951, 92nd Street Y recital, included Jane Dudley, William Bales, Alvin Beam, Rena Gluck, Billie Kirpich, Donald McKayle, Muriel Manings, Anneliese Widman, David Wood.

18. An extensive literature exists on the complex relation of blacks and Jews, though not yet in dance. For more information see Salzman *et al.* (1992).

19. For a fuller discussion of the role of the 92nd Street Y in the modern and postmodern dance world see Jackson, (1997).

References

Anon. (1952), *Theatre Arts*, clipping, Dance Collection, New York Public Library, February: 82.

Aleichem, S. (1949), *Collected Stories of Sholom Aleichem: Tevye's Daughters*, New York, Crown Publishers.

Berk F. (ed.) (1975), *The Chasidic Dance*, New York, American Zionist Youth Foundation.

Desmond, J. (ed.) (1997), *Meaning in Motion: New Cultural Studies of Dance*, Durham, Duke University Press.

Dzhermolinska, H. (1951), 'The Village I Knew', *Dance Magazine*, March.

Franko, M. (1995), *Dancing Modernism/Performing Politics*, Bloomington, Indiana University Press.

Gellerman, J. (1972), 'With Body and Soul: An Introduction to the Ecstatic Dance of the Hasidim', MA thesis, Ohio State University.

Graff, E. (1994), 'Dancing Red: Art and Politics', *Studies in Dance History*, 5: 1, Spring: 1–13.

Harris, J. (1996), 'From Tenement to Theater: Jewish Women as Dance Pioneers: Helen Becker (Tamiris), Anna Sokolow, Sophie Maslow', *Judaism*, 45: 3, Summer: 259–76.

Hickman, E. (1944), 'Sophie Maslow Looks for Concept of Universal Emotion in Dancing', *Asbury Park Sunday Press*, clipping, Dance Collection, New York Public Library, September 24, np.

Horosko, M. (1991), *Martha Graham: The Evolution of Her Dance Theory and Training 1926–1991*, Chicago: A Cappella Books.

Horst, L. (1949), 'Two Premieres at Festival: Group Composition and Solo', Clipping, Dance Collection, New York Public Library, August 17, np.

Hobsbawm, E. & T. Ranger (1983), *The Invention of Tradition*, Cambridge, Cambridge University Press.

Jackson, N. (1997), *Converging Movements: Modern Dance and Jewish Culture at the 92nd Street Y, 1930–1960*, Ann Arbor, UMI.

Johnson, P. (1987), *A History of the Jews*, London, Weidenfeld & Nicolson.

Josephs, S. (1996), 'Ageless Movement', *The Jewish Week*, June 7: 45.

Jowitt, D. (1977), 'Transformers, Villages, and Xmas Phalluses', *Village Voice*, 6 June: 77.

Kirshenblatt-Gimblett, B. (1992), 'Making Difference', unpublished paper presented at the American Anthropological Association Annual Meeting, 2–6 December, San Francisco.

———— (1995), 'Introduction', in M. Zborowski & E. Herzog, *Life is with People: The Culture of the Shtetl*, New York, Schocken Books.

Krevitsky, N. (1950), 'American Dance Festival', *Dance Observer*, August–September: 102.

Lapson, D. (1937), 'The Chassidic Dance', *Dance Observer*, November: 109–10.

Liebman, A. (1979), *Jews and the Left*. New York, John Wiley.

Lloyd, M. (1946), 'This Changing Modern Dance', *Christian Science Monitor*, clipping, Dance Collection, New York Public Library, 2 February, np.

Manning, S. (1993), *Ecstasy and the Demon*, Berkeley, University of California Press.

Martin, J. (1929), 'The Dance: A Unique Art Ballet', *New York Times*, clipping, Dance Collection, New York Public Library, 9 June, np.

———— (1936), *America Dancing*, New York, Dodge Publishing.

———— (1939), *Introduction to the Dance*, New York, W. W. Norton.

McKayle, D. (1993), *Speaking of Dance: Donald McKayle, Conversations with Contemporary Masters of American Modern Dance*, produced and directed by Douglas Rosenberg, American Dance Festival.

Myers, G. (nd), 'Ethnic and Modern Dance', in *American Dance Festival: The Black Tradition in American Modern Dance*, New York, American Dance Festival: 24–25

Platon, V. (1949), 'Thoughts on a Dance in Progress', *Jewish Life*, November: 34–6.

Prevots, N. (1986), 'Benjamin Zemach – from Darkness to Light', in *Israel Dance*, Tel Aviv: 22–30.

Pritzker, D. (1956), 'Maslow Dancers Blend Two Eras in Concert Form Here', *YMHA Bulletin*, 28 November: 1.

Salzman, J., A. Back & G. Sorin (eds) (1992), *Bridges and Boundaries: African Americans and American Jews*, New York, George Braziller in association with the Jewish Museum.

Terry, W. (1951), 'A Jewish Community in Dance: "Passional", to Bartok score', *Herald Tribune*, clipping, Dance Collection, New York Public Library, 4 February, np.

Trolin, C. (1979), *Movement in Prayer in a Hasidic Mode*, Austin, Sharing Company.

Zinberg, I. (1978), *The Haskalah Movement in Russia*, Cincinnati, Hebrew Union College Press.

5

Dancing Latin

William Forsythe's Challenge to the Balletic Text

Jennifer Jackson

William Forsythe is one of the most provocative choreographers in classical ballet in the 1990s. Both he and his ballets attract debate and divide opinion. Those who consider the brutal athleticism and disruptions of his quasi-deconstructionist choreography a rude assault on ballet classicism are countered by others who regard his choreography as revitalising the form and who are excited by the dancers' bravura performances in a high-tech context. Forsythe is variously characterised as a classicist with roots in the formalist work of Balanchine, as a post-structuralist influenced by the theatrical expressionism of Bausch, and as a highly skilled technical showman whose brand of postmodernism engenders an 'aesthetic distance from life' (Klotz 1988: 231). The debate revolves around the difficulty of locating his work within a single artistic and theoretical framework. Thus, if only one perspective is brought to a reading of his ballets, another potentially productive set of texts and intertexts may disappear. A linear reading would require the viewer to choose to situate his ballets within a system of classical ballet, *or* as a study in expressionism, *or* as a development of the modernist experiment with pure form. A more complex position would be to regard these works as historical and cultural commentary, only intelligible if viewed within the framework of postmodernism, where an understanding of the interplay of styles is not only legitimate but becomes a prerequisite.

In this chapter I examine an ostensibly formal work, *Steptext*, to explore Forsythe's allegiances to ballet classicism and modernism on the one hand and to post-structuralism and postmodernism on the other. Given the difficulty of defining the choreographer's overall artistic or theoretical position, the question is posed of how the signs, sets of texts and intertexts are rendered legible, and how far the reader is free to play imaginatively amongst the dancing material and cultural texts.

To locate the discussion firmly on dancing territory, the specific focus adopted for reading *Steptext* is scrutiny of the movement codes and choreographic structures. Privileging the formal properties of the ballet in this manner is an obvious strategy for reading a work based on a balletic vocabulary, just as knowledge of the artistic and sociocultural context for this work is helpful for locating the specific choreographic intertexts at play. But it is a reading which sees *Steptext* as a challenge to the balletic text, and that positions the work itself as a deliberate reconsideration of the institution and traditional vocabulary of ballet, its repertoire, conventions and culture. By this means, space is opened up for the intrusion of new texts and references. The dance text can be seen as a collection of its fragmented components that denies the possibility of an ultimate transcendental meaning, but which displays certain characteristics and qualities, evoking associations and responses that raise other texts and questions, which can in turn be interpreted as carrying many meanings. By drawing out characteristics observable in the text alongside the contextual considerations, the readings offered are based on a structural analysis of the dancing text and my interaction with it. As a preamble to the discussion of themes emerging, some background information about the choreography follows.

Steptext in Context

Since his first professional choreography in 1976, Forsythe has attracted many commissions, but in Britain his work was hardly seen before the success of *In the middle, somewhat elevated*, staged in 1992 by the Royal Ballet. *Herman Schmerman* was their next Forsythe acquisition, originally created in 1992 for New York City Ballet's Diamond Project. When the Royal Ballet secured their own Forsythe premiere on 27 April 1995 the 'new' ballet, *Firstext/Steptext*, was typical of the choreographer's controversial and deconstructionist experiments with balletic and theatrical form: it was a partial hand-me-down. Juxtaposing pieces written ten years apart, Forsythe challenged not only the establishment and Opera House audience's notions of ballet, but also the concepts of 'finished' work and author/ity, by presenting an earlier work, *Steptext* (1984), and injecting twenty minutes of new choreography before it. The choreography for this part, *Firstext*, was credited not just to himself, but also to two of his colleagues from the Frankfurt Ballet, Dana Casperson and Antony Rizzi. In their programming for the 1996/97 season, the Royal Ballet revived *Steptext* but jettisoned *Firstext*, the prized original material that was created with company dancers in 1995 by the Forsythe team.

Works such as *Steptext* and *In the middle, somewhat elevated* are 'academic'[1] in their exploration of principles of balletic technique or *danse d'école*. They are articulate ballets which Meisner characterises as 'essentially pure, virtuoso dance' (1995: 48). Each of these works can be programmed as discrete entities, and they punctuate the repertoires of major ballet companies worldwide. They also each form part of a longer work, *Artifact* (1984) and *Impressing the Czar* (1988) respectively, created for the Frankfurt Ballet, the company Forsythe has directed since 1984. These works in their entirety, together with pieces such as *Alie/n a(c)tion* (1992) and *Eidos: Telos* (1995), are ballets of a quite different order, and could perhaps be characterised as dance-theatre since they are written in a language that does not translate easily into the repertoires of other balletic institutions. They subvert performance convention and manifest themselves as fragmented theatrical spectacle. Taken together, *Steptext* and *Alie/n a(c)tion* for example, illustrate contrasting aspects of Forsythe's output, the formal and the social/analytic. Where *Steptext* focuses on the formal properties of ballet and its conventions, *Alien a(c)tion* examines and embraces technology, theatrical convention and the culture of the 1990s in the construction of the dance event. In *Steptext* Forsythe pushes the boundaries of existing balletic codes of dancing from within a given and precise framework of rules. In *Alie/n a(c)tion* he blurs social boundaries between dance codes. But whatever his overt concerns and use of theatrical and dance conventions, Forsythe's works always raise questions that indicate the potential for the reader to take a multiplicity of interpretative stances.

Steptext is derived from the second of the four parts in *Artifact*, Forsythe's first production as artistic director and chief choreographer of the Frankfurt Ballet, premiered on 5 December 1984. *Artifact* followed the full-length *Gange – Ein Stuck über Ballett* (1983), also created for the company and a similarly subversive probe into the formal properties and conventions of ballet and theatre. Forsythe's tenure with the Frankfurt Ballet is noted for his bold realignment of the company's repertoire with a modern sensibility.[2] Atypically for an international ballet troupe, Forsythe's use of improvisational methods and his aesthetic preferences require individual creative and physical contributions from each dancer. The dancers who flock to work with him are no uniform gaggle. He encourages the development of personal style and incorporates improvisation at varying stages into both the making and the performance of his pieces. He works to decrease the traditional hierarchical role of the choreographer as author of a closed text, and to 'create a company of interdependent artists' (Constanti 1995: 28) who are all active themselves as creators and performers.

Forsythe himself is responsible for the simple staging for *Steptext*, which consists of a prop (a white free-standing board inscribed with a graphic symbol), distinct lighting states, and practice uniform for costuming the four dancers – three men and a woman.[3] The music is a recording of the Chaconne for solo violin from Bach's D-minor Partita, interrupted sporadically while the movement continues unaccompanied. Forsythe 'styles himself as a designer and architect, who merely puts diverse materials and building bricks together' (Gradinger 1993: 515). His interest in current cultural philosophical writing, especially the work of Derrida, Foucault, Lyotard, Baudrillard and Barthes, is manifested in his experiments with dance and theatrical form. Reference to the influence of his study of Laban's space harmony theories on his choreography also emerges in the literature. His work straddles American formalism and European (especially German) dance theatre, reflecting (although a native of America) his ready identification with both American and European sensibilities. As a dancer with Stuttgart Ballet during the 1970s, Forsythe would have been exposed to many works by Cranko and Bausch, but he cites Balanchine's choreography as his paradigm. Like Balanchine, Forsythe made a significant shift of locality in his twenties, leaving his 'home' and finding a sympathetic environment on another continent in which to live and work. Gradinger suggests another parallel:

> Where Balanchine, [his] great model, has blown away the cobwebs from the classical, taking elements of jazz, folk, and Broadway into his style, Forsythe has ventured into funk, break-dancing, and 'Afro' dance.
>
> (Gradinger 1993: 515)

Steptext, however, evokes associations with the formalist work of the great Russian choreographer – ballets such as *Agon* (1957) and *Apollo* (1928), rather than *Who Cares?* (1970) or *Western Symphony* (1954). Through his uncompromising emphasis on stripping ballet to reveal its form, Balanchine changed the perceptions of ballet audiences this century, and it is the departure from the traditional nineteenth-century balletic text in the formal terms of structure and vocabulary that arouses interest in the work of both artists. In *Steptext* there is no conventional narrative. Its subject is ballet, or more precisely an interrogation of ballet – of the form, its conventions, the potentialities and limits of its technique, its manners and its presentation in a theatrical context.

Both choreographers position their 'home' brand of movement (classical ballet) in a wider cultural and artistic framework. Whereas Balanchine's ballets are located within the contemporaneous preoccupations of modernism and of the abstract expressionists of his adopted America, Forsythe reorders the balletic elements in *Steptext* in a way that resonates with current philosophical discourse, and in particular with the European writers cited above. In her paper on American theatricality in German dance, Jeschke characterises Forsythe's work thus:

> By quoting the constituent/contributory components of the balletic code in order to consider them – through deconstruction – as theatrical means, Forsythe experiments with ballet as an artefact.   (Jeschke 1992: 203)

Questions arise. Where is Forsythe's enquiry, in which post-structuralist method meets classical sensibilities, leading the balletic form? What are the implications of his methods for devising/making ballets for how they might be read? Which interpretative strategies might the reader adopt to illuminate the text? How far can the reader, herself, take on the role of constructing the text?

Language and the Balletic Text

Fischer suggests that many titles for Forsythe's pieces 'already embody the meaning and goal of their respective ballets', citing *The Loss of Small Detail* (1987) and *Artifact* (1984) as examples. In these works, 'Forsythe's examinations . . . are occupied with the ballet in and of itself and formulate, so to speak, a meta-language on dance' (1990: 52).

Linking 'step' with 'text' clearly indicates that here, too, the title telegraphs the work's preoccupations: with dance (and ballet) as language, as a system of signification and communication. Balletic vocabulary comprises a body of named steps, precise and recognisable moves signified by French terminology.[4] The word 'text' makes literal and metaphorical reference to the literary concepts of textuality and intertextuality and is indicative of Forsythe's concerns with postmodern and post-structuralist discourse. Talking about ballet in terms of language, although problematic, suggests that ploughing the linguistic terrain for further illumination of Forsythe's choreography may prove fruitful.

Saussure's much-quoted distinction between *langue* and *parole*, or 'language' and 'speech', has underpinned many versions of critical theory,[5] language being 'the theoretical system or structure of a language', and speech referring to 'the actual day-to-day use of that system by individual speakers' (Sturrock 1979: 8). Sturrock links this notion with Chomsky's distinction between 'structure' and 'event' – 'between abstract systems of rules and the concrete, individual happenings produced within that system'. He makes a further link to 'synchronic' and 'diachronic' axes of investigation, as radically different possibilities embodied in studying a language as 'a system functioning at a given moment in time, or as an institution which has evolved through time' (*ibid.*).

Forsythe describes concepts pertinent to his own methods of dance-making in terminology borrowed from such studies of verbal and written language, referring to 'speaking dance' (Forsythe 1991) and to ballet as 'a kind of Latin' (Forsythe 1990), which would indicate the choreographer's interest both in events at a given moment in time and in structures which persist through time. This appears to lead the reader simultaneously along rather different routes – on the one hand towards viewing *Steptext* in the context of the immediate uses of the vocabulary, and on the other, of the broad institution of ballet – which accounts for some of its intertextual productivity.

In an anthropological approach to reading dance symbols or signs, Kaeppler says that the construction of meaning is usually associated with the concept of communication. She too refers to Chomskian and Saussurian concepts, positing that competence or knowledge (*langue*) in a specific dance tradition enables the viewer to understand actual rendering (*parole*) of particular movements.

> Communication involves both structure and meaning – syntax and semantics – that are tied to specific cultural traditions. The movement dimensions of activities convey or communicate information in a symbolic medium that is . . . a significant part of uniquely human social and cultural systems . . . Movements convey conventionalised information only to those who understand the cultural and social constructs of which they are a part.
>
> (Kaeppler 1992: 156)

Exploring the analogy of ballet with Latin, within this notion of reading signs, obvious associations emerge. There is, firstly, the shared characterisation as 'classical', and secondly, classification as language, both Latin and ballet comprising rigorous syntax, grammar and a precisely articulated vocabulary. In a postmodern context, what emerges from this juxtaposition of 'languages' are problematic connotations – of fixed ideals, roots and linear development. Latin, the source and origin of the modern 'romance languages' and taxonomies of professional and academic disciplines, is immutable, 'dead', and no longer spoken 'actively'. Ballet, with its origins in the court etiquette of Louis XIV's time, can be viewed in the same way. It can also be argued, that ballet (like Latin) has informed many twentieth-century modern dance languages and the taxonomies of movement created for instance by Graham and Cunningham. In the popular imagination, ballet is emblematic of a nineteenth-century romantic image of woman, and even in the late 1990s, at the dawn of the new millennium, historical 'classics' more than a hundred years old dominate the repertoires of most major ballet companies. Traditionally viewed, ballet's heritage can be traced back over nearly four hundred years of an evolving technique that is underpinned by the strict principles and vocabulary first codified when Louis XIV established the Académie Royale de la Danse in 1661. The link at that time with the Renaissance (the most significant revival of art and aesthetics of ancient Greece and Rome), is historically significant as the source of the balletic aesthetic. 'Classical' denotes the rules of harmonic proportions and rational ordering of form which are characteristics of an understanding of that aesthetic, while 'ballet classicism' is evident in those ballets that exhibit classical qualities through their dance form. The high point of ballet classicism is generally seen to have occurred at the end of the nineteenth century and is epitomised by Petipa's ballets, in particular *The Sleeping Beauty* of 1890 (Macaulay 1987a: 6).

Revolutionary as *Steptext* may appear to conservative ballet-going audiences, its vocabulary is clearly situated somewhere along the continuum of Western 'classical dance'. Kirstein, who writes from an historical perspective, draws a neat linear thread across the language of ballet and history:

> Ballet's vocabulary . . . depends on muscular and nervous control deriving
> from four centuries' research in a logic combining gross anatomy, plane
> geometry and musical counterpoint . . . The root of ballet-training in the five
> academic foot-positions established some three centuries ago is not arbitrary.
> These determine the greatest frontal legibility and launch of the upper body
> as silhouette framed in a proscenium.   (Kirstein 1983: 240)

In an interview with Birgit Kirchner in 1984, Forsythe presents another view
of ballet language and history, saying,

> I like classical dance. I think it's a nice, neutral language. You look at a ballet
> and you read history. I look at a ballet and all I see is history.
>   (cited in Kirchner 1984: 6).

Here, Forsythe appears to make problematic the distinction between classical
dance and ballet, and thus between synchronic and diachronic perspectives.
Elsewhere he alludes to 'actively spoken' language and Latin, highlighting the
idea of *parole* and *langue*, discrete moment and the historical linkage. The
chemistry of holding these pairs of terms together is potentially unstable – and
therefore highly productive in intertextual terms.

The idea of 'classical dance' being a neutral language or system of symbols is
deeply problematic. From an anthropological perspective, Ward suggests that

> the reality of any dance activity cannot be reduced only to its particular
> physical movements. Rather these movements obtain their reality from the
> meaning context from which they emerge.   (Ward 1993: 26)

From a philosophical viewpoint the movement symbols of 'classical dance'
rest on a highly specific cultural context. In his book *A Measured Pace* (1995),
Sparshott twins ballet with opera, and argues that they are both

> elaborate forms of stage presentation of which the forms and destinies are
> closely joined; they have a special importance because they belong to the
> privileged domain of the fine arts as part of the cultural 'establishment'. Both
> of them are forms of opulent display; it is expected that they will be elabo-
> rately mounted and richly dressed, that the principal players will be extrava-
> gantly paid and will be celebrities. Both are addressed to the ruling classes:
> companies and buildings are likely to be Royal, or civic, or national. Each is
> expected to lose money, to be the creation of extravagant patronage, and to
> survive on lavish gifts from public funds.   (Sparshott 1995: 273)

Highly complex associations, inherent in the balletic text, surface as intertexts for the ballet reader, raising questions for both audiences and creators, for example, of the extent to which the aesthetic is fixed or labile; the nature of the discourse Forsythe proposes between steps and text (*langue*) in *Steptext* (*parole*); the nature of Forsythe's dialogue with ballet as a language of signification in contemporary art and with ballet as an institution; the possibilities open to the reader in her 'dance' with Forsythe's steps and text.

A starting point for the consideration of such issues is Eco's writing on the problem of alienation facing the artist who is 'installed in a language that has already done so much speaking'. Eco posits that the artist

> tries to dislocate this language from within, in order to be able to escape from the situation and judge it from without. Since language can be dislocated only according to a dialectic that is already part of its inner evolution, the language that will result from such a dislocation will still, somehow, reflect the historical situation that was itself produced by the crisis of the one that preceded it. (Eco 1989: 154)

An artist such as Forsythe seems to address just this problem and to create through his work an intellectual and artistic discourse on it.

Scene Setting: Lights and Architectural Action

Through an analysis of the paradoxes arising from the texts set in motion by the scene setting, the music and the dance steps in *Steptext*, it is possible to create a series of interrelated readings.

Structural and staging aspects of *Steptext* fly in the face of cultural expectations of establishment ballet. Forsythe's scenic approach appears frugal. He designs his own lighting, he says, 'because it's cheaper' (Meisner 1995: 51), and the dancers wear simple costumes: black tights, sleeveless T-shirts and grey ballet boots for the three men, and red leotard with regular pointe shoes for the woman. The choice of costuming, styled on the dancer's everyday wear in the studio, evokes Balanchine's practice of revealing the form of the dancer's body, and underlines an overriding preoccupation in the work with pure movement vocabulary and shaping the body. The staging is simple but theatrical in a way that owes more to European dance theatre than to Balanchine's formalism. The setting consists of a single prop (a free-standing white rectangular board like a small stage flat) and half a dozen lighting states. The flat, as a functional object, demarcates another backstage area, upstage centre, from which the dancers make many entrances. Proportionally its borders resemble that of a computer screen; the dancers carry dance 'information'. Inscribed on the flat is a graphic motif consisting of two parallel lines running vertically and then deflected along opposite diagonals. By extending the diagonals to bisect an imaginary central vertical, a central axis emerges, from which numerous different combinations of the vertical to horizontal could project. Aspects of the movement vocabulary that disturb the centre of balance and play on the vertical axis in *Steptext* resonate with the simple geometry displayed.

This graphic image also alludes to numerous non-balletic artifacts, notably to architectural or notation sketches. The notion of the choreographer as an architect of spatial design, and the potentially rich parallels between designing dance and buildings,[7] prompts the investigation of contemporary architects. David Libeskind's[8] work, exploring new relations between the vertical and the horizontal (Kultermann 1966: xviii), is evoked, as is that of Oswald Mathias Ungers. In a study of the history of postmodern architecture, Klotz says that Ungers 'introduced movement by means of axial displacement, or by placing a form in a manner that violated the rules of harmony' (1988: 231). Unger's concern with mediating a position between freedom and obligation highlights the factors which meet at a point in time – on the one hand this ballet is dependent on the roots and ideologies of classical ballet for its first existence, and on the other, it fashions a new life, liberated from its outmoded conventions and incompatibilities with the modern world. Plausible comparisons may be drawn between Unger's isometric projections that bring the illusion of another dimension onto a flat plane and one of Forsythe's systems for generating movement material, which he calls 'universal writing' and describes as a kind of three-dimensional 'writing' with points of the body in space (Forsythe 1990). Here the influence of Laban becomes evident. In his development of space harmony theory in *Choreutics* (1966), Laban examines and establishes links between architecture and movement of the body in space:

> Space is a hidden feature of movement and movement is a visible aspect of space . . . When we wish to describe a single unit of space-movement we can adopt a method similar to that of an architect when drafting a building. He cannot show all the inner and outer views in one draft only. He is obliged to make a ground-plan, and at least two elevations, thus conveying to the mind a plastic image of the three dimensional whole.			(Laban 1966: 4–5)

The intertextual thread is woven through the disciplines from architecture to music, and evident in the setting and choreographic concept. Deliberate violation of the rules of performance interrupts the notion of linear flow and development and invites the viewer to re-examine not just the choreography but the construct of theatrical practice. In music, vertical and horizontal axes are used to represent sound events – vertically for a chord, for example, or horizontally for a melody. In parts of the ballet, Forsythe chops up the recording of the music, breaking the horizontal musical line to produce discrete vertical events that subvert the classical unity of Bach's music itself and the expectations of harmony in the relationship of ballet and music. Forsythe says '*Steptext* is a good example of a simple exercise in on and off' (cited in Driver 1990: 93) and he has created a world where lighting states, as well as the music and dance partnerships explored later in this chapter, commence or are interrupted abruptly or vertically, at the flick of a switch.

Light plays as much a part in the choreographic structure as the physical movements of the dancers, stimulating inferences that sometimes uphold and sometimes subvert balletic convention. Juxtaposing gloom and photographic glare, sudden blackout and sharp shadow, Forsythe carves the actions and manipulates the viewer's gaze (exercising the kind of focusing power normally available only to a film or television director) to create atmosphere and mood. Traditional expectations of neat staging and of framing the action with a clear 'beginning' are disturbed by the fragmented opening in *Steptext*. Playing with concepts of unity, Forsythe places the first dancer on stage at the 'beginners' call with house lights up and the audience filing in. All four dancers have entered and start dancing before the house lights go off, and a solo beam downstage illuminates a *pas de deux* for two men. Mid-way through the ballet the lights suddenly fade to blackout while the music continues. The dancers are in mid-sentence, so to speak, when the stage lights lift. A minute prior to the notional end, the house lights suddenly brighten again, flooding the border separating auditorium and performing space.

Each lighting state suggests a different hierarchy of space. At one point in the central duet (bars 141–53), the woman, supported centre stage in an upright stance by her partner, travels forward centre stage *en pointes* with the precise delicacy associated with conventional ballet choreography in *pas de deux*. The movement recalls Ashton's use of supported *jetés* lightly skimming the floor, which are a motif in ballets such as *Symphonic Variations* (1946) and in the *pas de deux* for the Queen of the Air and Her Consort in *Homage to the Queen* (1953).[9] Choreographically it constitutes a notable contrast to the surrounding material, but by painting the stage with light that stops short of centre stage – the space the dancers occupy – the phrase is curiously linked with an obfuscated balletic past. Pockets of darkness accentuate the drama of an aggressive exchange, for example at the end of their last duet (bar 225). The impact of the second man's virtuosic, vigorous and oiled solo (bars 233–40) is deflected by the sudden flood of light engulfing the audience and the stage. Gloom in the man's solo (bars 154–75) creates a tangible sense of tension, a diminished power, as he grapples with the problems of focusing to execute a series of fast steps and changes. Forsythe's purposeful placing of dance patterns disrupts the regular frontal presentation of dancers' moves. Geometry on stage is defined for both viewers and performers by the play of light, subversion of standard patterns and additional points of exit and entry.

In other works, such as *Alie/n a(c)tion* and *Eidos: Telos* the dancers manipulate a range of large-scale props and barriers which form an integral part of the choreographed space. In *Firstext/Steptext* drapes fly in and out through the action, blurring the barriers between scene and scene change. This is 'theatre disrupting theatre' (Meisner 1994: 31), a conceit Forsythe employs often to create spaces in which the relationship between the performance and the reader can be redeveloped, where the reader can construct her textual relationships – verticality and horizontality, architecture of the body, space and time, and theatre – each theatrical artefact moving towards and leading away from the ballet at once.

Classical Time, Musical Dances

As with the 'neutral' label for balletic language, the labels 'classic', 'classicism' and 'classical' can serve as barometers implying both the durability and transcendent value of a work. Macaulay has written extensively about dance classicism, drawing attention to Diaghilev's view that classicism is not a fixed notion, but an evolving one. Diaghilev recognised in Balanchine's *Apollo* a classicism that he had not seen since Petipa. Although he admired Petipa's works, in particular *The Sleeping Beauty* which displays an 'architectural classicism' in its essentially musical or 'symphonic' structure, Diaghilev considered classicism to be 'a means – but not an end' (Macaulay 1987a: 8). Balanchine's interests in the function of the vocabulary and the dancer led him to reorientate classicism in terms of purer geometric and formal considerations in the body, and thus to link, transcendentally, with Plato's pure forms. His departures from the models of the nineteenth century are described well by Scholl:

> Where Petipa and Diaghilev's choreographers regarded costumes, decor and music as essential features of their ballets, Balanchine settled on a simpler formula. The human body and its movement in time through space came to be primary: time (expressed through music) and space would become the fundamental conditions of dance composition.   (Scholl 1994: 115)

Steptext exhibits Forsythe's debt to the twentieth-century classicism of Balanchine in the concentration on qualities such as legibility, speed and internal musical interest, and an overriding focus on dancing that is primarily about itself. This focus on dancing is clearly expressed in works such as *Apollo* and *Agon* (and *The Four Temperaments* [1940] which also references classical Greece). The importance that Balanchine attached to the relationship between the dancing and music is highlighted, for instance, by the way in which he continued to refine *Apollo* after its premiere, stripping away anything that was extraneous to that relationship. Macaulay reflects Balanchine's concerns when he writes that 'dance has its centre in its union with music' and that musicality is essentially a 'classical impulse' (1997: 30).

Forsythe, however, challenges the classical concept of unity in ballet as a marriage of music and dance. In *Steptext* the classical experiment is extended into new terrain through the interrogation of the temporal, the 'musical', aspect of ballet choreography. Provoked by this enquiry into 'time' in space, a new music and dance relationship emerges – that manifests in the aesthetic, in the dynamics of the movement, and ultimately in the overall structure of the work.[10] Forsythe's experiments, which are informed by current philosophical thought, lead the reader both away from Macaulay's notion of the classical in dance and towards another of his propositions – that 'classicism is more philosophical than technical' (1987b: 71). By this Macaulay appears to suggest that a choreographer's ideas about morality or philosophy become discernible in her or his choreographic world – that is, in the web of relationships s/he weaves across dancers, sound and space. Forsythe's very choices in structuring these relationships reflect a different moral universe from that which is associated with a classical world. He departs from the notion of what may be considered classical in the relationship of music and dance and releases the ballet from its tradition, thus revealing aspects of a modern world and contemporary morals.

The music Forsythe chooses for *Steptext* is from Bach's D-minor Partita, a recording of the Chaconne for solo violin interrupted at points during the dance. Reviewing the Frankfurt Ballet's repertoire (including *Steptext*), Doris Hering refers to Forsythe's 'touching fidelity to the formations of classical ballet and the stability of a composer like J. S. Bach' (1988: 28). After Thom Willems, his regular collaborator, Bach is Forsythe's most frequent choice of composer. The Chaconne, seldom played with its preceding four dances, is part of a set of three sonatas and three partitas for unaccompanied melody instruments, completed in 1720. Of the partitas, the second, the D-minor, is considered the 'heartpiece' and the Chaconne itself the brilliant gem of a masterwork. Geiringer describes it as a

> gigantic set of interconnected variations on a harmonic pattern derived from a simple, four-measure bass. The variations usually appear in pairs, the second one subtly enhancing the content of the first.   (Geiringer 1967: 309)

Numerical patterns are common to both the choreography[11] and the musical composition.[12] Forsythe builds the choreography around four dancers, predominantly in overlapping duets. But he selectively disregards linear musical development both in his choreographic response and in the manner in which he chooses to present the music, thus reworking the idea of a unity between dance and music in classicism. Brief anguished snatches of the opening bar of the Chaconne are heard initially. Then the recording plays continuously after the woman's first appearance, but stops abruptly at intervals during the ballet. Several bars are sometimes repeated when the music recommences, before it

plays through to its conclusion. Viewed conventionally, this hallowed composer's music has been vandalised. From the perspective of the deconstructionist
investigation of ballet, the rearrangement of the recording is both artistically
succinct, and a violent act.

Acknowledgement of the traditional relationship between music and balletic
method, where the timing of the action interlocks with the music, is indicated in
some sequences of repeated phrases of movement and music, for example, when
an undulating *rond de jambe* motif performed by the woman (from bar 77), is
repeated after the music has been almost imperceptibly interrupted (at bar 82).
With the recommencement of the music (at bar 77), the dance is repeated to
mirror the precise relationship established before. Correspondences are also
evident between the music and the structure of the various dance partnerships
in the way significant changes in the solo or duet groupings of the dancers
sometimes coincide with musical developments.

Departures from convention can be seen at the level of overall structure.
Movement, not music, appears to be the dynamic force that propels the action.
The 'time' lines of individual phrases are prescribed by the movement material,
as is evident in the repetition of the following memorable sequence after the
rond de jambe motif: with immense impetus, control *and* relaxation, the woman
lunges into a deep *relevé penché en pointes* holding her partner's hand, is pushed
so that the grasp is released, her torso turns *horizontal* to the floor and she falls
back to be caught under the armpits, and then swooped around like a chair
swing. On the repeat of the *penché* pattern, each man sequentially partners the
woman in this challenging feat of balance. The reader may recall the same
virtuosic concept in the promenade that Aurora and her Princes make in the
Rose Adage from *The Sleeping Beauty* Act I. But in *Steptext,* the balancing act
focuses not on negotiating a sculptural shape through judicious geometric arrangement of the limbs, but on judicious use of force and energy to negotiate
extreme changes in the thrust of the body's weight. The sequence is exciting,
dangerous, and the reader sees it played, then replayed. Implicit in the musical
and visual replay is an example of manipulation of the musical material for
choreographic purposes. The radical shift of emphasis in the dynamic intention
behind the movement, which Forsythe engineers, gives rise to qualities of movement quite alien to traditional ballet. Dynamic interaction of the musical character with particular dance passages can be read as implying particular meaning in
the dancers' relationships. During the long central *pas de deux,* the change of
key from minor to major (bar 133), the contrast of the soaring exhilarating
arpeggios (bar 89) with snatched fragments of music (bar 120), coupled with the
way the dance explores the extremities of body shape and stage space and seems
to reach for high musical moments, lend the passage the air of a conventional
climax. Tenderness and lyricism, qualities commonly associated with ballet, are
evoked very briefly by a sustained and partnered *rond de jambe,* but the moment

The dancers tilt off the balletic vertical, with a shared centre of gravity. (Deborah Bull and Adam Cooper in *Steptext*).   Photo: Leslie E Spatt

is soon disturbed when the dancers resume a combative relationship, alien to the classical harmonies.

Forsythe provokes a fresh contract between the Bach and ballet, inviting the reader to review concepts of musicality and dynamics. The polyphony and rich textures of the Chaconne, embellishments typical of music of the Baroque, are also general artistic characteristics, exemplified by *trompe l'oeil*, of the period.

Geiringer (1967: 307) suggests that both require the working of the inner ear or eye, just as Forsythe's processes do, with their extraordinary proliferation of movement. For Sulcas, Forsythe's work is analogous to 'looking through a microscope at the composition reveal[ing] a hitherto unimagined beauty and complexity of structure' (1991: 32).

Dancing Steps: Competing and Conflicting Texts

Seen within the spectrum of Forsythe's work, *Steptext* sits securely at the formal end.

> His is a reflection on the technical premises of the ballet: muscular perception, the function of internal joints, space . . . He articulates in a dance language that has a contemporary flair (high tech), expressing nothing more (or less) than the dance itself.   (Jeschke 1992: 203)

Such expressions are often taken to imply that there is no overt 'content' or 'expression' in modernist explorations of abstract form. But the idea that there are traces of conflicting texts inherent within the dancing steps is worth exploring further.

Much of the movement content in *Steptext* can be described effectively in balletic terminology, but it is the addition of those words from contemporary dance techniques and everyday behaviour that seems to capture the aesthetic and dynamic qualities of the dancing. Tilt, lean, elongate, extend, distort, undulate, snap and stride, all appropriately describe actions integrated into balletic method to forge the movement material. Forsythe's explorations are clearly concerned with an expansion of a grammar and code that he considers to be usefully neutral but, simultaneously, he uses to subvert aspects of convention and structure that are apparently straightforward. Actions are inflected with emotionally evocative overtones to comment and impact upon ballet's institutional and cultural status, making the language far from neutral.

Contrasting movement codes operate in *Steptext*: a gestural and pedestrian mode of behaviour, and a very vigorous athletic dancing based on balletic principle. The dancers switch on and off, abruptly and apparently automatically, between everyday street walking, balletic sequences and the gestural code, actions which make Jeschke's description seem too straightforward. The gestures consist of curious arm signals performed by the men at intervals throughout. As a counterpart are actions reminiscent of 'signing', precise movements of the forearms only, as if restricted to a box in front of the chest. Executed initially by the woman, the men respond by reflecting the 'box' gestures back to her later.

A clue to deciphering the men's arm signals comes half way through the ballet, as the second man is about to partner the woman (at bar 115). As he approaches her, he waves his arms from side to side passing through the positions he may adopt, to execute a supported 'finger turn' for instance. These arm moves are like the ones he uses again to partner the woman, and also like those of the third man, who, on quitting actual partnering, continues to move his arms as if transposing or 'marking' the actions needed to partner.

Repetition in dancing, especially in the act of creating a new work and the acquisition of a technique, leaves trace lines within the body, a kind of 'muscle memory' or multi-muscular pattern, known as engrams. 'Constant, exact repetitions or practice will produce an engram, a condition where individual muscles or movements are not consciously considered' (Howse & Hancock 1992: 19). An essentially technical device, vital for building a dancer's competence, is presented here as a component of the artistic product. 'Marking' (a dance shorthand for rehearsing moves in order to commit them to memory) is juxtaposed with virtuosic ballet, a combination which roots the *Steptext* enquiry in the fundamental physiological potentialities and limitations of the ballet dancer's body as well as in ballet's own silent languages. Both understandings become traces in an intertextual reading.

Forsythe tests the limits of balletic principle in *Steptext* by challenging a central tenet of ballet, *en dehors*, or turning out. Aesthetically, *en dehors* derives from the open fluid stance of antique Greek and Roman sculpture. Visually and physiologically it expands the ballet dancer's silhouette and frees her to achieve height in linear extensions by extreme rotation in the hip joints. Forsythe plays with this concept of freedom to exploit movement along a multiplicity of planes. The technical foundation of his choreographic investigations are in ballet, and the obviously balletic action in *Steptext* exhibits all the polar characteristics associated with his style. His explorations of extreme points of balance, broken lines, the radical tilt of the torso off the balletic vertical, the articulation of the hips to facilitate broader *degagé* and the verticality in the limbs (with torso tilt) derive from a balletic comprehension of movement: by sustained but rapid *transference of weight* with control the dancers negotiate their balance and their (often shared) centre of gravity. Implicit in the resulting vigorous, athletic dance, very much of its time, are concepts of danger and necessarily, therefore, of trust, which resonate with the risk-taking contemporaneous dance techniques, dubbed 'Eurocrash', expounded by choreographers such as Wim Vandekeybus. Its mechanics, however, are distinct from those of the new dance. Release into fall and recovery, the analytic foundation of many modern dance techniques, are not part of the lexicon of action words in *Steptext*.

If, as Kirstein argues, 'ballet simulates a conquest against gravity of aerial space' (1983: 243), Forsythe's treatment of the form topples this key philosophical ideal in ballet. He exposes the duality of balletic ideology in which physical and perceptual properties appear to differ, through concealing effort to present lightness and lift. Removing these illusions of ease may serve to liberate lines of

The central duet of Steptext, showing the woman supported 'like a handbag' from her partner's elbow. (Deborah Bull, Adam Cooper.)   Photo: Leslie E Spatt

communication to the percipient, opening up the possibility for the viewer to engage imaginatively with the sensations of the dance, with its visceral qualities, with the realities of its extreme workings and with the dancers' engagement with their own normally disguised physical effort. For instance, in the central duet (at bar 122), the woman lands weightily from a high circling supported *jeté*, in a huge fourth position *en pointes* which she maintains effortfully, tacitly protesting, while her partner drags her across the floor in a rigidly held pose from his arm; he then struggles to turn, supporting her stiff body like a handbag hanging from his elbow. The peculiar and unpredictable elements juxtaposed here, the centrifugal force of the soaring leap, the palpable awkwardness of the drag and the comedy of the 'handbag' hold, combine to create a fresh passage of dance that flaunts effort and challenges what Scholl suggests is 'ballet's primary problem, the struggle to overcome gravity' (1994: 117).

When Balanchine choreographed *The Four Temperaments* in 1940, 'acknowledgment of gravity was a commonplace' in contemporaneous modern dance, and Scholl posits that in this ballet Balanchine was similarly experimenting with the body's weight (1994: 118). *The Four Temperaments* takes as a theme the ancient Greeks' belief that the body comprehends our temperaments: Melancholic, Sanguinic, Phlegmatic and Choleric. A motif is developed through the work where the woman is dragged along the stage, her legs in *jeté arabesque* skimming the floor, while she clutches the man's torso. In his play with the concept of verticality and elevation, Forsythe both acknowledges Balanchine's celebration of the body weight, and extends it by expanding the classical silhouette through a freer use of the arms and torso. Conventional use of *port de bras* determines that the arms are always held slightly in front of the body, embracing the audience, while radical play around the centre of gravity in *Steptext* determines that the arms reach out to balance the legs. Undulation in the torso impels the arms into spontaneous, reflexive action.

In *Steptext* the play with the paradox that places perceptual and physical properties in opposition to each other opens up other philosophical texts. The illusion of ease touches on the Cartesian concept of dualism that distinguishes thinking substance (mind) from extended substance (matter) and Plato's world where 'forms' and 'ideas' are attributed with a greater substance and reality than concrete objects which are real in the physical dimension. In reflecting on the separation of mind and body, the reader may be drawn to a prevailing theme in twentieth-century art, the dichotomy which places formalism and expressionism, Apollo and Dionysius, mind and matter, at opposite ends of a pole. Reconciliation of these opposites, in transcendence and transformation, leads back to both the goal and theme of traditional ballet; the geometric form to which the body impossibly aspires. Transformation is explored thematically in narrative, as in Tchaikovsky's *The Nutcracker* by Petipa (1892) or in Nureyev's 1968 production, where the character of Clara literally transforms from gawky girl into ballerina as part of the drama. The dancer's ultimate goal becomes the subject matter and form of the choreography. Heppenstall expands on the idea of transformation as the dancer's ultimate technical goal in his *Apology for Dancing* (1936):

> It is a struggle between a wastefully complex muscular system, designed for a limited range of animal acts and offices, and the economy, the simplicity, in line and mass of the postures and movements – the Physical Ideas – to which his body, as a material of Art, aspires. And the result is not a triumph of Mind over Matter, but the emergence of non-cerebral matter into such a condition of subtlety and sensibility that it can itself be called Mind.
>
> (Heppenstall 1983: 288)[13]

Competing texts are held simultaneously within the concept of duality and transformation. Rejecting the romantic, the metaphysical notion of transcending the technical demands so that the body dissolves into effortless expression, Forsythe shares with Balanchine an 'understanding of the dancing body's materiality' in choreography (Scholl 1994: 115). In his study of Balanchine's manipulation of material between movement and stasis to make architectural dance statements, Scholl comments on the choreographer's ability 'to transform the commonplace and unlovely into things of beauty' and 'celebrate the transcendent powers of [his] arts' (*ibid.*: 122). Where the notion of transcendence in *Steptext* is apparent, however, is not in the sculptural design of material objects but in the manifestation of qualities of effort and energy that the reader constructs. The idealist illusion of ease disappears. 'Fleshing out' the dance's physicality, the art form becomes less visual, more visceral – and the distance between dancing the dance and reading the dance is transcended. Seeing the body's effort, the physical sensation of the dancing is what the reader is stimulated by and engages with; what she also may recognise is a notion of humanism today, defined by Maurice Merleau-Ponty as

> no longer anything decorous or decorative . . . [and that] no longer loves man in opposition to his body, mind in opposition to its language, values in opposition to facts.   (cited in Eco 1989: 154)

The thread winds back to Saussure's insight that 'language is a form not a substance' (Sturrock 1979: 10), to Plato's theory about the value of ideas over material objects and thus returns full circle to a post-structuralist denial of such binarisms.

The Antithesis of Classicism: Fragmented Structures

Steptext leads the viewer into a fragmented world of interrupted episodes and multiple interactions. The *pas de deux*, often the heart of a classical ballet, is the structural device Forsythe manipulates not to create a formulaic display of duet, solos and coda, but layers of duet and solo events which occupy the temporal and spatial landscape erratically. It is also a rich framework in ballet for exploring intimate relationships, particularly between the sexes – the discourse of love and conflict in physical form.

The premise upon which the *pas de deux*[14] material is founded, examining interdependent strength, control and balance in the partnership to discover and reveal the increasingly extreme plastic possibilities between two human forms, is the same as that for the groundbreaking *pas de deux* in Balanchine's *Agon*.[15] As in *Steptext* there is no dramatic narrative, but *Agon* presents a series of unwinnable games of dancing skill, in which the dancers employ wit, humour, physical strength and daring to create drama and tension. Forsythe's and Balanchine's dances employ a similar range of qualities to suggest meanings that reach beyond the strictly formal properties. Statements of tension, friction, comedy, trust and danger are inherent in the performance of the movement material, which is alternately strident, jagged, sensual, sustained, distorted, angular and

The angular, combative relation between the sexes in *Steptext* (Deborah Bull, Adam Cooper).

Photo: Leslie E Spatt

expansive. In the long central *pas de deux* of *Steptext* in particular, the dancers' intimate understanding of their shared work enables them to embrace a breathtaking range of qualities, from the sensual to the mildly comic to the dangerous. The danger and tension in the *pas de deux* of both *Agon* and *Steptext* underline their sexual nature, the play of sexual attraction and 'sizing up' between potential partners. Risk, and therefore fear, accompany the loss of control that is courted implicitly in the sexual act – qualities with which the dancers contend in dancing these steps.[16]

Forsythe's exploration of the *pas de deux* elicits unusual movement material and defines the woman's role in this work. In certain respects her usual primacy of place is confirmed by her costuming (she wears red to the men's grey or black) and her slighter feminine build is acknowledged in that she does not physically take her partner's weight. Whilst these aspects of the presentation of woman conform to expectations of traditional roles, the sharing of weight and strength integral to achieving the extremes of counterbalance, the physical risk, and her authority, which extends to initiating or ending the dances, paint anything but an ethereal, restrained or demure picture of a female classical dancer. Instead of transcendent sylph, the woman in *Steptext* has emerged from the sexual revolution moving with assertiveness and confidence, comfortable with expressing a range of qualities with an obviously physical body. And unlike the women in many of Balanchine's ballets, who are revered and commodified in their plastic beauty, the female protagonist in *Steptext* takes decisions, initiates movement and literally 'pulls her weight' within a partnership.

Reading the movement language together with structure – juxtaposing different movement codes against disintegrated music – the social world of *Steptext* can be seen. In the spatial and temporal arrangement of the duets and solos the choreography makes no concessions to the traditional balletic formality surrounding the virtuoso solo or *pas de deux*, or to the code of manners, embodied in ballet's shapes, for maintaining an implicitly respectful distance between participants. In nineteenth-century repertoire the *pas de deux* invariably begins with a solemn greeting or *révérence* derived from the vocabulary of movement.[17] The staccato dynamic characterising the *Steptext* woman's boxed gesture code that borders her different partnerships suggests a formal device for the dancer to change her dancing partner, without recourse to the niceties of balletic mannerism.

Within the structure of the ballet, the men dance solo and in duets or *pas de deux*. One of their *pas de deux* is especially noteworthy because of the way it is framed – a sustained supported *adage* near the beginning of the ballet is performed in silence and lit by a slim beam from the downstage left wing, and is one of only two occasions during the main body of the ballet where there are no more than two dancers on stage. The woman never dances solo. So, despite her visible show of strength and initiative in partnered movement, her place is read, within the structure, as dependent upon the male dancers; ultimately one is led back to questions of control and power, conflict and contradiction in gender relationships. The male and female dancers jockey for power. Traditionally 'feminine' qualities, compassion and sensuality, are seen fleetingly; aggressive, predominantly 'masculine' qualities surface readily.[18] In this world, relationships begin and end abruptly, often punctuated by a symbolically sharp movement or gesture.[19] It is difficult for the reader to settle into following the linear development of one partnership within the ballet. Instead, threads lead outside the ballet to a social world that resonates not with a romantic ideal, but with the gritty reality of a contemporary society, to tension between the genders, to dangers in sexual relations, to both fear and trust and – implicitly – to the interdependence of opposites, within the self as in partnerships.

Conclusion

This intertextual reading presents a Forsythe who, informed by his own interests in postmodern analytical thought, reveals the processes by which ballet is conventionally constructed on systems of theatrical dancing; ballet here is the subject of an intellectual scrutiny alien to traditional procedure and more typical of analytic postmodern dance. That *Steptext* is a bold experiment with the conventions of theatre and ballet is clearly a shared reading; but, not surprisingly, this work does not find favour with all critics and audiences. While enjoying the kinaesthetic qualities of Forsythe's work, some critics wonder at its 'mystifying hollowness' (Hering 1988: 33). The kind of post-structuralist and postmodernist devices that he employs engender analytical detachment and emotional disengagement, while simultaneously generating viscerally rich ballet that the reader can almost touch and feel. Ironically, the contradictions in the work, its conflicting, coexisting texts, are central to its drive.[20]

Forsythe focuses with the singularity of Balanchine on the formal properties of ballet and its conventions, extending Petipa's and then Balanchine's classicism into new terrain. Boundaries of an existing code of dancing are pushed to forge an expanded aesthetic. The vocabulary celebrates effort, and acknowledges gravity as a means of enlarging power and range, taking the interrogation of balletic principle in verticality and elevation from balance to breaking point. Intertexts from different corners of contemporary dance culture and philosophical enquiry converge. In the intertextual confluence the reader discovers both evidence of and the subversion of classicism. Elegance and rigour are hallmarks in the structure of the enquiry into making situated contemporaneous art from historically generated vocabulary: the resulting material text moves away from classicism to discord and disunity, to become an open and unstable text. The reader can also trace the thread in the intertext of balletic concepts through to Platonic theory, Cartesian duality and Forsythe's vocabulary with contemporary humanism, glancing off conflicting postmodern strategies.

While philosophical and human conditions are overtly explored in longer pieces of the order of *Alie/n a(c)tion*, works such as *Steptext* appear 'academic' on the surface (Forsythe, in Odenthal 1994: 25), as pure exercises in modernism. It is by ploughing the balletic text and drawing out threads in the formal components that meaning can be created beyond the poetic abstract. Contradictory worlds occupy the intertextual landscape – intellectual ideas alongside the social considerations of gender relations, democracy and autocracy – all are manifested in this most physically extreme and sexually potent of dances. Most significantly, Forsythe is engaged in the discourse of innovation from a traditional base; he writes for a contemporaneous ballet and is in dialogue with ballet as an institution. His method for establishing modern materiality is to scrutinise the system and to plumb the richness of the balletic heritage. By fragmenting and decentralising balletic and musical components, and rephrasing them in a new dynamic relationship that leads to a world outside the immediate context, Forsythe attempts to divorce balletic technique from aspects of its ideology and history that are incompatible with a notion of reality in a modern world. *Steptext*'s dances dispense with the manners and postures of the imperial court, subvert the hierarchies that determine the reproduction of nineteenth-century works in large ballet companies, and overturn historically situated and redundant principles of balletic form. Attention is drawn to dance as action and energy, not sculpted object – 'actively spoken' and colloquial, not courtly dancing.

Interest in the material dancing text testifies to the resilience of the balletic components in the face of this onslaught of deconstruction, and provokes debate on the suitability of this movement language for formal enquiry. Productivity in the text and intertext is the result of the meeting of contraries – visible effort and transcendence, system and writing, colloquialism and formality, male and female, synchronic and diachronic axes of investigation, verticality and horizontality – in time and space, in choreography.

Notes

1. Historically, the use of 'academic' in relation to classical ballet denotes knowledge and understanding of *danse d'école*, or the principles and set of classroom steps or vocabulary that form the basis for technical training in pure form of the classical ballet dancer. Kirstein considers that the balletic concept of the five 'academic' foot positions with *en dehors*, or turning out, determines the frontal 'legibility' of the silhouette of the body in the frame of the proscenium arch (1983: 240). Accurate exposition of ballet steps is commonly referred to as 'articulate' footwork. Words such as 'legible', 'academic' and 'articulate' are terms also used in the linguistically-focused postmodern dance where movement is treated as 'language', a set of socially constructed practices.

2. With the support of Frankfurt's intellectuals, artists, musicians and architects, Forsythe quickly dispensed with presenting 'classics' and instead built his programming around his own work and that of choreographers he admires, such as Jan Fabre, Amanda Miller and Stephen Petronio. Public approval testifies to the success of his uncompromising policies and experiment. The international recognition exemplified by Frankfurt Ballet's annual residencies at the Châtelet in Paris and the worldwide demand for Forsythe's ballets are indicators of the interest his work attracts.

3. Raymond Dragon Design is credited alongside Forsythe for design of the costumes in the Royal Ballet's production.

4. 'Step' in ballet terminology is *pas*. This term can denote a specific individual movement, such as a *pas de bourrée* (running step), and an aspect of structure, such as *pas de trois* (trio or dance for three people).

5. Sturrock (1979: 12) posits that Saussure's insight into language fundamentally informs the work of Barthes, Foucault and Derrida.

6. Macaulay (1987a: 8) suggests that in ballets such as *The Sleeping Beauty*, Petipa's choreography achieves something of the formal perfection in the music of the great classical composers Haydn, Mozart and Beethoven.

7. See Scholl's analysis of Balanchine's choreography with reference to architectural concepts (1994: 105–33).

8. Another contemporary architect, Daniel Libeskind, is a friend of Forsythe's. His design for the Jewish Museum in Berlin was realised in 1997 and represents a

Star of David, partly deconstructed and remade to introduce new dimensions on to the flat silhouette (Glancey 1997: 10).

9. The viewer's perception of lightness in this type of lift belies the strength required by the man to sustain the woman's 'dead weight' in a constant position just above the floor. By contrast, the technical demands of spectacular lifts above the head are premised as much upon complex co-ordination and timing in the relationship between two dancers, as on actual physical strength.

10. Time is the aspect that Forsythe continues to explore in ballets such as *Eidos: Telos* (1995) that makes direct reference to *Apollo*; clocks dominate the visual and aural scene in *Alie/n a(c)tion* and *Eidos: Telos*.

11. Here Forsythe's experiments with technologies such as CD-ROM to formulate choreographic material, and his appreciation of the impersonality of ballet cohere in his interest in the anonymity of systems. He calls ballet 'a very complex mechanical structure with the beauty of mathematics' (cited in Meisner 1995: 50).

12. Bach's fascination with mathematical structure and number symbolism is a well researched and much debated topic (Tatlow 1991).

13. The idea was current at that time. Mabel E. Todd's seminal book *The Thinking Body*, published in 1937, was an examination of the effect of psychological and mental processes on human movement.

14. For clarity of analysis I distinguish between a duet as a dance for two people which has clear formal spatial relationships but where there is no physical contact, and *pas de deux*, a dance for two people which also involves weight bearing and physical contact.

15. *Agon*, which is Greek for contest, is the last of Balanchine's trilogy of collaborations with Stravinsky which reference classical Greece, following *Apollo* (1928) and *Orpheus* (1948). *Apollo* is also interesting in the context of *Steptext*: both ballets employ a dancer of one sex and three of the other, and play with gendered issues of power and control in the choreography.

16. Dunnant writes about the connection of female fear with eroticism in 'Waking the Dead', coinciding with publication of her book *Transgressions* (1997).

17. The final *pas de deux* in Act III of *The Sleeping Beauty* (1890) and *Coppélia* (1870) begin in a similar manner with the male and female dancers entering from opposite sides, to greet each other sharing centre stage. They proceed by walking forward and their dancing steps start with an elaborate choreographic greeting.

18. Representation of gender in dance performance and of the 'feminine ideal' in ballet is the subject of recent writing influenced by feminist and film theory, for example Adair (1992) and Foster (1995). Burt (1995) examines representations of masculinity and the male dancer in twentieth-century theatre dance arguing that the limited ways in which cultural forms present images of men uphold patriarchy and the power imbalance between women and men.

19. See McRobbie's comments on Harvey (1989) in which 'Harvey takes up the notion of the temporary contract as the hallmark of postmodern social relations' (1994: 29).

20. Postmodernity is linked with the emptiness of late twentieth-century life in texts by Jameson (1984) and Harvey (1989). In her critique of postmodernity and cultural studies, McRobbie refers to Jameson's view that postmodernism is 'associated with the emergence of broken, fractured shadow of a "man"' (1994: 27).

References

Adair, C. (1992), *Women and Dance: Sylphs and Sirens*, London, MacMillan.
Burt, R. (1995), *The Male Dancer*, London, Routledge.
Constanti S. (1995), 'The Royal Ballet – What's the Big Idea?', *Independent*, 18 May: 28.
Driver, S. (1990), 'A Conversation with William Forsythe', *Ballet Review*, 18, 1: 86–97.
Dunnant, S. (1997), 'Waking the Dead: Wayward Girls and Wicked Women', *Guardian*, 7 June: 10–11.
———— (1997), *Transgressions*, London, Littlebrown.
Eco, U. (1989), *The Open Work*, London, Hutchinson Radius.
Fischer, E. (1990), 'Aesthetic Norms and Today's Social Taboos: The Effect on Innovation and Creativity', *Ballett International*, 1: 49–52.
Forsythe, W., S. Paxton & M. A. de Mey, (1990), *I Think the Body Likes to Move*, video directed by A. Quirynen, Vlaams Theater Institut, Holland, Ministerie van Onderwus/Dienst Media en Informatietechnologie.
———— (1991), Taped interview by J. Castanau, *Ballet 2000*, Madrid, Teatro de la Zarzuela, 8 November.
Foster, S.L. (1995), 'Harder, Faster, Longer, Higher – A Postmortem Enquiry into the Ballerina's Making', in J. Adshead-Lansdale & C. Jones (eds), *Border Tensions: Dance and Discourse*, Proceedings of the Fifth Study of Dance Conference, Guildford, National Resource Centre for Dance: 109–14.
Geiringer, K. (1967), *Johann Sebastian Bach, the Culmination of an Era*, New York, Oxford University Press.
Glancey, J. (1997), 'Prepare to be Outraged', *Guardian*, 15 September: 10–11.
Gradinger, M. (1993), 'Forsythe, William', in M. Bremser, L. Nicholas & L. Shrimpton (eds), *International Dictionary of Ballet*, Detroit, St James Press: 513–5.
Harvey, D. (1989), *The Condition of Postmodernity*, Oxford, Blackwell.
Heppenstall, R. (1983), 'The Sexual Idiom' (1936), in R. Copeland & M. Cohen (eds), *What is Dance?* Oxford, Oxford University Press: 267–88.
Hering, D. (1988), 'Frankfurt Ballet, City Centre Theatre', *Dance Magazine*, October, 28, 32–3.
Howse, J. & S. Hancock (1992), *Dance Technique and Injury Prevention*, London, A & C Black.
Jameson, F. (1984), 'Postmodernism, or the Cultural Logic of Capital', *New Left Review*, 146: 53–92.
Jeschke, C. (1992), 'American Theatricality in Contemporary German Theater Dancing: John Neumeier and William Forsythe', *Proceedings of the Society of Dance History Scholars*, Riverside CA: Society of Dance History Scholars, 201–6.
Kaeppler, A. (1992), 'Theoretical and Methodological Considerations for Anthropological Studies of Dance and Human Movement Systems', *Ethnographica*, 8: 151–7.
Kirchner, B. (1984), 'Good Theatre of a Different Kind', *Ballett International*, 8: 6–7.
Kirstein L. (1983), 'The Aria of the Aerial' (1976), in R. Copeland & M. Cohen (eds), *What is Dance?* Oxford, Oxford University Press: 238–43.
Klotz, H. (1988), *The History of Postmodern Architecture*, Cambridge, MA, MIT Press.
Kultermann, U. (1966), *New Architecture of the World*, London, Thames & Hudson.
Laban, R. (1966), *Choreutics*, London, MacDonald & Evans.

Macaulay, A. (1987a), 'Notes on Dance Classicism', *Dance Theatre Journal*, 5, 2: 6–9, 36–39.

———— (1987b), 'Notes on Dance Classicism', in J. Adshead (ed.), *Choreography: Principles and Practice*, Report of the Fourth Study of Dance Conference, Guildford, National Resource Centre for Dance: 63–79.

———— (1997), 'Further Notes on Dance Classicism', *Dance Theatre Journal*, 13, 3: 24–30.

McRobbie, A. (1994), *Postmodernisrn and Popular Culture*, London, Routledge.

Meisner, N (1994), 'Frankfurt Ballet', *Dance and Dancers*, 516: 31.

———— (1995), 'Dangerous Beauty', *Opera House*, 1: 48–51.

Odenthal, J. (1994), 'A Conversation with William Forsythe', *Ballett International*, 2: 23–7.

Scholl, T. (1994), *From Petipa to Balanchine*, London, Routledge.

Sparshott, F. (1995), *A Measured Pace: Towards a Philosophical Understanding of the Art of Dance*, Toronto, University of Toronto Press.

Sturrock, J. (1979), *Structuralism and Since: From Lévi-Strauss to Derrida*, Oxford, Oxford University Press.

Sulcas, R. (1991), 'The Poetry of Disappearance and the Great Tradition', *Dance Theatre Journal*, 9, 1: 5–7, 32–3.

Tatlow, R. (1991), *Bach and the Riddle of the Number Alphabet*, Cambridge, Cambridge University Press.

Ward, A. (1993), 'Dancing in the Dark: Rationalism and the Neglect of Social Dance', in H. Thomas (ed.), *Dance, Gender and Culture*, London, MacMillan: 16–33.

6

Mark Morris's *Dido and Aeneas*

Carol Martin

The reader is given here the opportunity to construct her/his own reading from a series of intertexts. The traces of material presented give an outline of the work in sections: the time frame of the action with a brief narrative; a selection of dance texts which Carol Martin created; her own 'reader perspective'; selected statements of dance critics on Dido and Aeneas; and theoretical statements on intertextuality. You are invited to create your own route through these texts, bringing your own text/thoughts/memories to join them in intertextual play.

DANCE/OPERA STRUCTURES

Table 1 . Solo, Duet, Trio and Ensemble Structure

Act I (Nos. 2–13)	Act II (Nos. 14–28)	Act III (Nos. 29–39)
Solo (aria)	*Solo* (recit.)	Solo + Ensemble (aria)
Solo (aria)	Ensemble (chor.)	Solo (instr.)
Duet (recit.)	Solo (recit.)	Duet (recit.)
Ensemble (chor.)	Ensemble (chor.)	Trio (recit.)
Trio (recit.)	Trio (recit.)	Ensemble (chor.)
Duet/Ensemble) aria)	Ensemble (chor.)	*Ensemble (instr.)*
Solo (recit.)	Duet (aria)	Trio (recit.)
Ensemble (chor.)	Ensemble (chor.)	Ensemble (chor.)
Solo (recit.)	*Ensemble (instr.)*	Duet (recit.)
Duet (aria)	*Duet (ritor.)*	Solo (aria)
Ensemble (chor.)	Solo + Ensemble (aria)	*Ensemble (chor.)*
Ensemble (chor.)	*Solo* (aria)	
	Solo (recit.)	
	Solo + Ensemble (aria)	
	Solo + Ensemble (recit	

As can be seen, nearly half of all dances are, or include, ensembles, rendering this movement 'chorus' a particularly significant structure. The brackets illustrate the way in which these group dances link the scenes (in italics) and acts, a thread which brings a level of structural coherence. Present throughout the work except for 'The Grove' scene (No. 23), the dance 'chorus' function as observers and, like their Greek prototype, comment on events. The ensemble is also a 'rounding off' structure with two consecutive group dances ending four of the six scenes. This is a translation of Purcell's passages for chorus followed by instrumental music for 'dances' (Nos. 13, 22, 34) from which Morris produces an extended group dance.

The second most dominant feature in this hierarchical arrangement is the solo, a choreographic reflection of the lead soprano, mezzo-soprano and tenor passages in Purcell's score. This is the opening structure for each act, a form associated with setting the scene, characterisation and reflection. As the choreographic equivalent of the soliloquy, the solo also contributes to the individual/group contrast vital to the production of meanings. All characters have solo passages through which their status as separate from the group is identified.

Table 2. Structuring a Narrative of *Dido and Aeneas*

Score Item	Time	Text shown on screen	Music/dance form	Narrative
Overture and Act I: The Palace	0'00''-16'07''			
1 4/4 Adagio then Quick	1'50"	Film and dance credits	Overture/ whole cast	Brief synopsis of the story followed by credits and introduction of characters and cast. Ends in tableau. D and B seated upstage centre. CH seated across back of stage.
2 4/4 Allegretto	1'08"	THE PALACE 'Shake the cloud from off your brow'	B + chor. aria/ solo + ens.	A conversation between D, Queen of Carthage and her sister B: the arrival of the Trjan prince AN and the passion it has aroused in D are revealed.
3 3/4 Slow	3'49"	'Ah! Ah! Ah Belinda...'	D aria/solo	
4 4/4 then 2/4 Andante	0'35"	'Grief increases by concealing ...'	B, SW recitative/duet	
5 3/4 Allegro	0'14"	'When monarchs unite...'	chorus/ensemble	
6 4/4 Andante	1'55"	'Whence could so much virtue spring'	D, B, SW recitative/trio	The CH celebrate the prospect of a union between two great empires but D fears the intensity of her emotions.
7 3/4	1'36"	'Fear no danger to ensue...'	B, SW aria + chor./ duet + ensemble	The two women try to allay her fears.
8 4/4 Andante	0'49"	'See, see, your royal guest appears...' AN recitative/solo	AN recitative/solo	Urged by the council of her court, D listens to AN pledge his love but reminds him that his destiny lies elsewhere.
9 2/2 Allegretto	0'34"	'Cupid only throws the dart...'	chorus/ensemble	The Trojan is prepared to follow his heart and the CH, led by B, proclaim the work of Cupid.
10 4/4	0'23"	'If not for mine for Empire's sake...'	AN recitative/solo	AN begs for pity.

AN = Aeneas B = Belinda CH = Chorus D = Dido SW = Second Woman S = Sorceress W1 = First Witch W2 = Second Witch SL = Sailor

Score Item	Time	Text shown on screen	Music/dance form	Narrative
11 4/4 Quick	0'50"	'Pursue thy conquest love...'	B, SW duet aria/duet	The two women urge D to accept AN.
12 3/4 Allegro Vivace	1'15"	'To the hills and the vales...'	chorus/ensemble	The court prepares for a hunting party and dance to celebrate the triumph of Love. The clouds have lifted and D's happiness is shared by all.
13 3/4 L'istesso Tempo	1'08"	THE TRIUMPHING DANCE	chorus/ensemble	The lovers depart.
No Music	0'11"	No Text	ensemble	The silence that follows is disturbed by the noise of doom and the gathering storm.

Act II: The Cave (Act II Scene I: The Cave) 16'08"–23'46"

Score Item	Time	Text shown on screen	Music/dance form	Narrative
14 2/2 Non Troppo Lento	1'57"	'Wayward sisters, you that fright...'	S recitative/solo	The S beckons her sister witches to appear.
15 3/4 Allegro	0'15"	'harm's our delight...'	chorus/ensemble	The nature of this kingdom of darkness is revealed.
16 2/2 Non Troppo Lento	0'34"	'The Queen of Carthage whom we hate...'	S recitative/solo	The plot to lure AN away from Carthage and destroy D is concocted and savoured with glee. The S will send one of her cronies to the hunting party disguised as Mercury. There the deceitful messenger will deliver Jove's command – that AN must leave Carthage and his Queen.
17 3/8 Vivace	0'11"	'Ho ho ho ho ho...'	chorus/ensemble	
18 4/4 Non Troppo Lento	1'08"	'Ruin'd ere the set of sun...'	S, W1, W2 recitative	
19 3/8 Vivace	0'09"	'Ho ho ho ho ho...'	chorus/ensemble	The coven join in laughter.
20 2/2 Allegro	1'06"	'But ere we this perform...'	W1, W2 duet arti/duet	The two witches suggest a storm to ruin the hunting party and separate.
21 3/4 Moderato	1'17"	'In our deep vaulted cell...'	chorus/ensemble	AN from D for the bogus message. The Witches will prepare the dreadful charm.
22 4/4 Allegro	0'51"	ECHO DANCE OF FURIES	instrumental/ensemble	The S leads her coven in an ungainly dance.
No Music	0'10"	No text	S image	The silhouette of the S fades into total blackness...

The Grove (Act II Scene 2: The Grove) 23'47"–24'33"

Score Item	Time	Text shown on screen	Music/dance form	Narrative
23 2/2 Allegro	0'46"	No text	instr. Ritornelli/duet	Alone together, the ill-fated union is consummated.

Score Item	Time	Text shown on screen	Music/dance form	Narrative
The Hunting Party (Act II Scene 2: The Grove) 24'34" – 32'15"				
24 3/4 Allegretto	1'35"	'Thanks to these lonesome vales...'	B + chor. aria/	Led by B, the CH conjure images of the realm of Diana the Huntress. A story within a story, the SW narrates the legend of Actaeon, devoured by his own hands after spying on Diana's nakedness.
25 4/4 Allegretto	1'57"	'Oft she visits this lone mountain...'	SW aria/solo	
26 4/4 Moderato	0'34"	'Behold upon my bended spear...'	AN recitative/solo	AN displays his own prowess but D hears a storm approaching and B urges a hasty return to court.
27 4/4 Allegretto	0'44"	'Haste, haste to town...'	B + chor. aria/ solo + ens.	
28 4/4	2'41"	'Stay Prince...'	SP recit./ AN solo + ens.	AN is deceived by the spirit of the sorceress disguised as Mercury who relays a message from Jove commanding the Trojan to leave Carthage immediately.
No Music	0'10"	No text	AN image	AN turns and walks upstage.
Act III: The Ships (Act III Scene 1: The Ships) 32'16"–38'18"				
29 3/4 Allegro Molto	1'36"	'Come away fellow sailors...'	SL + chor./solo + ens.	AN's turmoil (and D's impending heartbreak) are highlighted by the boisterous antics of the sailors as they prepare for voyage.
30 2/2 Allegro	0'44"	THE SAILORS DANCE (no text)	instrumental/SL solo	
31 4/4 Moderato	0'57"	'See, see the flags and streamers...'	W1, W2 duet recitative/duet	In a final glimpse of the underworld, the death of D is acted out with a wicked enthusiasm by the S and her two favoured crones.
32 4/4	0'34"	'Our next motion must be the storm...'	S, W1, W2 recit./trio	
33 4/4 Allegro	0'35"	'Destruction's our delight...'	chorus/ensemble	An orgy of celebration reminds us that this victory has been easily won.
34 4/4 Pomposo	1'23"	THE WITCHES DANCE (no text)	instrumental/ensemble	

Carol Martin

Score Item	Time	Text shown on screen	Music/dance form	Narrative
No Music	0'13"	No text	S image	
The Palace (Act III Scene 2: The Palace) 38'19"–52'48"				
35 4/4 Adagio	4'12"	'Your council is urg'd in vain...'	D, B, AN recitative/trio	D meets her fate with strength, dismissing AN's explanations and rejecting his offer to stay.
36 2/2 Sostenuto	0'56"	'Great minds against themselves conspire...'	chorus/ensemble	The CH reflect on the tragic outcome.
37 4/4 Grave	0'57"	'Thy hand Belinda...'	D recitative/D + B duet	Forsaken and longing for Death, D takes leave of her sister.
38 3/2 Larghetto	3'33"	'When I am laid...'	D aria/solo	In a final lament she seeks remembrance without pity.
39 4/4 Larghetto	4'48"	'With drooping wings...'	chorus/ensemble	The CH entreat the Cupids to watch over D's tomb. They depart, leaving B beside the body of her sister. A final image of sisterhood, mourning, life and death, victim and survivor.
No Music	0'03"	No Text	Silence/D + B image	
THE END		Production Credits	Blank	THE END

Dance intertexts

Morris refers to the processions found in the first acts of the ballets in 'The Triumph-
-ing Dance', an instrumental section of Purcell's score (no. 13) in which Dido and
Aeneas proceed up an invisible aisle, the essential image of 'betrothal' (made
even more explicit, 'marriage'), needed for the later depiction of 'betrayal'. But
Morris's procession is anything but regal: he swings his hips like a catwalk model,
jumps up and down the 'furniture' (a low bench at the side of the stage) and, of
some significance, walks
ahead of his man. Another
borrowing is 'the mime
scene': Dido, sitting on her
'throne' pondering on her
own feelings is, simulta-
neously, pondering 'he
loves me, he loves me not',
the well-known scene in
which Giselle (1841) picks
off the petals of a daisy.
Belinda, like Siegfried's
mother, is pressuring Dido
to marry (for more or less
the same reasons) but the
notion of marriage–
children–lineage is deconstructed by the male sex/
female gender ambiguity.

Theoretical Intertexts

'The concept of intertextuality requires that we
understand the concept of text not as a self-
contained structure but as differential and
historical. Texts are shaped not by an imma-
nent time but by the play of divergent temporalities.

Texts are therefore not structures of presence
but traces and tracings of otherness. They are
shaped by the repetition and the transformation of other textual structures.

These absent textual structures at once
constrain the text and are represented by and
within it; they are at once preconditions and
moments of the text.'

(Frow, 1990: 45).

Dido contains depictions
of the supernatural in the
tradition of the 'ballet blanc'
(*Giselle* Act II, *Swan Lake*
Acts II and IV, *La Bayadère* Act IV). The use of all-black costumes in a 'ballet noir'
is, thus, one of the more explicit of Morris's subversions. The Sorceress has
precedents in the female-as-witch figures, Myrtha (*Giselle*) and Odile (*Swan Lake*).
Both are evil 'beauties' (the former performed by a leading soloist, the latter by a
principal ballerina) rather than hags, a characterisation of feminine power which
Morris subverts and parodies.

A more direct reference to the nineteenth-century ballet repertoire can be
found in Morris's last work in Belgium, *The Hard Nut* (1991). A deconstruction of
the Tchaikovsky/Ivanov ballet *The Nutcracker* (1892), this intertext, along with
Swan Lake (1877) and *The Sleeping Beauty* (1890), completes a reference to the
hierarchical codes of the imperial Russian ballet.

Critics' Intertexts

Acocella's statement: 'Morris doesn't cover his traces. You can see what he was looking at: in Dido, Indian and Indonesian dance . . .' (1993: 249).

Dance Intertexts

The dualism of the Dido/Sorceress role deserves further consideration. If Dido's vocabulary is reminiscent of Graham's *Lamentation* (1930) then the Sorceress's ungainly, acrobatic antics call to mind a work by another modern dance pioneer, Mary Wigman's *Witch Dance II*.

Through the portrayal of two 'courts', good (The Palace) and evil (The Cave)

Theoretical Intertexts

'What is relevant to textual interpretation is not in itself, the identification of a particular intertextual source but the more general discursive structure (genre, discursive formation, ideology) to which it belongs. This has implications for the kind of knowledge we should expect to be relevant to the readings of texts. It suggests that detailed scholarly information is less important than the ability to reconstruct the cultural codes which are realised (and contested) in texts.' (Frow, 1990: 46)

Morris refers to the opening act of that paradigm of ballet classicism *The Sleeping Beauty* (1890) in which Princess Aurora's christening is interrupted by the wicked fairy Carabosse and her freakish entourage. The reference deepens when one considers the fact that the role of Carabosse was originally danced by a man (the Italian 'maestro' Enrico Cecchetti), a tradition continued today.

Critics' Intertexts

Jann Parry of the *Observer* wrote, 'The question of gender soon recedes in importance', but then goes on to say that 'Like Graham, his movements are spare and graphic, like Duncan, he has the courage to exploit his sincerity, at the same time knowing and naive' (1992). Alastair Macaulay of the *Financial Times* also compared Morris to Graham, saying, 'Mark Morris . . . is the greatest modern-dance creator of dramatic female roles since Martha Graham' (1989). And Dale Harris of the *Wall Street Journal* reiterated the comparison to women dance pioneers: 'Blending what looks like elements from Greek vase painting, photographs of Isadora Duncan, the early solos of Martha Graham and Nijinsky's *L'Après-midi d'un faune*, Mr. Morris has invented a style of movement that goes beyond the archaic to the primeval' (1989) (Morris 1996: 150).

A Reader's Perspective

A familiar terrain of 'already writtens' . . . (to me) . . .

The two intertexts to be considered here are drawn from the nineteenth-century ballet repertoire. Divided in terms of geographical location and by genre, the Coralli/Perrot ballet *Giselle* (1841) belongs to the French romantic ballet whilst *Swan Lake* (1877) is a product of the relocation of ballet to St Petersburg and the emergence of a Russian classical school. This apart, both works reflect the influence of European Romanticism in an underlying dualism between two 'worlds', the 'real' and the spiritual. In the structure of *Dido and Aeneas* (1989), this is alluded to through the two settings of a Palace and an underworld. Further, the role of Odette/Odile, a good/evil dualistic structure performed by the same dancer, is quoted in Morris's portrayal of both Dido and the Sorceress.

Looking across the three works, the first acts emerge as representations of 'real life' and of the hierarchies on which that life is founded. A summary of the 'real life' acts reveals the extent of Morris's quotation and deconstruction:

Looking at the summaries of the first Acts from *Giselle* (1841), *Dido and Aeneas* (1989) and *Swan Lake* (1877), a level of deconstruction can be read into Morris's 'real world'. Here, the family image of mother/daughter (*Giselle*) or King, Queen, son and heir (*Swan Lake*) plays alongside the image of a tormented 'Queen' in a court with no King and no heir. Albrecht must marry, Prince Siegfried must marry, and so must Dido. The illusions of 'reality' ('nature' or court), an essential contrast to the illusions of the 'fantastic', are deconstructed by a minimalist set with an almost empty floorspace which signifies not 'reality' but the artifice of theatre and performance. Giselle and Siegfried 'belong' in their settings, the one as a beautiful innocent peasant girl, the other as a handsome prince and heir. Dido is neither a girl nor innocent, but a man/woman, a King, Prince and 'Queen'. The traditional contrast in colour is also lost, the 'real' world, like the unreal, is monochrome, there is no escaping from one's 'life' because life (autobiography) and fantasy (fiction) are intertwined.

Theoretical Intertexts

'The theory of intertextuality insists that a text . . . cannot exist as a hermetic or self-sufficient whole, and so does not function as a closed system. This is for two reasons. Firstly, the writer is a reader of texts (in the broadest sense) before s/he is a creator of texts, and therefore the work of art is inevitably shot through with references, quotations and influences of every kind . . . Secondly, a text is available only through some process of reading; what is produced at the moment of reading is due to the cross-fertilisation of the packaged textual material . . . by all the texts which the reader brings to it. A delicate allusion to a work unknown to the reader, which therefore goes unnoticed, will have a dormant existence in that reading. On the other hand, the reader's experience of some practice or theory unknown to the author may lead to a fresh interpretation.' (Worton & Still, 1990: 1–2)

Carol Martin

Dance Intertexts

There are aspects of Dido's first solo which emerge as an explicit reference to Martha Graham's early solo *Lamentation* (1930). The seated position with legs open is one such reference (Graham's work is, similarly, performed sitting on a bench) and though the sheath of lilac stretch fabric is missing, the taut quality is represented in the angular arms and flat hands. The verticality is in contrast to Graham's rocking torso but the position is only part of a solo in which Morris bends, leans, leaves and returns to the bench, all features of the Graham solo.

Both dances are expressive of torment, Graham's solitary, minimalist almost dehumanised figure, a reflection of the political and economic crisis of the American 'depression', of women's struggle against the oppression of patriarchy and of the wider context of expressionism in the arts.

On one level, Morris's dance offers a characterisation of Dido's suffering through translation (often literal) of Nahum Tate's libretto. On another level wider discourses can be reconstructed. One can, for example, bring in other related intertexts. Graham as Medea in *Cave of the Heart* (1946), as Jocasta in *Night Journey* (1947), as Joan of Arc in *Seraphic Dialogue* (1955), the mother of Orestes in *Clytemnestra* (1958). What emerges is the classical tradition of the tragic heroine, the betrayed lover, wife, mother, destined by Fate to sacrifice/suicide.

Critics' Intertexts

'In *The Hard Nut* Morris examines gender in a different way than in *Dido and Aeneas*. Instead of centring the work on his own body (in *The Hard Nut*, he dances only two small roles), he uses his entire company to create a proliferation of gender identities. He also creates a more overtly parodic kind of theatre, often through the use of drag. He especially plays on ballet's highly developed vocabulary of male and female steps and conventions which stress heterosexual roles and male domination.' (Morris 1996:150)

Theoretical Intertexts

'The form of representation of intertextual structures ranges from the explicit to the implicit. In addition these structures may be highly particular or highly general; they may be of the order of the message or of the order of the code. Texts are made out of cultural and ideological norms; out of the conventions of genre; out of styles and idioms embedded in the language; out of connotations and collacative sets; out of clichés, formulae, or proverbs; and out of other texts.' (Frow 1990: 45)

Dance Intertexts

Another intertext can be identified in references to the classical Indian dance genre. This takes the form of similarities, where the gesture appears as a combination of Western and Indian dance codes. One such reference is the asymmetrical raised arms of the position accompanying the words 'Aeneas' or 'The Trojan Prince'. The position bears a remarkable resemblance to a picture of the dancer Indrani, a renowned exponent of Kuchipudi dance-theatre, in Judith Lynne Hanna's text *Dance, Sex and Gender* (1988). As noted by the author, this dance form is now kept alive by women (playing both male and female roles) but was originally performed by dancers and actors from the male Brahman (priestly) caste. In relation to Morris, one could read this as *a man being a woman performs a position performed by women performing as men.* The quotation is a prime example of the irony which permeates this work. Other examples can be found, including the 'shimmering' hands with which a classical Indian dancer denotes 'river', performed by Dido in Act III Scene 2 ('Thus on the fatal banks of the Nile, weeps the deceitful crocodile'). One suspects that the snapping hand which 'bites' the wrist of the other hand on the word 'crocodile' has, similarly, Eastern, if not Indian, origins. References to the classical Indian dance genre bring another layer of meanings to Morris's gender ambiguity. As Hanna's (1988) subtitle 'Nonwestern Travesty' suggests the dances of India (and the Far East) contain various traditions of gender imitation. In the classical tradition there are masculine (*tandava*) and feminine (*lasya*) styles which can be performed and developed by dancers of both sexes. In Odissi, young boys dance dressed as girls ('Gotipuas'); in Kathakali, men perform as both men and women (as they do in Japanese Kabuki theatre). The tradition of 'devadasis' in Bharata Natyam is exclusive to female dancers who dance the stories of gods, goddesses and humans, switching freely between roles. The tradition is alluded to in a scene from Act II (subtitled in Morris's dance 'The Hunting Party') in which Dido and Aeneas are entertained by a courtier.

Theoretical Intertexts

'Intertextual analysis is distinguished from source criticism both by this stress on interpretation rather than on the establishment of particular facts, and by its rejection of a unilinear causality (the concept of 'influence') in favour of an account of the work performed upon intertextual material and its functional integration in the later text.' (Frow 1990: 46)

Dance Intertexts

As detailed by Acocella (1993), Morris's works are permeated with references to gender, sex and sexuality. Of significance to this study is the notion of intertextuality between these dances. Using Acocella (1993) as an intertext alongside my analysis it is possible to identify at least one intertext with some confidence in Morris's *Deck of Cards* (1983). The following interpretation of the earlier work would seem to offer great potential to the reading of *Dido*: 'This is not a drag act. Most drag acts, by dint of their energetic but always imperfect imitation of one sex by the other, reaffirm the separation between the sexes. The point of a drag act is that you can still tell the difference: gender is permanent, immovable. Morris, however, is not trying to conceal the difference. He is saying that the two can exist in one body.' (Acocella 1993: 94)

Critics' Intertexts

In her recent study of gender in Morris's work, Gay Morris (1996) draws on Judith Butler's notion of gender as performative arguing that 'Morris's treatment of gender in these two works [*Dido* and *The Hard Nut*], particularly his multiplication of identities and his use of parody and hyperbole as critical tools, suggested parallels with Judith Butler's gender theory' (Morris 1996: 141). She offers an interesting interpretation of Morris's Dido: 'He has often been called androgynous because of his size, muscularity, and substance of his body, considered "masculine", combined with an extreme flexibility and soft, fatty quality that is read stereotypically "feminine". Morris consciously emphasizes and uses these differing aspects of his body as an element to upset dichotomous gender categories' (Morris 1996: 145).

Dance Intertexts

Traces of Pina Bausch's *Café Müller* (1978) can be identified in the Morris work through a shared music source in Purcell's famous aria commonly known as 'Dido's Lament' (No. 38). In both works, the haunting soprano voice is accompanied by the image of a woman in pain, Bausch's gaunt, sunken-eyed sleepwalker and Morris's betrayed Queen resigned to suicide.

Critics' Intertexts

Considering his age, Mark Morris has had a prolific and accomplished career. His works reflect a range of imagination and musicality that are a comfort to those who look for someone to carry on the classical, formalist traditions. At the same time some of his movement vocabulary and choices of subject matter fly in the face of many traditional concerns. (Cohen 1992: 251)

A Reader's Perspective

Let me go back a bit – Dido is also the Sorceress and Morris changes from tormented Queen to woman-as-demon. Reading Morris as Sorceress, allusions to this women/demon association can be found throughout the cave scenes (Act II Scene 1 Act III Scene 1) in the grotesque vocabulary, the spasmodic gestures and the use of the floor, all aspects of Wigman's *Witch Dance*. This Hades is ruled by a powerful witch who is also a siren figure: her power is signified through, amongst other things, a hierarchical use of space, her centrality in a 'court' which parodies the ordered symmetry of Dido's palace.

His witch is younger, more agile and sexual, more Cruella de Ville than Carabosse, more Morticia than Madge, more 'way out' than Shakespeare's 'weyward sisters'. These references to Walt Disney (*101 Dalmatians)* and American television (*The Addams Family*) are performed with an explicit level of camp (exaggerated use of hips, 'limp' wrists, flicking the hair, head lowered with eyes looking up). Morris's Sorceress is too young for a hag or pantomime dame, the wrong sex to be the siren, too camp to be persuasively malevolent. S/he is also a 'popular' image and, thus, from a variety of angles, western theatrical traditions are deconstructed.

We first see the Sorceress lying on her front across the width of the bench throne. We cannot see her face, her head and arms appear lifeless, and we wonder if she is asleep or dead. As she begins to move it becomes apparent that this is no benign awakening but a crawl back from the ashes at the bottom of the stake. What follows is revenge, a plot to destroy her persecutor, Carthage's powerful and illustrious Queen. This reading brings the notion of revenge alongside 'fate the Sorceress, like Carabosse and Madge has been wronged and plans the ruin of the wrong-doer.

Mark Morris and Ruth Davidson
as Dido and Belinda.
Photo: Cylla von Tiedemann

A Reader's Perspective

A man sits with his legs wide open, hands emphatically pointing towards his penis, an image of the phallus complicated by a robe, the face of Clara Bow and glinting fingernails . . .

Gay Morris (1996) considers whether Dido might be seen as a drag act, comparing Acocella's 'imperfect imitation' criteria with Butler's notion of drag as a means of revealing the 'imitative structure of all gender through hyperbole and parody' (Morris 1996: 461). Like Morris, I would agree that in *Dido*, the level of parody is subdued (certainly in relation to the performance of her alter ego); however, as evident in the Astaire/Rogers couple dance overtones at the end of Act I (The Triumphing Dance), it is never entirely absent.

Acocella's use of the terms 'sex' and 'gender' is somewhat confusing. I would want to define 'drag' as the imitation of the latter (socially constructed) rather than the former (biologically determined). I would also want to introduce the terms feminine and masculine as two facets of this 'cultural performance'. Vocabulary remains a problem in discussions of gender but the point I want to make is that although genitalia may be (but of course, are not necessarily) 'permanent' or 'immovable', gender, as something constructed, has the potential for deconstruction, or change. This is nothing new but I am tempted to move towards more recent notions such as 'sexual difference', the notion that male and female are biologically different but can 'wear' the same gender or, conversely, that two women or two men, can be sexually different. A more radical issue, still, is the recent challenge to the facticity of 'natural difference' in which even the biological reality of men and of women is being questioned (see Hood-Williams 1996).

Dance Intertexts

Giselle (1841) Act I
A vineyard in the Rhineland – ruled by a Duke
Theme of betrothal (Albrecht and Bathilde)
'Extras' – villagers, couples
Mainly decorative colour – reds, golds, greens – 'nature'
Mime scene – 'he loves me, he loves me not'
Procession – entrance of hunting party
Pomp – ceremony surrounding above
No explicit representation of evil

Swan Lake (1877) Act I
A palace ruled by King and Queen
Theme of betrothal (Siegfried must marry)
'Extras' – courtiers, princesses etc.
Colour – royal blues (or reds) and golds
Mime scene – the Queen indicates that Siegfried must marry
Procession – entrance/exit of King and Queen
Pomp – ceremony surrounding above
No explicit representation of evil

Dido and Aeneas (1989) Act I
A palace ruled by Dido a 'Queen'
Theme of betrothal (Dido and Aeneas)
No 'extras' – chorus integrated
No colour – monochrome
Mime scene – 'Ah! Belinda'
Procession – 'The Triumphing dance'
Pomp – ceremony surrounding above
No explicit representation of evil

Critics' Intertexts

Susan Manning offers an interesting interpretation of Wigman's work in terms of gender/power: 'But although her solos reversed the misogyny of turn-of-the century cultural representations of woman as witch, they reinforced the special association between women and demonism and posited a sphere of female power separate from the sphere of male power' (Manning 1991: 12).

Theoretical Intertexts

'Jenny poses the problem of this disparity of forms of intertextual representation by asking whether one can properly speak of an intertextual relation to a genre. Such a relation is not strictly a relation to an intertext, and it would 'mingle awkwardly structures which belong to the code and structures which belong to its realisation'. But he immediately concedes that it is not possible to make a rigid distinction between the levels of code and text: 'Genre archetypes, however abstract, still constitute textual structures', and conversely reference to a text implicitly evokes reference to the set of potential meanings stored in the codes of a genre.' (Frow, 1990: 45–6)

A Reader's Perspective

I see Morris as the Queen of Carthage on her throne, I see Graham's 1930 essay on grief. My first reading takes the image of Morris as Dido seated on a bench/throne in the first solo. There are several points of interest in this soliloquy: the verticality and poise, the angular wrists, the opening of the legs. The black robe, Morris's physique, make-up, hair and painted fingernails are equally significant. This body is strong, regal and confident and yet the facial expression is one of melancholy.

In line with Frow's (1990) theoretical concepts, Graham's *Lamentation* (1930) is identified here as an 'absent textual structure, both a precondition and moment' of the Morris text.

Mr Mark Morris (33) wears a dress. Miss Graham (36) does not. Both have their own gender agendas: on the other hand, perhaps rewriting 'masculine' and 'feminine' is the same thing?

Theoretical Intertexts

'The identification of an intertext is an act of interpretation. The intertext is not a real and causative source but a theoretical construct formed by and serving the purposes of a reading. "There are no moments of authority and points of origin except those which are retrospectively designated as origins and which, therefore, can be shown to derive from the series for which they are constituted as origin." The prehistory of the text is not a given but is relative to an interpretive grid.' (Frow, 1990: 46)

Mark Morris as Dido with
Guillermo Resto as Aeneas
Photo: Cylla von Tiedemann

A Reader's Perspective

Myrtha is 'Queen of the wilis'. Is Morris playing on
words here? After all, these 'wilis' don't belong to
men . . . and is he referring to homophobic notions of the 'unnatural' in this
depiction of the 'supernatural'?

The general narrative structure of betrothal/ betrayal/female suicide which
underpins both ballets is reflective of a preoccupation with death (particularly
suicide) associated with romanticism. However, it is significant that in *Dido* the
structure is played with. Morris deconstructs the betrothal/sex metaphor by
putting sex 'firmly on the map'. Intercourse and masturbation are the 'unseen'
and 'unmentionable' of nineteenth-century ballet and, of course, Tate's libretto.
And yet, Morris chooses *not* to depict suicide; we see Giselle stab herself, Odile
jumps into the lake, but Dido just lies down. Thus, in the Morris work, the
preoccupation with death is displaced in favour of a study of love/sex distinctions, topics on which Morris has talked publicly, and which form the titles of
two of the chapters in Acocella's 1993 biography. Of equal significance, the
traditional power relations in these ballets, male victimiser/ female victim and
female dancer/male dancer, are fragmented into a complex terrain. Image of
feminine power, beauty Queen, siren or hag, will always be deconstructed by
Morris's body. The dominance of the ballerina and the resulting subordination
of the male dancer are equally challenged when a male dancer dances the
Odette/Odile role.

A Reader's Perspective

... have reached a place where East meets West and West meets East ...

A woman stands in the centre of the seated party, a *devadasi* outside the temple recounting a story of the Gods with her arms, her hands, her face ... only this is not one of Lord Krishna's exploits but the story of Diana and Actaeon. The dancer, storyteller, mystic, is both the Huntress and the Hunter, warning of the perils of love but to whom – Dido or Aeneas? Who is the hunted and who is the hunter here?

Introducing these intertexts, the terrain widens and several intertextual borders emerge. One consideration is the friction between the highly codified symbolic gestures of these Eastern classical forms and the explicit portrayals of sexual acts, for example the Sorceress's mimed masturbation (Act III Scene 1). The combination of these two codes, the traditional/acceptable and the radical/unacceptable is a subversive device challenging the 'reader' to reconsider the notion of what can and cannot, should and should not, be included in Western theatre ('art') dance. The same tension arises in the juxtaposition of the enactment of sexual acts to a Baroque score and in the placement, side by side, of Indian classical dance, firmly rooted in Indian music structures, and the essentially contrapuntal structure of Purcell's music.

A man masturbating as a woman to Purcell, interfacing traces of Bharata Natyam storytelling with Restoration drama, the Baroque and ancient myth and creating a situation of double travesty are all intertextual complexities through which 'Dido' and 'Mark Morris' are (re)constructed.

Critics' Intertexts

'Such differences between Europe and America are even more pronounced in the case of modern dance. In America, modern dance has had a far smoother development than in Europe. It is now considered a form completely apart from ballet, and its basic medium, like that of American ballet, is dance, not theater. Though in recent years young, experimental dance makers have gone in for a great deal of talking and videotape-showing, most American modern dance choreographers still focus primarily on movement ... But German dance-theater is far more theater than dance, as can be seen in the work of Pina Bausch, director of the Wuppertal Dance Theater and, since the seventies, the leader of the *Tanz-theater* movement ... Where Mark Morris fits into this picture should be obvious. He is squarely in the American tradition.' (Acocella 1993: 207)

Conclusion

By juxtaposing different types of intertext, the potential for multiple readings is revealed as considerable. Logistically, the 35 discrete statements presented allow section-to-section or intertext-to-intertext comparisons, each of which will create a different intertextual border. This was not, however, a random procedure but an acknowledged interpretative act, the result of several trial attempts within a fixed framework. Extracts from the 'already written' linear essays were cut up, placed on the floor, arranged and rearranged in relation to the section headings. In setting these boundaries I have sought to address the complex issue of limitation and freedom in interpretation, an issue which continues to dominate the theory and practice of 'reading' dance. In this instance, the section headings were fixed as a regulating device without which the exercise could not be usefully contained.

Having studied the strips of text alongside the original essays, the value of the later reading emerges in the diversity of 'routes' across the map. Only a small percentage of these were addressed in the original writings despite their combined length of 10,000 words. An example can be found on p. 136: if one moves from the reading under 'Dance/Opera Structures' to Jann Parry's claim that 'the question of gender soon recedes in importance' (cited in Morris 1996: 150) and, perhaps, on to Alastair Macaulay's contradictory 'Mark Morris . . . is the greatest modern-dance creator of dramatic female roles since Martha Graham' (cited in Morris 1996: 50). The relationship between the formal symmetry and closure of the operatic structure and the instability of meaning in relation to gender is hardly a revelation. However, the presence of these specific intertexts on these particular pages provides a possible starting point from which to follow this particular form/gender line of enquiry.

One of the more radical implications of intertextuality is the notion of 'divergent temporalities' identified by Frow. In part, I take this to mean the suspension, or elimination of any notion of chronological/linear order and development. Thus, in addition to considering traces of Graham's work as 'moments' of Morris's text, the opportunity is given to locate *Dido and Aeneas* (1989) within an intertextual reading of Graham's work. Rereading Graham in the light of Morris's performance (and, indeed, any other post-Graham developments) would seem an interesting perspective. In my own experience, this is easier said than done since the tendency is to revert to cause-and-effect ways of thinking. The chart format, if nothing else, exposes the organising principles which intertextuality challenges as well as those without which it cannot be seen to operate/exist/give meaning.

Perhaps the greatest difference between this deconstruction and the original texts is in the spatial patterning of intertexts. The uniformity of the chart design, the equal space given to intertexts within the same category is intentional. The desired effect is the image of superficiality, never successfully achieved within the linear essays. The intention was to avoid any notion of depth, of one intertext being any more of a 'truth', any more acceptable, than another. In this respect, the tabular design would seem to lend itself to this image of 'flatness': it has, in effect, 'widened' and 'evened out' my previous interpretations. This newly constructed surface appears as an even terrain; however, the arrangement of content within the intertextual borders reveals my own preferences, interests, decisions, as the reader who completes the act of interpretation.

References

Acocella, J. (1993), *Mark Morris*, New York, Farrar Straus Giroux.

Cohen, S.J. (2nd edn, 1992), 'Mark Morris, the Hidden Soul of Harmony', from *The South Bank Show* (London, 1990), in S.J. Cohen (ed.) *Dance as a Theatre Art: Source Readings in Dance History From 1581 to the Present*, Pennington, NJ, Princeton Book Company: 251–6.

Frow, J. (1990), 'Intertextuality and Ontology', in M. Worton & J. Still (eds), *Intertextuality: Theories and Practices*, Manchester, Manchester University Press: 45–55.

Hanna, J. Lynne (1988), *Dance, Sex and Gender: Signs of Identity, Dominance, Defiance and Desire*, Chicago, University of Chicago Press.

Hood-Williams, J. (1996), 'Goodbye to Sex and Gender', *Sociological Review*, vol. 44, 1: 1–16.

Manning, S. (1991), 'The Mythologization of the Female', *Ballett International*, vol. 14, 4: 11–14.

Morris, G. (1996), '"Styles of the Flesh": Gender in the Dances of Mark Morris', in G. Morris (ed.), *Moving Words: Re-Writing Dance*, London, Routledge: 141–58.

Price, C. (ed.) (1986), *Dido and Aeneas: An Opera*, New York, W. W. Norton.

Sweete, W. (director) (1995), *Dido and Aeneas* (film), broadcast Channel 4, 26 December 1995.

Worton, M. & J. Still (eds.) (1990), 'Introduction', in *Intertextuality: Theories and Practices*, Manchester, Manchester University Press: 1–44.

7

Too Many Cooks Mix the Metaphors:
Marin and Spink, and the Sandman Link

A Recipe for Deconstruction

Deveril Garraghan

For Starters

'When you don't know how to deal with a story, you put stereotyped situations in it because you know that they, at least, have already worked elsewhere' (Eco 1988: 449). Choreographing dance, like any art, is a matter of combining a number of elements to create an end product of some sort. In many ways it can be like cooking. You must learn or discover the basic techniques before preparing any food. Even the most adventurous cooks have their favourite simple ingredients, methods and dishes. As you become a more experienced cook, you are able to utilise more and more of these techniques to produce a large number of recipes. There will be times when you have to rely on tried and tested ways of cooking ingredients, both old and new to you. When you don't know how to deal with a dish, you put familiar ingredients in it because you know that they, at least, have already worked elsewhere. Making a dance is like making a dinner. Watching a dance is like eating a dinner: it needs to be ingested, digested and assimilated. This paper is an attempt to do these things to two seemingly unrelated dance works. They are Ian Spink's *Heaven Ablaze in his Breast* (1990) and Maguy Marin's *Coppélia* (1994).[1]

Ingredients

All manner of things can be used as the main ingredient, but for this recipe take a short story, as dense in imagery and symbolism as you can find. A tale that touches a nerve in the reader; that is about human beings, their fears and their condition in a dark, timeless, ethereal world. The story must mix love and death and instil in the reader a sense of confusion: Do I really know what love is? Can

I ever fully know or love another without uncertainty? Is love really as blind or as deadly as that?

In this chapter two works that are both derived from the same base ingredient – *The Sandman* by E.T.A. Hoffmann, first published in 1816 – are the focus.[2] The two cooks, Spink and Marin, are the principal selectors of the ingredients for their dances. The processes by which they chose and combined the materials were the result of their previous experiences. Ian Spink (born 8 October 1947), originally of Melbourne, Australia, moved to England in 1978. Trained in ballet, he performed for the Australian Ballet (1969–74) and New South Wales Dance Company, before forming the Ian Spink Group after emigrating. Works such as *De Gas* and *Canta* (both 1981) were subsequently filmed for television in 1982. In the same year, Spink formed Second Stride with Siobhan Davies and Richard Alston. With pieces such as *New Tactics* (1983), *Further and Further into Night* (1984) and *Bösendorfer Waltzes* (1986), Spink established himself as an artist keen on cross-arts collaboration, as evident in choreography for the English National Opera, Scottish Opera and Opera North; work with theatre companies, including the Royal Shakespeare Company, and with playwright Caryl Churchill on National Theatre productions of new plays, for example, *Lives of the Great Poisoners* (1991). Since 1987 he has been the artistic director of Second Stride.

Maguy Marin (born 2 June 1951), grew up in Toulouse, France. She started dancing at the age of eight, danced at the Strasbourg Opera Ballet, and went to study at Béjart's Mudra School in Brussels. At Mudra she participated in the formation of the splinter-group Chandra, and was strongly influenced by Carolyn Carlson, for whom she danced briefly. Between 1972 and 1976 she danced with Béjart's Ballet du XXe Siècle. She choreographed *Yu-ku-ri* (1976) for the company, and the next year won first prize at Nyon for her piece *Evocation* (1977). In 1978 she won another first prize in the International Choreography Competition in Bagnolet for *Nieblas de Nino*, and formed Ballet Théâtre de l'Arche, with Daniel Ambash. In 1981 the company took up residence in Créteil, near Paris, where they still remain, and in 1984 changed their name to Compagnie Maguy Marin. Marin's pieces for her own company include *May B* (1981), *Babel Babel* (1982), and *Eden* (1986, commissioned by the Centre National de Danse Contemporaine d'Angers). Marin has choreographed for other companies, for example, the Paris Opéra Ballet, the Lyon Opéra Ballet and the Dutch National Ballet.

Both Marin and Spink have produced works that span a range of theatre genres. Following Béjart's philosophy of dance as total theatre, Marin includes text in many of her pieces and combines dance styles that avoid easy categorisation. Spink too has experimented with mixing many elements of performance, and it is difficult to determine whether his productions are dance, opera or theatre.

This examination of the differences and similarities between Spink and Marin's treatment of *The Sandman*, and its progeny *Coppélia*, uses as its basis the principles of intertextuality: the infusion, in complex ways, of references to many other sources. Barthes has written that the

> intertextual in which every text is held . . . is not to be confused with some origin of the text: to try to find the 'sources', the 'influences' of a work is to fall in with the myth of filiation; the citations which go to make up a text are anonymous, untraceable, and yet *already read*: they are quotations without inverted commas.   (Barthes 1977: 60; emphasis in original)

While some of the dances' 'sources' are known, they serve only to explore the further connections that knowing what they are produces.

It must be stressed, however, that this examination is a highly personal tasting, drawing on this reader's experiences. The sources Spink and Marin can be said to refer to are derived from films, psychoanalysis and art. Images are modified and new ones made which may resemble their starting point or not, or may convey pictures which Spink and Marin had not intended. For example, early on in *Heaven Ablaze in his Breast*, one of the characters revealed as Nathanael reclines on a settee (see note 34), bringing to my mind 'The Death of Chatterton', the 1956 painting by British pre-Raphaelite artist, Henry Wallis. This painting was based on the suicide of the young poet, after being spurned by Horace Walpole and failing as a writer. As noted below, another viewer may not make this connection.

The two dances are analysed here in their made-for-television form, where the techniques of the medium produce a distinctive range of possibilities for the choreographer. For example, television is well suited to presenting states of mind, through cross-cutting and montage of images, providing the audience is capable of deciphering the relationships between the images. Eco describes the modern audience in just this way, as coming from a 'culture of instinctive semioticians', able to read the multitude of signs presented to them in rapid succession on the screen (1988: 455).

Using the structure of Hoffmann's story, Spink created a work that practically defies categorisation. In conjunction with Vocem Electric Voice Theatre, Second Stride (with Spink as choreographer) produced the piece in 1989 as a stage show, and in 1990 it was remade as a television piece (directed by Peter Mumford) for the BBC's 'Dancemakers' series, presented by Judith Mackrell. The television version differs from the stage version in many respects (to be expected when transferring material from one medium to another). The work has an operatic use of text, and spoken/sung words are taken directly from *The Sandman*, as are other images; and the movement is based on both ballet technique and everyday gestures.

Marin's *Coppélia* was originally produced for the Lyon Opéra Ballet as a stage show in 1993. However, it deviated in many respects from the traditional stage versions of the ballet. Marin used Délibes' score to follow the structure of the earlier productions, but she dispensed with the third act. Her setting for the dance is a modern French suburban estate. The exact time is not explicit, and it could just as easily be set in the 1960s as the 1990s.[3]

Method and Serving Suggestion

When you have the story, tear it up, and remove any parts that don't take your fancy. Throw the pieces in a pot and mix in a liberal amount of your own ingredients. Season to taste and pour the mixture into a receptacle of your own choosing and cook until just right. Serve it hot or cold, and tell its consumers some of its ingredients, but do not give away all your secrets. Allow the consumers to try to discern the tastes for themselves. Some will deliberate over what went into it and make guesses based on previous experiences, while those with less developed senses will miss its subtleties. No one will discover all the ingredients and methods used in the creation of your presentation.

Spink and Marin have created new works of art from the broken up ingredients of other works of art, most prominently, the story of *The Sandman*. Both choreographers draw the audience's attention to the story through their supporting material and through the pieces themselves. However in Spink's programme, according to David Hughes (1990), there was too much material forcing the reader to see an intended set of meanings, rather than allowing the freedom of interpretation that Spink appears to advocate: 'everyone can find different things to look at and think about and they can argue about what it all means' (Spink, cited in Mackrell 1992: 68). It is not only the connection with the original story that is of importance, just as significant are the other points of reference in the works that make them open and highly suitable for a free intertextual reading.

Much theoretical writing has outlined strategies for interpreting 'texts' (the work of art, in this case a dance piece) that, perhaps deliberately, 'borrow' from other sources. This borrowing, or more properly 'quoting', from previous works produces a multi-layered text. The process of interpretation takes into account this multi-dimensionality, termed intertextuality, and examines the interplays between works of art, the creator and the reader.

Barthes writes,

In the multiplicity of writing, everything is to be *disentangled*, nothing *deciphered*; the structure can be followed, 'run' (like the thread of a stocking) at every point and at every level, but there is nothing beneath.

(Barthes 1977: 147)

These interpretations do not follow and complete a rigid and linear analysis of the dances' components. The passage of food through the alimentary canal is usually uni-directional. However, the tastes and textures of the food have associations with past sensations and events that open up a string of reminiscences in the brain.[4] The taster, or in the case of art, the reader, attributes meanings to these stimuli, thus creating a unique web of connections. This analysis does not so much 'forget meanings' as not assert or proffer all the possible meanings. Another reader would find other '*avenues* of meaning' (Barthes 1994: 262) and construct a different set of connections.

The analysis demonstrates how Marin and Spink's employment of intertextual techniques opens up initially linear narrative works into a maze of interrelated pathways that can take the readers in tangential directions. The starting point for any reading might primarily be either the text or the reader. In this chapter it is the text.

The Chief Ingredient

Marin acknowledges the influence of the E.T.A. Hoffmann story in the stage production's programme, and also the lineage of the ballet up to her version.[5] Over the opening image of *Heaven Ablaze*, Spink tells the audience that it is 'based on "The Sandman" by E.T.A. Hofman [sic].'[6] This short story is regarded as a classic example of German Romantic fiction, by a writer whose life was as fantastic as his stories.

Ernst Theodor Wilhelm (later changed to Amadeus, after Mozart) Hoffmann was born in 1776, the son of a Prussian state advocate. In the course of his life he studied (and practised) music, art and law, and was a member of a number of government offices. He got into trouble on many occasions for his satirical drawings and writings. 'Hoffmann was a two-sided, schizophrenic kind of man . . . [his] personality informs all his fictions' (Hollingdale 1982: 7). In 1812 he began composing *Undine* (after the fairytale), which has since become a popular opera in Germany. It was performed in Berlin in 1816, the year in which the first volume of *Nachtstücke* (the opening tale in the volume was 'Der Sandmann') was published. Hoffmann also wrote the story that was later to become the source of the ballet *The Nutcracker*.[7] He escaped a legal action brought against him in 1822, because of illness and subsequent death through alcoholism. *The Sandman* has been a source of inspiration to choreographers, composers, writers, psychoanalysts and film-makers ever since. What follows is a synopsis of the story, highlighting the major images used by Spink and Marin.

Although mainly narrated by a 'friend' of the central character, Nathaniel, the tale opens with three letters from Nathaniel himself. In the first, he recollects that his mother would send him to bed early, due to the visits of the

Second Stride in Ian Spink's *Heaven Ablaze in his Breast.*

mysterious lawyer, Coppelius, with the threat that the 'Sandman' was coming. Nathaniel's nurse explains that the Sandman

> is a wicked man who comes after children when they won't go to bed and throws handfuls of sand in their eyes, so that they jump out of their heads all bloody.
> (Hoffmann 1982: 87)

Nathaniel's fear of the Sandman is further compounded by his belief that Coppelius is the legend incarnate, and this is 'proven' when the boy hears the lawyer say, 'Eyes, bring eyes!' (*ibid.*: 91). Coppelius grabs the terrified Nathaniel and almost puts out the boy's eyes with red-hot coals, but is prevented by Nathaniel's father. A year later, Coppelius is present the night Nathaniel's father is killed in a freak explosion, but the lawyer vanishes without trace, leaving Nathaniel mentally disturbed.

The letters are written when Nathaniel has grown up, and gone away to study. He has become engaged to Clara, the daughter of a distant relative who, with her brother Lothario, lives with Nathaniel's mother. Nathaniel, however, falls in love with a woman he views through the glass door in the flat of his

tutor, Spalanzani. He can also see her from his room through a telescope purchased from an optician and 'dealer in barometers' (*ibid.*: 85), the repellent
Coppola. Nathaniel forgets his fiancée, Clara, so strong is his new love for the
beautiful Olympia, daughter of Professor Spalanzani. Nathaniel attempts to win
the affections of the enchanting Olympia, blind to the fact that she is not real,
but a mechanical doll with glass eyes, which reflect only what is in front of
them.[8] He stumbles onto an argument between Spalanzani and Coppola, the
inserter of Olympia's eyes, who runs away with the now obviously insentient
doll. Spalanzani is furious and throws Olympia's removed eyes at Nathaniel
who becomes insane and tries to strangle the doll's creator.[9]

To Nathaniel, the optician Coppola is the reincarnation of Coppelius, and in
turn, the Sandman. The 'eyes' that Coppola sells, in reality, spectacles and spy-
glasses, renew the grown-up Nathaniel's fears and cause him to become unstable again. But, having recovered from this incident, he becomes betrothed to
Clara again. While sightseeing in a tall tower he looks into the telescope purchased from Coppola (which he finds in his pocket), to see an object in the
distance. Inexplicably, he is thrown into a screaming display of insanity and
meets a violent death.[10] Coppelius mysteriously appears to prevent the villagers
from saving Nathaniel, but then he disappears 'into the crowd' (*ibid.*: 124). The
tale ends on a happy note, with Clara settling into a contented relationship with
an affectionate, calm man.

A Feast for the Eyes

It is not difficult, even from a brief description, for the importance of the 'eyes'
to emerge in the story of *The Sandman*.[11] Detailed attention to the meanings of
the eyes in psychoanalysis and symbolism is common, and two meanings especially connected to *The Sandman* can be found in Freud's essay, 'The Uncanny'
(1955: 217–56), and in Møller's reading of *The Sandman* which explores the eye
as symbol: 'To Freud, then, the eye in Hoffmann's narrative is a metaphor of
sexual difference. The eye represents the male organ' (Møller 1991: 114).

Møller continues, expanding, improving and supplementing Freud's dichotomous reading (masculinity and castration, represented by 'woman'; reality and
the supernatural; life and death; his obsession with the Oedipal story) by adding
another dimension:

> the relationship between surface and depth and between appearance and
> being ... The eye is the medium through which one reads – or misreads –
> the outside world.   (Møller 1991: 115)

Spink and Marin use the eye (or related images like the window, the curtain,
the blindfold and optical instruments) as a motif or sign throughout the piece. In

both dances, the eye plays an essential part in the development of the story lines. In *Coppélia*, Swanilda and Franz see Coppélia on the balcony; and in *Heaven Ablaze* Nathanael sees Olympia through the glass door. It is the simple act of looking that prompts the narrative; the desire to satisfy curiosity and lust through closer inspection. Marin's Swanilda, when viewed by Coppelius, seems to be the catalyst for the entrance of Coppélia. Coppola and Coppelius, in *Heaven Ablaze* and *Coppélia* respectively, are linked with focal apparatus. Spink's Coppola spills a suitcase full of spectacles onto Nathanael's desk and 'sells' him a phallic telescope. Coppola shines a light into Nathanael's eyes, and checks his sight. In *Coppélia* Coppelius is seen looking into a microscope (using montage to show the youths playing football like cells under the lens); he examines cine-film with a magnifying glass; he has his glasses removed by the youths; and he is a photographer and film-maker.

The Ma(r)in Meal of the Day

Marin's publicity mentions *West Side Story* (the 1961 film, choreographed by Jerome Robbins) in its description of *Coppélia* – 'un peu West-Side Story' – and this source seems to be directly quoted in the first half of the piece.[12] In *West Side Story* there is a recurrent motif of a wire fence within which the youths fight amongst themselves, symbolising society's constraints. In *Coppélia*, the youths stare defiantly through the same kind of fence; the subject of their gaze is not known, maybe it is the audience itself. The conflict which occurs behind the fence in *Coppélia*, is not only between the males, but is also a battle of the sexes.

A further cinematic influence is cited in the Opéra de Lyon programme for the ballet, and is even more relevant to the filmed version. *A Short Film About Love* (1988), by Krzysztof Kieslowski, is part of his *Dekalog* (1988) series based on the Ten Commandments. In this film an adolescent, Tomek, falls in love with Magda, a woman who lives in an apartment opposite. He views her with a telescope, and eventually gets into her flat. When confronted by Tomek, Magda (in a bath robe) invites him to touch her in an overtly sexual manner. Tomek does, and it is too much for him; he leaves rather hurriedly, his illusions shattered. The thematic similarities between this, *The Sandman*, and *Coppélia*, are clear: objectification and voyeuristic viewing of women can lead to disaster for the men involved. When the woman turns the tables on the man, she emerges victorious.

It is unlikely that Marin, a French choreographer, escaped the influence of the *Nouvelle Vague* (New Wave) cinema movement, which was a reaction to the old, 'realistic', mainstream *cinéma de papa*, of the 1950s.[13] The New Wave film-makers (such as Truffaut, Godard, Chabrol, Rohmer and Rivette) changed the form of the film; they fragmented story-lines and made *mise en scène* the focus.

Their films are about young people, city life (the city was even made into a 'character', with filming taken out of the studio into the streets), and little themes concerning individuals. Lovell says of New Wave cinema:

> Its heroes are neither personally or socially integrated . . . they are marginal men, disaffected intellectuals, students . . . Interest centres exclusively on immediate face-to-face relations.   (Lovell, cited in Cook 1985: 41)

The films draw attention to the fact that they are films, which were 'as much about the process of film-making as . . . about desanitising the sacred cows of the bourgeoisie' (Hayward 1993: 209) – with direct camera address and reference to Hollywood movies. But as Lovell implies, the New Wave films are inherently sexist, based on the male self with women defined by and through men.

It is possible to trace these ideas in Marin's *Coppélia*. Coppelius is the marginal man who doesn't fit into society; he constructs the female through the use of film and photography. The youths are constructed as living dull lives in the city suburbs; all they have to do is play football, court each other and bully old people. But Marin also seems to subvert many characteristics of the *Nouvelle Vague*, while simultaneously applying its techniques, to present a surface that appears to share its stylistic conventions. A parallel can be found in Jean-Claude Gallotta's video-dance work *Un Chant presque étient* (1987), a study of a male relationship set in the Gare de L'Est in Paris. The setting for *Coppélia* is a French suburban estate; the action moves from the car park and concrete square to inside one of the apartment blocks, and then to the inside of the heads of Coppelius and Franz. The characters are nothing out of the ordinary, except for the enigmatic and too-perfect Coppélia. The story is simply a love story, although the details are a little unusual, and for the two central lovers there is a reconciliation and a happy ending.

Variety is the Spink of Life

Films (and the processes of cinema) and visual art are among the most prominent sources in Spink's works. Spink's use of film, often as a primary source, can be seen in his earlier works, for example, in *Further and Further into Night* (1984) which used Hitchcock's film *Notorious* (1946). Mackrell writes that because of his 'formalised treatment, little was left of the original story, although the designs remained faithful to the style of the film' (1992: 112). *Heaven Ablaze* too has a strong relationship with the cinema, with Spink and McDonald looking to pictures of thirties film stars and movie sets for inspiration.[14]

As with Marin, Spink's own specific references are unknown. McDonald (in the 'Dancemakers' introduction to *Heaven Ablaze*) indicates that he referred to early German films, while developing his designs.[15] The visual style, mainly produced through lighting, is reminiscent of the German cinema of the 1920s. Other similarities are the use of broken illumination and sets, and the framing of shots to show the psychic states of characters (attributed to the German director Pabst especially). In *Heaven Ablaze* Spink makes use of the same techniques as Pabst and the Expressionist film-makers, who were keen employers of mirrors and reflections; of the double (or *doppelganger*) to show split personality; and shadow, inspired in turn by romantic and gothic writers such as Hoffmann. Similarly the oscillation between the sombre, morbid rooms inhabited by Nathanael (or imagined by him), and the bright, open rooms untouched by his neurosis, is yet another device of Pabst and the Germans.[16]

Heaven Ablaze 'is shot through with echoes of German art and history' (Stumpfl 1989: 17). McDonald (in Mumford 1990) cites among his influences, the Biedermeier artists of 1815–48 Germany in the construction of *mises en scène*. The style of the interiors was taken directly from paintings of the period, which had 'a lyrical homely taste [in its] portrayal of bourgeois existence' (Vaughan 1980: 21). The final shot of the piece is of Klara and her happy family standing, in tableau, before a painted landscape. 'Hoffmann's constant references to seeing things more clearly are mirrored in scenic paintings of far distances' (Stumpfl 1989: 17). The still image suddenly breaks as the credits roll and figures move, fidgeting self-consciously, finally walking forward to be frozen once more, this time mechanically, as silhouettes.

The effects (for example, intense fore/background split, and the use of half-light, with a brighter concentration as a focus for emphasis) are like those of Caspar David Friedrich, an artist who was a contemporary of Hoffmann. Vaughan has written of Friedrich's work that 'there were few . . . who recognised that Friedrich's paintings were less acts of self-indulgence than penetrating attempts to bring some submerged experience to consciousness' (Vaughan 1980: 66). Friedrich's attitudes towards art's purpose are uncannily like Hoffmann's (although not so surprising when it is remembered that both were German romantics with a taste for the melancholic, symbolic and spiritual/psychological), and like Spink's. The latter is often also accused of being hard to understand or even self-indulgent in the extent of allusion in his work, when that to which he alludes is too well-hidden, or too intellectual, for a particular reader's taste.

What a Dish!

In life and in art people are constantly presented with pictorial images, for example, signs, advertisements, works of art and photographic studies of others' lives. The presentation of the human being is one form of imagery, with the larger proportion of these showing the female as subject.[17] Spink refers to the

'representation of women as two-dimensional figures, completely unreal, fuel-
ling male fantasies' (cited in Stumpfl 1989: 17). The star system of the cinema
industry is probably the most infamous promulgator of sexist imagery and by
referencing it in his piece, Spink is drawing on something that most of the
audience could be expected to recognise.[18] However, whereas Marin uses the
same imagery and processes to challenge and invert these ideas, Spink only
perpetuates the image of the *femme fatale*, the vamp, who does nothing but
cause a man's death, setting her in opposition to the boring, loyal woman who
cannot exist outside domestic relationships with men and family. Thus the
position of women within Western patriarchal society and its cultures is shown,
tied up with the dominance of men in the power structure; women's portrayal in
art serves not only to illustrate but to reinforce men's power over women. In
Heaven Ablaze, Spink's Klara is seen icing a cake, and Nathanael's mother is
also seen baking. Spink's Olympia exists only to look beautiful and sing when it
is deemed appropriate by the men around her. The men gain a sense of power
and sexual excitement by this means.[19]

The inspiration for the poses and the costume of Olympia can be seen in the
actress Louise Brooks, in Pabst's film *Pandora's Box* (1928).[20] In Brooks's character, Lulu, there is an ideal role model for the representation of Olympia. She is
highly attractive and seductive, and is the archetypal *femme fatale*, luring men
to their death. However, the characters of Olympia and Coppélia in both these
dance works (particularly as portrayed by Gabrielle McNaughton in Second
Stride's production) bear a more striking resemblance to platinum blonde actress Jean Harlow than to Brooks's dark, waif-like Lulu. In such films as *Platinum Blonde* (1931), *Dinner at Eight* and *Bombshell* (both 1933), Harlow epitomised feminine beauty.[21] Underlying Harlow's image is the question of the
representation of 'the ideal woman', and its production in society and by artists.
Just as Marin's Swanilda is brunette and her Coppélia is fair, Spink's Klara is
dark, and dowdy compared to his blonde, ultra-feminine Olympia.[22] In *The
Sandman*, the narrator says that 'Clara could not possibly be called beautiful . . .
[but] all were enamoured of her wonderful Magdalen hair' (Hoffmann 1982:
102). It can be no coincidence that Mary Magdalene, the patroness of frail and
penitent women, is sometimes represented with dark hair, 'but it should be
luxuriant, fair and golden' (Clement 1994: 224). Which colour did Hoffmann
intend us to visualise?

Marin's Swanilda has dark hair and wears unisex clothes. She openly shows
her emotions, often in an aggressive, physical manner: she throws herself onto
Franz to try and get his attention and when this fails (repeatedly), she scowls,
shrugs off his feeble attempts to placate her and runs away. When Coppelius
first sees Swanilda, she is eating an apple – the act of Eve that opened her eyes
to her nakedness – and he creates the opposite to this earthy, rebellious, unfemi-
nine image of woman.

As well as revealing two extremes of female stereotyping, Coppélia and Swanilda can also be seen as representing Berger's two sides of being a woman in Western society: 'surveyor' and 'surveyed' (1972: 46). Berger's oft-quoted statements relate the act of looking in everyday life to the perception and creation of self:

> *Men act* and *women appear.* Men look at women. Women watch themselves being looked at . . . The surveyor of woman in herself is male: the surveyed female. Thus she turns herself into . . . an object of vision: a sight.
> (Berger 1972: 47; emphasis in original)

Coppelius watches Swanilda, and it is a result of projecting the image of his ideal woman onto a real woman to create Coppélia on the balcony, even if only in the minds of Franz, Swanilda and himself. If Swanilda and Coppélia are taken as uncanny doubles of one another, then when Swanilda watches Franz looking at Coppélia, she is watching herself being watched. Swanilda, as 'surveyor of woman in herself', is costumed in 'masculine' attire as though to emphasise her position as the 'surveyor'. Kaplan questions whether the gaze is always male, arguing that the process of looking involves one person taking a dominant role of spectator and the other taking a submissive position. In Western culture these positions are so bound up in gender that the former role, regardless of who is looking, is known as 'masculine' and the latter as 'feminine'; this keeps 'the whole [cultural] structure intact' (Kaplan 1983: 29). Marin's intention could be to advocate a reversal of positions in society as 'a safety valve for the social tensions that the women's movement has created by demanding a more dominant role for women' (*ibid.*: 30).

Metz stresses the act of looking as central to the cinema, which removes the need for any other physical activity (except the even more passive activity of hearing). Theories about the 'look' (the physical act) and the 'gaze' (the ways in which pleasure is obtained from looking) have become popular. Cinema and theatre share many similarities, but it has been argued that cinema differs from theatre in the relationship it has with the audience. The live aspects of theatre (here read also dance) mean that the audience and performers share the same space and, in some ways, the same physical experience. But in film the relationship is more complicated. The performers in a live show are fully aware that they are being watched at that particular moment; whereas film actors, according to Metz, are exhibitionistic while simultaneously behaving as though they are not being watched (cited in Cook 1985: 247).

In *Coppélia*, the dancers look directly at the camera, drawing the spectator into the action. The filmed Coppélia also looks directly through the camera at the spectator (Franz, Coppelius, the audience). What precisely does this do to the way she is perceived? Mulvey, a feminist film-maker and psychoanalytic critic, suggests that women as seen in films are fantasies of men, who practise scopophilia: 'using another person as an object of sexual stimulation through sight' (1990: 32).[23] The men for whom they act as image are present both in the film and in the audience; and within many films, so as not to disturb the narrative flow, the women appear as 'showgirls':

> the gaze of the spectator and that of the male characters in the film are neatly combined without breaking narrative verisimilitude. For a moment the sexual impact of the performing woman takes the film into a no-man's-land outside of its own time and space.   (Mulvey 1990: 33)[24]

This is the case in *Coppélia*. Coppelius is the creator of the film, and of the fantasy woman within it, *and* the spectator deriving 'visual pleasure' from the dancing Coppélia. Marin invites us to ask: 'Qui est Coppélia? Un rêve. Le rêve d'un vieil homme . . . Coppélia, femme à deux dimensions, star et dépositaire des fantasmes communs à tout le voisinage' (Opéra de Lyon 1993: 7).[25] Other men in the audience are able to share Coppelius's action of looking, along with Franz, and the dance moves from the two men watching a home movie of Coppélia, into being in a dream world inhabited by Coppélias, returning almost seamlessly into the 'real' world of simply watching a film. Coppelius's transition out of the dream into his conscious state involves looking out of the window in the dream and seeing Franz and Swanilda outside his apartment.

What happens when Coppelius and Franz are asleep, and apparently in the dream world, seems to turn Mulvey's male gaze phenomenon around. This inversion of the gaze and thence of the power relations begins even before Coppelius and Franz get drunk. Coppélia is assumed to be the physical product of Coppelius, in the form of a mechanical doll (as in the ballet *Coppélia* and in *The Sandman*), but when he and Franz begin to watch the film the 'doll' loses the mechanical qualities it had when being watched by Swanilda and Franz. Of course, it is now the unruly Swanilda in the guise of the doll. Coppélia is no longer an object of restraint; she eats and throws fruit, and most importantly she beckons to the men, urging them towards the screen. The two men have begun to lose control. The film, which is assumed to have been made by Coppelius, now has a mysterious director who, through Coppélia, is commenting and controlling the time and space occupied by the characters. Now the relationship is more like a theatrical event, the actor in the film, instead of 'behaving as though she is not being seen, or able to see the voyeurs' (Metz, cited in Cook 1985: 247), looks at the characters and eventually controls their actions. The people in the film, presumably made some time earlier, interact with the spectators. The two actions (filmic and 'real') are perfectly synchronised, a situation impossible or purely coincidental ordinarily. It would not be normal to take seriously the beckoning gestures of a person in a film from outside it, but Coppelius and Franz do not question that it is they themselves who are actually being addressed.

Finally, after getting the two men drunk (a practice usually associated with scheming men intent on taking advantage of intoxicated women), Coppélia, who has now multiplied into many Coppélias, can wreak her (their) revenge for having been objectified for so long. The sequence following Coppelius's and Franz's collapse into sleep, the climax of the piece, shows them subjected to a humiliating chain of events. If it *is* a dream, whose unconscious is shown? How exactly should this sequence be read?

Can be Grilled or Freud

Brooks (1994) and other literary critics have written that traditionally the use of psychoanalysis focuses on three objects: 'literature as mise-en-scène of unconscious fantasies [of the fictional characters], as expression and artistic elaboration of its author's repressed wishes . . . as that which allows the reader to enjoy his own fantasies and rework his own psychic conflicts' (Møller 1991: 6). The first of these is discussed in relation to *Coppélia* and *Heaven Ablaze*.[26] Although a major criticism of the use of psychoanalysis in literary interpretation is that it often purports to have 'the last word, the final hermeneutic power' (Brooks 1994: 23), the intention here is not to proffer a definitive reading of any dance. Just as there are a number of 'objects' which could be analysed, there are a number of distinctive approaches to their analysis. In the two works under consideration, these mostly stem from Freud's theories of psychoanalysis and include the post-Freudian framework set up by Lacan.

Freud's methods of analysing dreams (see Freud 1953) and the symbols contained therein are similar to the ways in which he and other analysts have studied literary texts:

> Freud works from the premise that all that appears is a sign, that all signs are subject to interpretation, and that they speak of messages that ultimately tell stories that contain the same *dramatis personae* and the same narrative functions for all of us.
> (Brooks 1994: 23)

Freud's theories on sexuality and the Oedipal complex have also been appropriated by critics such as Mulvey, because Freud attempted to show how the power relations between the sexes are formed. Freud's phallocentric view places woman at the centre of his structure: 'it is her lack that produces the phallus as a symbolic presence' (Mulvey 1990: 28). Woman is seen as the embodiment of castration, yet at the same time an object of desire for men, in whom she produces ambivalent thoughts: love/hatred, want/fear and life/death. In films, men control these thoughts by having control over the images of the women in them (see Mulvey 1990). In dreams, Freud says, repressed wishes and fears are shown, usually in a 'symbolic disguise' (Jung 1960: 240).

> The processes of cinema mimic in many ways those of the unconscious. The mechanisms Freud distinguishes in relation to dream and the unconscious have been likened to the mechanism of film . . . if psychoanalysis is a tool that will unlock the meaning of dreams, it should also unlock that of films.
>
> (Kaplan 1983: 34)

In the 'dream' sequence of *Coppélia*, then, it can be said that what is seen is the repressed unconscious of the bewildered, eye-rubbing Coppelius (and Franz, and heterosexual men in general), in which a desire to be seduced by many women who all personify the image of 'ideal beauty' is found.[27] The use of point-of-view shot – 'a shot in which the camera assumes the spatial position of one of the characters . . . in order to show us what s/he sees' (Cook 1985: 244) – within *Coppélia* is restricted to six instances in the dream sequence. The technique is used for many purposes in films, one of which is to indicate the psychical state of the person it is connected to: Coppelius's views of Coppélia's body show us his obsessive and objectifying character (see Dworkin 1981: 113); his spinning-in-the-chair views are one of the ways in which Marin inverts the processes of wish-fulfilment and control.

A basic study of the symbolic references in the dream sequence of Marin's *Coppélia*, before looking at the power inversions which occur, shows a link with a male unconscious.[28] The costume of Coppélia is made up of fetish objects: the wig, the distinctive red fitted suit, and stiletto shoes. By Freud's definition, the fetish is a sign of castration, 'a substitute for the woman's (the mother's) penis that the [man] . . . does not want to give up' (Freud 1961: 152–3). Fetish objects are usually feminine objects that prompt in a man the same reactions as do the female genital organs (Dworkin 1981). According to Freud, 'the female genitals are symbolically represented by all such objects as share their characteristic of enclosing a hollow space which can take something into itself' (Freud 1963: 156). Freud links the head to the male genitals, so therefore, wigs and hats are symbols of the female. Shoes are similarly 'feminine' objects, and in the dream sequence they are used to tease the two men. The Coppélias take off their stiletto shoes and place them by their hips and on their shoulders, emphasizing the undulating pelvis, and the breasts. The heels, however, often point forward aggressively towards the men, turning the feminine shoe into a dagger-like symbol of masculinity. Coppelius even strokes a shoe as it moves swiftly past him: he can barely touch that which he so desires. Another symbolic representation of the male genitals (and of male power) is the gun. The dream sequence contains the only fully audible words of the piece. As Franz tries to escape, he is stopped by a Coppélia who points and says, 'Is that a gun you have in your

Maguy Marin's *Coppélia*, with the Ballet de l'Opéra de Lyon.   Photo: Gerard Amsellem

pocket? Or are you just glad to see me?' The women then laugh and Franz is pushed back into the room to dance. Coppélia at this moment has full control over the men and uses the male preoccupation with the penis to belittle them further, by being derisive about the main symbol of manhood so that even Franz, a virile young man, is made impotent.

In the dream it is clear, at least to the off-screen audience, that half of the Coppélias are men dressed as women. Coppelius and Franz are seemingly unaware of this, which provides the first example of inversion. The processes underlying transvestism and how cross-dressing onstage affects the audience are extremely complicated, and would provide substantial material for further study in relation to Marin's *Coppélia*. Coppélia (her image and being) was the product of Coppelius, literally a 'man-made woman'. As a result there is a masculine side to the doll's construction; Coppelius sees himself, or rather a likeness of himself as represented by the men in the guise of Coppélia. To say that the manifestation of 'male' Coppélias in Coppelius's dream is a sign of his latent homosexuality may be taking a reading of Marin's dance a little too far, but further questions can be asked as to what transvestism does to an interpretation of the piece. The male-to-female transvestite is a sign of female sexuality without the possibilities of reproduction, in much the same way that the 'mechanical'/'fantasy' doll is. Coppelius has suppressed the futility he knows exists in loving Coppélia, and it is through the dream that he begins to realise this. He lets Coppélia go, and all he can do is watch as she runs away in the dream/film-world which she inhabits. Franz too realises his stupidity in loving Coppélia and returns to Swanilda.[29]

This insight of Coppelius and Franz is brought about through a further inversion: the two men are stripped, dressed-up and made to dance for the Coppélias. This is particularly interesting in terms of the 'gaze', for not only does it allow Marin to include the traditional dances that feature in the original (without breaking the narrative as such), but it also makes the women possessors of the 'gaze', placing the men in the position of object.[30] The process of cross-dressing further complicates the issue because we see Coppelius in the attire of a female Spanish dancer, and Franz in a kilt, a confusing garment for it is a 'feminine' skirt worn by men, currently in vogue with designers such as the Frenchman, Jean-Paul Gaultier.[31] Thus an intricate series of role-reversals occurs, all designed to reduce the men to an extremely low position. Here Marin is on shaky ground because it could be said that she is guilty of creating an equally oppressive gaze.

Discussing the *femme fatale* in cinema, Doane writes,

the difficulties in thinking female spectatorship demand consideration . . .
what is there to prevent her from reversing the relation and appropriating the
gaze for her own pleasure?   (Doane 1990: 44)

To summarise Doane's argument, which takes into account Mulvey's theories on male power in the 'look', Erens writes that 'spectatorship revolves around questions of proximity and distance' (1990: 5). The female spectator is in an unusual situation, because 'she *is* the image' (Doane 1990: 45), she must either become overly involved or be guilty of narcissism when viewing another woman. Doane says that the way to avoid these options is for women to become like men (for example, dressing as men) and assume the dominant position, to distance themselves from the image. But many women perform another type of 'masquerade' by 'over-doing the gestures of feminine flirtation ... flaunting femininity' (Doane 1990: 49). This then becomes a front, a manufactured image of womanliness that serves to create another form of distance between a woman and her image. In *Coppélia*, Swanilda assumes the costume and role of Coppélia, which removes her from the narcissistic position she occupied in relation to it.[32]

Out of the Frying Pan into the Fire

In Spink's *Heaven Ablaze*, death linked to the concept of the 'ideal woman' is a major theme; death caused by a psychopathological obsession and the morbid fears of a man unable to come to terms with the death of his father. Much has been written on obsessional neuroses and imagery to explain psychological states. In the *Dancemakers* introduction, Spink made specific reference to the writings of Freud, and this can be felt in the treatment of Hoffmann's story.

Of relevance here is Møller's assertion that

> Freud is on the verge of suggesting that the ultimate source of the uncanny is the death instinct itself. The uncanny is the drive toward the end (which is also the beginning), operating through the compulsion to repeat.
>
> (Møller 1991: 135)

From beginning to end, Spink emphasises the uncanny through repetition of a particular image. The opening image of *Heaven Ablaze in his Breast* is of a fire; then an arm is seen throwing a book onto the fire. It becomes apparent that the fire has been made from the pages of books. Spink's piece is based on a story that contains many references to fire and burning. Spink's title seems to be a play on lines from the tale itself, transformed to make Nathanael the focus of the piece (presumably the title refers to his breast), rather than Hoffmann's mythical Sandman.[33] Spink also removes the role of the narrator. Just as the theme of burning is repeated in *The Sandman*, the theme is returned to in *Heaven Ablaze*. Later on, the burning pages are superimposed over Michael Popper dancing (as Nathanael). The titles introducing Part 2 have the flames behind them also, and an intra-textual connection is made as the audience is informed, expositionally, that Nathanael returned 'from home to find his lodgings burnt to the ground'. The burning books are seen again in the penultimate section, this time free of any visual overlapping of images. Spink continually inserts shots of the fire into the action of Nathanael, Klara and Lothar out walking. There is a juxtaposition between the initial serenity of the scenes in the open air with the raging intensity of the burning books.

Repetition of often disturbing images is seen as a symptom of obsessional neuroses in Freudian theory.[34] Spink repeats the image of the fire, alerting the audience to the mental state of his Nathanael. Spink also represents the fractured nature of the protagonist's psyche by having two performers playing the same role (one as singer, one as dancer).[35] This neurosis began after a childhood incident involving Nathanael's father in a fatal explosion. Nathanael connects the figure of the Sandman with the diabolical visitor Coppelius, and this is reinforced, in the story, by the latter trying to blind the young Nathaniel with glowing coals from a furnace. In Spink's piece, this element of the story is replaced with Coppelius brandishing a pair of scissors in front of Nathanael's eyes. The scissors are also a possible symbol of castration, represented by the Sandman's ability to put out eyes. Since the earliest times, fire has stood as a symbol for man's passion (specifically 'man's'),

> or, as we should say, as a symbol of the libido. The warmth that is radiated by fire calls up the same sensation that accompanies a state of sexual excitation, and the shape and movements of a flame suggest a phallus in activity.
>
> (Freud 1964: 190)

Man's control over fire is also his control over sex. In fire there is a disturbing duality. If its power can be harnessed it is a useful tool. However, if the controlled flame becomes a conflagration, 'it implies the desire to annihilate time and to bring all things to their end' (Cirlot 1971: 106), like the fires of Hell, which signify eternal damnation. The symbol of sexual desire is transformed into a destructive element: Nathanael's yearning for Olympia is the fire that controls and destroys him. In Scorcese's film *The Last Temptation of Christ* (1988), Willem Dafoe as Jesus sits in a dark circle to resist the temptation of the devil, a bright flame in the wilderness. In the Bible, it is God who is represented by fire, Jesus being baptised 'with the Holy Ghost, and *with* fire' (Matthew, 3:11). Scorcese's Jesus resists the fire of the devil (succumbing though to the temptation of sex); Spink's Nathanael sits in a circle of ashes but it is too late. The fire of passion has already burnt out, he is burnt out by it too. The ring of fire in *Heaven Ablaze* can be seen to represent the course of Nathanael's life: a vicious circle, intense but short-lived. It just leaves a scorched scar in the floor. Nathanael and Olympia dance in the black, extinguished ring and Nathanael, Christ-like, lies down alone in the middle of it. This comes just before the moment when Nathanael realises that Olympia is not a warm-blooded, living being, but a cold, lifeless doll. The once burning, consuming desire is now a cool, spent longing. Yet desire is still evident, with a potential to flare up again as mysteriously as it had done before. Nathanael is like a magical, reigniting candle, awaiting to be finally snuffed out by death. Indeed Spink uses candles in the second part of *Heaven Ablaze*, highlighting the fragile flame of life.[36]

The image of the burning books becomes more and more frequent in the montage that precedes Nathanael's fatal fall. It is the first thing he sees when he looks through the telescope sold to him by Coppola (in the story it is Clara he spies, which sparks off his re-descent into delirium and descent to death). The image becomes mixed with hallucinations of Olympia that drive Nathanael to attack Klara.

Nathanael's neurosis is not restricted simply to the recurring fear of the Sandman, it also manifests itself as an obsession with a woman, or rather, the man-made Olympia. Nathanael's demise can be seen as the result of self-destruction brought about by his obsession with a woman. This is a common theme in Hoffmann's life and stories, a theme which plays a major part in *The Sandman* and *Councillor Krespel* where Hoffmann 'is inscribed in the novel like one of his characters' (Barthes 1977: 161).[37] Hoffmann's obsessional personality is presented to us in the form of self-referential fictions featuring women who were out of his grasp. For example, Hoffmann's

> attachment to Julia Merc [one of his music students] was pathologically serious, and he was led to thoughts of suicide by the insuperability of the difficulties in the way of making her his.   (Hollingdale 1982: 10)

Hoffmann got into trouble because of his writing, and his obsessive personality manifested itself in his habitual drinking, which Hollingdale describes as 'self-destructive' (*ibid.*: 12). The dead author Hoffmann is reintroduced into *Heaven Ablaze*, as though resurrected. Spink, by replacing the narrator (that is Hoffmann) with Nathanael, reinforces the similarities between the writer and the fictional character. Hoffmann is now 'a guest' (Barthes 1977: 161) in this new work, a new mixture of the old. He is connected to a character in that new work of art (Nathanael in *Heaven Ablaze*), who in turn is based on a character in an older work of art (Nathaniel in *The Sandman*), who is seen as inspired by the life of the original author (Hoffmann). The circle is complete. Spink stresses the point that Nathanael is an aspiring writer through a number of motifs. These include the use of books; the hands writing, creating an image reminiscent of Escher's 1948 lithograph 'Drawing Hands' (Escher 1967, plate 69), Nathanael is also seen writing in his dream sequence; the typewriter is one of many anachronisms in the piece. In the second part, Nathanael walks on piles of books in order to get to Olympia, using the product of his art to reach his beloved both literally and figuratively.

In Spink's *Heaven Ablaze*, there is a strong relation between books (the act of writing) and death. The typewriter has a sword (another phallic symbol, strongly related to death) placed into it, producing a more modern representation of the martyr, Saint Boniface, apostle to the Germans. The burning books prefigure Nathanael's death, almost as though he can see his own death approaching. When he finally sees the burning books (real or imagined) in the spy-glass, he realises the moment is soon. All through the piece the books are present as a reminder of death. They are the major fire motif used by Spink (the ring of fire is not used as frequently) to replace the constant references to fire and heat used adjectivally and metaphorically by Hoffmann. The death of the father by explosion in mysterious circumstances is yet another instance that prefigures his son's violent end. The father died in the place of Nathanael, simply delaying fate.

While out walking, Spink's Klara and Nathanael climb a clock tower, a symbol of time, of fate. Nathanael and Olympia are seen wrestling in front of the large clock face, and as Lothar runs to Klara's aid, the incessant workings of the clock countdown to the end. As in Hitchcock's *The 39 Steps* (1935), the climax occurs on a clock tower with the hands of time present to increase the audience's sense of destiny. In Hitchcock's film, disaster and death are averted as a man stops the hands of Big Ben's clock. But in *Heaven Ablaze* there is no such reprise for Nathanael, as time continues unabated, and leads to death. When Nathanael looks through the telescope he sees not only into the distance, but into the future. Further into the future Nathanael can see an event which again links fire, books and death.

> On 27 February 1933, the Reichstag building in Berlin, home of the German government, was set on fire. It marked the start of the Nazi dictatorship and the death of many people.
>
> On May 10 [1933], in front of the Berlin Opera House, and opposite the main entrance to Berlin University, thousands of books were burned in a massive bonfire ... The burning of books and the killing of individuals, went on side by side. (Gilbert 1987: 38)

The word 'holocaust' means 'burnt whole', and has now come to represent a period of German history that most people would connect to persecution and suffering.[38] The persecution of intellectuals and artists (Jewish or anti-Nazi) and Nazi control of culture (indeed hatred of it) can be seen as being symbolically represented by the book bonfires. Spink (or Mumford) may or may not have consciously employed this image with the intention of causing an audience to make the connection; but in repeating the image he endows it with messages inviting readings by the audience. As Barthes says:

> All images are polysemous; they imply, underlying their signifiers, a 'floating chain' of signifieds, the reader able to choose some and ignore others.
>
> (Barthes 1977: 38–9)

Barthes' statements on the readers of texts and the ways signs are partially recognised has a strong bearing on how Spink's *Heaven Ablaze* can be viewed.[39] Thoughts of 'the Final Solution', triggered off by the use of one simple image, create an intense feeling of horror: the death of an individual can symbolise the suffering of many. All human beings share the same fate (death), but the manner in which that fate is met may have a consequence on the way the life is judged. It is a person's death that sums up his or her existence; it causes his or her worth to be assessed. In the case of Spink's Nathanael, his worth is symbolised by the burning books. His attempts at living by writing go up in smoke, his unrequited passion for a woman being the cause of death. 'The book is related . . . to the symbolism of weaving . . . The act of weaving represents, basically, creation and life' (Cirlot 1971: 31, 369).

The fabric of Spink's *Heaven Ablaze in his Breast* has a gold thread running through it. The gold (metal of the sun, represented on earth by fire) is in the form of the burning book imagery. Spink, as weaver, has made a tapestry with many textures. His patterns tell a story, but turn the cloth over and new patterns are revealed. Take it to pieces and the construction is made explicit. Flaws are found, but the colours and the types of thread are open to closer scrutiny. Each individual material has a source, its own stories, a background, which can be invented when it is seen in isolation. Many of the threads have been ignored in this reading, or simply touched on. There are innumerable elements to any intertexture. For Theseus, only one thread can be followed through the labyrinth at any one time, but we are free to reject Ariadne's aid and wander along pathways of our own choosing.

For Desert: Crumble

'Maguy Marin is free . . . Mistress of our emotions, she is free to open our eyes and to make us laugh once and forever at life's absurdities' (Babkine 1993). *Coppélia* makes us look at the roles and positions of people in society. But Marin, too, presents an intertexture of many elements, which can lead us in a wide variety of directions. Like Spink, she gives us pointers, but ultimately the route is chosen or found by the readers. All the readers need to do is keep their eyes peeled and follow their own senses.

Spink and Marin are like Hansel and Gretel, dropping crumbs to mark the way home. We are the hungry birds, who eat what we want to eat of the crumbs, until distracted by something more appetising. We cannot piece together the crumbs to make the bread as it once was; we can only imagine what it looked like, using the tastes and textures to help us. Intertextuality is like this. From stories to dance. From dance to food. From food to eyes. From eyes to women. From women to death. From death to fire. From fire to books. From books to weaving. From weaving to mazes. From mazes to stories. From stories to . . . who knows where? Shakespeare wrote,

> From women's eyes this doctrine I derive:
> They sparkle still the right Promethean fire;
> They are the books, the arts, the academes,
> That show, contain, and nourish all the world.

(Love's Labours Lost, IV.iii: 350–3)

Notes

1. *Heaven Ablaze in his Breast* (1990). Choreography, Ian Spink; Music and Libretto, Judith Weir; Design, Antony McDonald; Adapted for Television by Peter Mumford and Ian Spink. *Coppélia* (1994): Music, Léo Delibes; Choreography and *mise-en-scène*, Maguy Marin; Produced and Directed for Television by Thomas Grimm for RM Arts and Danmarks Radio in Association with BBC, RTP, ZDF/ARTC, 1994.
2. Note that the spellings of the names in the publication of *The Sandman* used for study differ from those used by Spink in his production. Marin used the names of the characters as given by Arthur Saint-Leon and Charles Nuitter in 1870.
3. This change of context allowed Marin to portray Coppélia as a home movie. On stage, a 31-minute film accompanied the entire first half, and was projected onto the cyclorama. The film contained views of the estate, and sometimes presented 'a larger-than-life image of the action on stage' (Merrill 1993: 86). In the second half, an 8-minute film (in the style of an amateur, Super 8 movie) of Coppélia is seen projected within Coppelius's apartment. In the television version, it is this film which is watched by Swanilda, Coppelius and Franz in the second half. The film does occasionally fill the television screen, increasingly so as Franz and Coppelius become drawn into the world of the filmed Coppélia.
4. Most people know what tasting (gustation) is, but few fully understand its workings. Humans are able to perceive a wide variety of flavours, through a combination of taste (see O'Mahoney 1987) and (predominantly) smell (see Jones 1987). The chemical responses are translated by the brain into a set of learned, descriptive evaluations. This process is taken to the extreme by expert tasters of wine, olive oil and tea, who develop a large vocabulary of responses to describe the nuances of each liquid. But someone must have experienced these sensations previously to enable them to refer to them. Combined with this adjectival response might be another memory, that reminds tasters of the first time they experienced that taste; who they were with, what they wore, the weather, etc. 'We do not perceive or remember in a vacuum. The context within

which we experience an event will determine how that event is encoded and hence retained' (Baddeley 1987: 464). Recall of a memory has to be triggered by something related to that which caused the remembrance in the first place. 'The nervous system contains many pathways that re-excite themselves ... [a memory] must endure for long enough to allow a record to be "printed" in the long-term memory' (Young 1987: 455).

5. The creators of the original *Coppélia* were, like Marin, also French, and the ballet was premiered in Paris in 1870. The qualities of *Coppélia* are comic and fantastic, which Poesio claims were reflective of Second Empire France with 'its aura of bourgeois prosperity (real or imagined) and its over-optimistic faith in progress' (1993: 889). Unfortunately this self-confident air was soon to be shaken in the Franco-Prussian War, which broke out shortly after the ballet's premiere in Paris. Saint-Léon and the original Swanilda (Giuseppina Bozzacchi) died in the siege of the city. In the first act, Dr Coppelius, the toymaker, makes a doll in the likeness of a woman. She, Coppélia, is so life-like and beautiful that when Franz sees her he is smitten and forgets his fiancée, Swanilda. In the second act, the spurned Swanilda decides to settle things by venting her anger on Coppélia. The true nature of Coppélia becomes apparent to Swanilda, who seizes her chance to take revenge on Dr Coppelius for deceiving Franz. She dresses as Coppélia and 'performs' for the old toymaker, by dancing and destroying his workshop. Franz admits his folly. The third act celebrates Franz and Swanilda's wedding.

6. The choreographers and their production team reference specific inspirations in the work and in, for example, the theatre programme, and interviews. Marin's programme and press releases contain much material on her sources. In the filmed version of *Heaven Ablaze* (1990), Judith Mackrell presented a number of brief interviews with the four main creators in which they spoke about the process of producing the piece.

7. *The Nutcracker and the Mouse King* was first published in 1819. Lev Ivanov choreographed the first ballet to Petipa's libretto and Tchaikovsky's music in 1892.

8. Kappeler writes, 'The demand for verisimilitude in dolls [in the nineteenth century] led to the manufacture of dolls with real rather than artificial hair, to dolls with orifices and with moving eyelids, and finally to the speaking doll. What is more, dolls are no longer toy children ... they are "young ladies", full-breasted, well curved and pouting, preferably blond' (1986: 78). Germaine Greer refers to the idealised stereotype of femininity as 'a doll' (1970: 60).

9. Olympia exerts much control over the men in the story, for 'she is pure surface, a mirror in which [the characters see] nothing but the reflection of [their] own desire. Her soul exists, quite literally, in the eye of the beholder' (Møller 1991: 115). There is an analogy to be drawn here with the concept of intertextuality, which is sometimes referred to as surface rather than depth analysis.

10. Hoffmann writes, 'Clara was standing before the glass! ... [Nathaniel's] eyes began to roll, fire seemed to flash and glow behind them' (Hoffmann 1982: 123).

11. The eyes were even important in the Saint-Léon *Coppélia*, which was subtitled 'La Fille aux yeux d'émail' (The Girl with the Enamel Eyes).

12. 'A little West-Side Story', remarks the press release, pointing out a possible source of inspiration for Marin. Some of Marin's choreography recalls this work, including the men's acrobatic manipulation of the women when it is dark. In the

1961 film, it is a man who is thrown by the opposite gang members.

13. The exact dates of the movement are debatable. Bordwell and Thompson (1990: 398) cite 1959 to 1964 and proffer appraisals of the New Wave. Earlier books on the subject include Graham (1968), Armes (1970) and Monaco (1976).

14. Spink first worked with designer Antony McDonald in 1981 on his piece, *De Gas*, which was inspired by the paintings of Degas. It was followed by *Bösendorfer Waltzes* (1986), which drew on the art of the Surrealists (as well as Fokine's ballet *The Firebird*) to create a piece made up of non-sequiturs and confusing cross-referencing of words, movements and objects. *Weighing the Heart* (1987) made allusion to artistic sources of a religious nature, creating a piece 'in an almost comic-strip fashion' (Mackrell 1992: 115).

15. Among these early German films are those termed Expressionist. Some confusion exists over the dates and canon of this small but influential movement (perhaps 'cinematic approach' is more apt). The generally considered starting date is 1919 with the production of Wiene's *The Cabinet of Dr Caligari*. The end depends on the definition applied to the movement. Salt (1979) writes that only six films from *Caligari* (1919) to Leni's *Waxworks* (1924) can be counted as examples (with the possible addition of Lang's *Metropolis* [1927] due to its expressionist acting). Again, Bordwell and Thompson (1990) give brief overviews of the movement. For more detail see Kracauer's much criticised *From Caligari to Hitler* (1947), Eisner (1969) and Barlow (1982). Also of interest are other books on Expressionism, which encompassed art, music, literature, theatre and dance, for example, Whitford (1970), Willett (1970) and Richard (1978).

16. Pabst 'moved away from expressionism and became a prime mover in a trend toward pessimistic realism in German cinema, noted for a keen interest in human psychology' (Katz 1994: 1048). He was particularly Freudian in his approach, working with some of Freud's assistants on *Secrets of a Soul* (1926). See Atwell (1977).

17. From Greer (1970) through Berger (1971) to Paglia (1991) runs the argument that in Western culture the production of images is male-dominated.

18. Gledhill (1985) gives a succinct overview of the concept and study of stardom. For discussions about the nature of stardom see Dyer (1979) and King (1986).

19. In its extreme, the reduction of woman to sexual object occurs in prostitution and in pornography, as Dworkin calls it, 'the graphic depiction of whores' (1981: 10); but it can be argued that in everyday life the woman is often viewed in a similar way, if with less violence.

20. Brooks also starred in Pabst's 1929 film, *Diary of a Lost Girl*. In both films, Brooks's characters face many vicissitudes and sexual experiences. Brooks, like some of her screen characters, lived a life with many ups and downs. Of interest to dance historians is to note that Brooks was originally a dancer under Ruth St Denis and Ted Shawn. She was reputedly the first person to dance the Charleston in London, and danced for Florenz Ziegfeld, before moving into cinema. After making films she once again returned to dance, this time in nightclubs and as ballroom dance teacher. Brooks lived a far from glamorous life as a shop assistant and alcoholic, taking up film studies and writing in her later years. See Paris (1990).

21. In 1930 Brooks was offered the lead part in *The Public Enemy* (1931), opposite James Cagney, but she turned it down. The part was given to the relatively

unknown Jean Harlow, who went on to become one of the cinema's greatest sex symbols.

22. Dworkin explains the love of blond women in terms of men's attraction to purity and cleanliness. Dark hair and skin are related, Dworkin argues, to filth, excrement, and that the 'fair' aesthetic is often connected to racism: 'the love of blonds is in fact as socially significant as, and inseparable from, the hatred of those who are seen to embody opposite qualities or characteristics' (Dworkin 1981: 114–5).

23. Mulvey's highly influential 1975 article on the functions and origins of the 'gaze', 'Visual Pleasure and Narrative Cinema' (see Mulvey 1990), has since been revised and contested, but for the purposes of this argument, the basic points of Mulvey's article are relevant.

24. Two recent examples are Verhoeven's *Showgirls* (1995) and Bergman's *Striptease* (1996). The settings for both films are 'erotic dance' clubs, making no attempt to disguise the blatant inclusion of naked women as subjects of the gaze.

25. 'Who is Coppélia? A dream? The dream of an old man ... Coppélia, a two dimensional woman, star and object of the collected [collective?] fantasies of the whole neighbourhood'. (My insertion.)

26. The other two hold some potential for investigation, but this chapter does not claim to study the choreographers' psyches (an interesting prospect), or to encompass the full range of reader responses. What does this chapter tell you about its writer?

27. 'In research on men's sexual fantasies, the two most popular themes were being seduced by a Red-Hot Woman and punishment/humiliation at the hands (actually at the feet) of a dominant woman' (Friday 1991: 87). '*One of the major themes in male fantasy is the abdication of activity in favour of passivity.* Role reversal' (Friday 1993: 268; italics in original).

28. I do not want to be guilty of presenting a one-sided phallocentric, masculine-defined reading of Marin's piece (although I feel that I am guilty of this. Being a man, what else can I offer?). It must be remembered that Marin is a woman and therefore is using these symbols probably with a conscious awareness for what they signify. Another reading might analyse Marin's *Coppélia* as simply a representation of her or another female's fantasy. Friday writes of the 'new woman's recognition of 'her assertive, angry self' (1991: 132), and of her ability to vent this anger. 'If a woman can reverse painful reality into fantasy and feel that revenge is complete, that is therapy' (*ibid.*: 134).

29. Attention is drawn to 'Uncanny Women and Anxious Masters: Reading Coppélia Against Freud' by Bergner and Plett (1996: 159–79). Bergner and Plett examine how the two sides of femininity, represented by Swanilda and Olympia, have been constructed; and the nature of masculinity embodied by Franz and Coppelius. They use Freud's reading of 'The Sandman' to question directly the relationship between the ballet and Hoffmann's story, and point to the roles of Clara and Swanilda as more important than Freud's work might suggest. It is the headstrong character of Swanilda that poses a threat to the men's masculinity, through her shattering of the male dream of perfect female passivity.

30. It is usually Swanilda in the guise of the doll who dances the solos with a Scottish hat and Spanish fan.

31. In Saint-Léon's ballet, and some subsequent productions, Franz was played by a

woman *en travesti*: a further complicating factor when examining the consequences of cross-dressing on the gender relationships in *Coppélia* as a dance throughout history.

32. Brennan writes that 'Freud's theory of narcissism presupposes an "identification" with oneself . . . Narcissism presupposes that one sees oneself as if one's image were reflected in a mirror. The idea of seeing oneself in a mirror is passive because it presupposes being seen. This means that the people concerned are in some sense visualizing themselves, and in this actively *directing their capacity for visualisation, or imagination, inwards* towards a passive end' (1992: 31; emphasis in original). According to most post-Freudian psychoanalytic theory, 'female 'narcissism' is a consequence of penis envy . . . a pathological disorder consequent upon her exclusion from power and subjective definition' (Waugh 1989: 43–4). See Freud 1957: 67–102.

33. In the description of Nathaniel's poem, Clara's eyes are ignited by Coppelius and 'sprang out like blood-red sparks, singeing and burning, on to Nathaniel's breast'. Nathaniel is then thrown into 'a flaming circle of fire'. Clara's voice is heard to say, 'those were not my eyes which burned into your breast; they were glowing-hot drops of your own heart's blood' (Hoffmann 1982: 105).

34. For Freud, neurosis results from a conflict between the ego and its id (the unconscious, instinctual part of the mind). The ego is 'the self' as it develops through childhood; it is responsible for self-love and narcissism, and all our decisions and perceptions. The superego is an idealised image and causes repression of any feelings of guilt that the ego may experience. It is easy to see Freud's interest in the story of *The Sandman*, and his connections between it and the Oedipus Complex and myth. Nathaniel's rivalry with his father is not resolved. Nathaniel feels guilty for his death. See Freud (1958), Dilman (1984).

35. Hoffmann's seminal literary use of the double in *The Sandman* representing, for example 'the "immortal" soul . . . [or] the uncanny harbinger of death' (Freud 1955: 235), is represented in Spink's piece in his use of two performers playing all the major roles.

36. Cf. 'And all our yesterdays have lighted fools / The way to dusty death. Out, out brief candle!' (Shakespeare's *Macbeth*, V.v: 22–3).

37. In 1814, Hoffmann published a collection of short stories entitled *Zeitung für die Elegante Welt*. One of the stories was *Die Automate* (*The Automaton*). The tale, coincidentally, 'combines the account of an ingeniously designed speaking figure with the story of a young man's love for a woman possessed of a beautiful expressive and highly trained voice – this element in the story relates to Hoffmann's love for Julia Merc' (Garland 1976: 50).

38. Kracauer, as the title of his 1947 book suggests, saw a connection between the early German films to the rise of Nazism. With hindsight he believed that the films contained premonitions of the totalitarianism of the 1930s. He argues that Hitler's ascent to power was the resolution of psychological dilemmas reflected in the nation's movies. However, Salt (1979) criticises Kracauer for generalising in the films without taking into account their true position in history and society.

39. See Barthes 1977: 158–60.

References

Allen, R.C. (ed.) (1992), *Channels of Discourse, Reassembled*, London, Routledge.

Armes, R. (1970), *The French Cinema since 1946: Vol. 2*, New York, A. S. Barnes.

Atwell, L. (1977), *G. W. Pabst*, Boston, Twayne.

Babkine, B. (1993), 'Liberty . . . Maguy Marin is Free . . .', press release, Créteil, Compagnie Maguy Marin.

Baddeley, A. (1987), 'Memory and Context', in R.L. Gregory (ed.), *The Oxford Companion to the Mind*, Oxford, Oxford University Press.

Barlow, J. D. (1982), *German Expressionist Film*, Boston, Twayne.

Barthes, R. (1977), *Image Music Text*, London, Fontana.

———— (1988), 'Textual Analysis: Poe's "Valdemar"', in D. Lodge (ed.), *Modern Criticism and Theory: A Reader*, Harlow, Longman.

———— (1994), *The Semiotic Challenge*, Berkeley, University of California Press.

Berger, J. (1972), *Ways of Seeing*, London, Penguin and BBC.

Bergner, G. & N. Plett (1996), 'Uncanny Women and Anxious Masters: Reading *Coppélia* against Freud', in G. Morris (ed.), *Moving Words: Rewriting Dance*, London, Routledge.

Bordwell, D. & K. Thompson, (1990), *Film Art: An Introduction*, New York, McGraw-Hill.

Brennan, T. (1992), *The Interpretation of the Flesh: Freud and Femininity*, London, Routledge.

Brooks, P. (1994), *Psychoanalysis and Storytelling*, Oxford, Blackwell.

Cirlot, J. (1971), *A Dictionary of Symbols*, London, Routledge & Kegan Paul.

Clement, C. E. (1994), *Legendary and Mythological Art*, London, Bracken Books.

Cook, P. (1985), *The Cinema Book*, London, BFI.

Dilman, I. (1984), *Freud and the Mind*, Oxford, Basil Blackwell.

Doane, M.A. (1990), 'Film and the Masquerade: Theorizing the Female Spectator', in P. Erens (ed.), *Issues in Feminist Film Criticism*, Bloomington, Indiana University Press, 41–57.

Dworkin, A. (1981), *Pornography: Men Possessing Women*, London, Women's Press.

Dyer, R. (1979), *Stars*, London, BFI.

Eco, U. (1988), 'Casablanca: Cult Movies and Intertextual Collage', in D. Lodge (ed.), *Modern Criticism and Theory: A Reader*, Harlow, Longman.

Eisner, L.H. (1969), *The Haunted Screen: Expressionism in the German Cinema and the Influence of Max Reinhardt*, Berkeley, University of California Press.

Erens, P. (ed.) (1990), *Issues in Feminist Film Criticism*, Bloomington: Indiana University Press.

Escher, M.C. (1967), *The Graphic Work of M. C. Escher*, London, Macdonald & Jane's.

Freud, S. *The Complete Psychological Works of Sigmund Freud*, London, Hogarth Press (Volumes referenced: Vol. V, 1953; Vol. XVII, 1955; Vol. XIV, 1957; Vol. XII, 1958; Vol. XXI, 1961; Vol. XV, 1963; Vol. XXII, 1964).

Friday, N. (1991), *Women on Top*, London, QPD.

———— (1993), *Men in Love*, London, BCA.

Garland, H. & M. (1976), *The Oxford Companion to German Literature*, Oxford, Clarendon Press.

Gilbert, M. (1987), *The Holocaust: The Jewish Tragedy*, Glasgow, William Collins.

Graham, P. (ed.) (1968), *The New Wave*, Garden City, NY, Doubleday.

Greer, G. (1970), *The Female Eunuch*, London, Paladin.

Hayward, S. (1993), *French National Cinema*, London, Routledge.

Hoffmann, E.T.A. (1982), *Tales of Hoffmann* (1816), London, Penguin.

Hollingdale, R.J. (1982), 'Introduction', in E.T.A. Hoffmann (1980), *Tales of Hoffmann*, London, Penguin: 7–15.

Hughes, D. (1990), 'Heaven Ablaze in his Breast', *Dance Theatre Journal* 7, 4 (February): 15, 29.

Jones, F. N. (1987), 'Smell', in R.L. Gregory (ed.) *The Oxford Companion to the Mind*, Oxford, Oxford University Press.

Jung, C.G. (1960), *The Collected Works of C.G. Jung Vol. 4*, London, Routledge.

Kaplan, E.A. (1983), *Women and Film: Both Sides of the Camera*, London, Routledge.

Kappeler, S. (1986), *The Pornography of Representation*, Cambridge, Polity Press.

Katz, E. (1994), *The Macmillan International Film Encyclopedia*, London, Macmillan.

King, B. (1986), 'Stardom as an Occupation', in P. Kerr (ed.), *The Hollywood Film Industry*, London, Routledge/BFI.

Kracauer, S. (1947), *From Caligari to Hitler: A Psychological History of the German Film*, Princeton, Princeton University Press.

Kuhn, A. (1982), *Women's Pictures: Feminism and Cinema*, London, Routledge.

Lodge, D. (ed.) (1988), *Modern Criticism and Theory: A Reader*, Harlow, Longman.

Mackrell, J. (1992), *Out of Line*, London, Dance Books.

Merrill, B. (1993), 'Baby Doll', *Dance Magazine*, LXVII, 9 (September): 86, 88.

Møller, L. (1991), *The Freudian Reading*, Philadelphia, University of Pennsylvania Press.

Monaco, J. (1976), *The New Wave: Truffaut, Godard, Chabrol, Rohmer, Rivette*, Oxford, Oxford University Press.

Mulvey, L. (1990), 'Visual Pleasure and Narrative Cinema', in P. Erens (ed.) *Issues in Feminist Film Criticism*, Bloomington: Indiana University Press: 28–40.

Mumford, P. (1990), 'Heaven Ablaze in his Breast', *Dancemakers*, BBC2

Opéra de Lyon (1993), *Coppélia* (Programme), Lyon.

Paglia, C. (1990), *Sexual Personae: Art and Decadence from Nefertiti to Emily Dickinson*, London, Penguin.

Paris, B. (1990), *Louise Brooks*, London, Hamish Hamilton.

Poesio, G. (1993), 'A Controversial Ballet: Reflections on Coppélia', *Dancing Times*, LXXXII (June): 889–91, 893.

Richard, L. (1978), *Phaidon Encyclopedia of Expressionism*, Oxford, Phaidon.

Salt, B. (1979), 'From Caligari to Who?', *Sight and Sound*, 48, 2 (Spring): 119–23.

Stumpfl, C. (1989), 'Living Doll', *Guardian*, 2 October: 17.

Vaughan, W. (1980), *German Romantic Painting*, New Haven, Yale University Press.

Waugh: (1989), *Feminine Fictions: Revisiting the Postmodern*, London, Routledge.

Whitford, F. (1970), *Expressionism*, London, Hamlyn.

Willett, J. (1970), *Expressionism*, New York, McGraw-Hill.

8

Locating Space

Dance and Architecture in Rosemary Butcher's *3d*

Libby Worth

To study a performance by Rosemary Butcher is to be confronted by a range of intriguing contradictions. In her dances sharp contrasts coexist of modern and postmodern; coldly abstract and richly emotional; collaborative and a single artistic vision; dance performance and visual art installation. *3d*, the performance primarily considered in this chapter, is no exception. It offers ample opportunity to explore some of the paradoxes inherent in Butcher's work.

In *Theatre as a Sign-System*, Aston and Savona point out the benefits for theatre studies of applying a semiotic methodology. The tendency to ally the study of theatre too closely to that of literature, they argue, has detracted from the 'doing' of theatre.

> Once the 'doing' of theatre is reinstated, then the notion of individual author-
> ship is also challenged, given that the 'doing' also requires the collaboration
> of the performers, director(s), technical staff, and so on, all of whom contri-
> bute to the making of the theatrical event.   (Aston & Savona 1991: 2)

While dance has not been subsumed into the study of literature in quite the same way, it was common for the choreographer to be regarded nevertheless as the singular 'author' of the dance. It is useful to counteract this tendency through a consideration of dance performance as 'doing', in recognition of the multiple texts that exist in each performance. The approach I have taken in the following chapter is to consider the dance, *3d*, from a variety of contextual angles and, as Janet Adshead-Lansdale has described in Chapter 1, to treat 'these partial perspectives . . . as threads of the intertextual web' (p. 18). The interventions of the many layers of texts in the work open up questions of power, control and conflict and do not encourage a singular cohesive reading. By exploring *3d* in this way, it is not my intention to underplay the importance of Butcher as 'author', but to acknowledge some of the many forces at work in the

creation of the piece. Indeed, I argue that part of Butcher's role is in maintaining
a balance between freedom and boundary, both in process and production as
shown by her persistent choice to negotiate the knife edges of improvisation and
interdisciplinary collaboration. I aim to maintain a similar balance between the
freedom of interpretation encouraged within intertextuality, while respecting the
boundaries set by the performance.

From 1989 to 1990 Butcher worked closely with architects on a series of three
performances, *d1*, *d2*, and *3d*, collectively known as the *d's*.[1] The last of these,
3d, was performed at the Tramway Theatre in Glasgow in September 1990, a
year after the *d's* project had begun. The environment for the dance had grown
from flat white lines on the floor in *d1*, to a huge scaffolding bridge which thrust
out across the space to a height of eighteen feet, combined with a ramp approach and dramatic lighting in *3d*. The choreography had similarly built up,
becoming a full-length work (almost one and a half hours) of great complexity
and energy (see Table 1 for a choreographic outline of the dance). This project
stands out within Butcher's canon of work. She had previously linked works
together, for instance *The Site* and *Imprints* (1983), but never made such a long
experiment on one stated subject matter, or on such a scale, extending over a
year. She had worked in outdoor city spaces in London and Bristol, but for this
project she chose the city and architecture as her subject, the inside of prominent city buildings as her sites, and the architects Zaha Hadid (*d1*) and John
Lyall (*d2* and *3d*) as collaborators. The multilayered connections with architecture, combined with the use of a strong repetitive rhythm reinforced (at times
driven) by the music of Jim Fulkerson, allowed Butcher a new range of possibilities for performance. *d1*, *d2* and *3d* were designed to be complete performances
in their own right, which would gain added interest if seen as a series. Their
distinctive qualities of intensive investigation of choreography and architecture,
use of vigorous rhythm and connection of dances across such distance and time
do not recur in Butcher's work. Her later collaboration with the architect John
Lyall ('Tension and Compression', in *Body as Site*, 1993) is on a smaller more
intimate scale, reminiscent of Butcher's pieces with the sculptor Heinz-Dieter
Pietsch rather than of the *d's*.[2]

In the following detailed examination of the making and performance of *3d*,
the focus is maintained on the association of dance with architecture. It is this
cross-media dialogue that remains crucial throughout the series. In the first
section of this chapter, 'Planning Dislocation', I argue that Butcher's collaboration in the *d's* extends beyond her work with the specific artists. Ideas drawn
from architecture as a discipline are evident within the planning of the performances. She described in interview (Butcher 1995) how her choreography was
'hugely influenced' by many of Le Corbusier's architectural ideas. During the
same planning period she became interested in the concept of ley lines. Both
these are employed to interrogate dance as an art form, as well as providing

stimulus for the subject matter and environment of the performances. Butcher was one of the first British choreographers to re-site dance both in terms of location and discipline. She moved away from traditional theatre venues and into intimate contact with other art forms. This form of dislocation is not superficial. It is a theme that can be traced into a further layer within the performance of *3d*, and occurs as one response to the complicated subject of contemporary city living. As the audience is similarly relocated both in terms of expected venue and proximity/level in relation to the performance space, the context, like the collaborators, plays an active role in any perception of the dance.

In conceiving the *d's* Butcher was already working across media and she began the choreography from that point. She needed architects and the musician, Fulkerson, in order to maintain the lively discourse essential to the piece. The term 'collaboration' has become so frequently used that it skates across vastly different methods of working. Like the language used to describe dance itself, this is indicative of a society that pays less heed to methods of co-working than to hierarchical process, as it pays less heed to movement than to the written word. In this attempt to unpick Butcher's methods in creating the *d's*, issues to do with oppositions of power and control, openness and experimentation emerge and are addressed below in 'Designing Uncertainty'. Although Butcher has experienced a wide range of close working relationships with artists, it is inappropriate to generalise from her experience with Hadid and Lyall, since each case is distinct. However, using *3d* as a basis, some insight can be gained into the choice Butcher continues to make to enter the ferment of collaboration. I suggest that Butcher deliberately seeks out the inevitable uncertainty that arises when several art forms are brought together in a single venture. She locates the importance of collaboration for her work within the mix of ideas generated in process, rather than, necessarily, in the final product that the artist makes. The theme of uncertainty, as a dynamic as well as an unsettling experience, emerges beyond process as a forceful element within the performance of *3d*.

Butcher's long-term dialogue with the visual art world perhaps stems from her own attitude to dance, that as an art form it is limited in what it can express. This view (a point she returned to repeatedly in talks given at the 1997 Royal College of Art retrospective of her work) is particularly puzzling in the light of her ability to choreograph dances that are highly textured and expressive of a wide range of human experience.[3] The critic, Nadine Meisner, takes a similar angle when she writes that Butcher's collaborations are an 'attempt to dislodge dance from a perceived rut' (1997: 25). Butcher is not alone in recognising the limitations of her art form. Other choreographers such as Yvonne Rainer have shared this view, but responded by taking a different direction. 'What the body can say without verbal language is limited, which is why I so frequently used language in my dances' (cited in Dempster 1995: 22).

However the type of limitation to which Butcher and Rainer refer does not contain the disparaging attitude towards the form noted by Elizabeth Dempster:

Dance has been represented as a secondary, derivative, diversionary and minor art, an art which does not generate its own meanings.

(Dempster 1995: 24)

Certainly Butcher has found variety and stimulation within her dialogue with the visual art world, but no one watching her dances could doubt the centrality of the movement in them. Yet the style of that movement has given rise to charges that complicate the issue further, through the suggestion that the limitation is self-imposed. For instance, the writer Stephanie Jordan asserts that, 'Butcher has derived more from minimalism over the years than we might have hoped' (1992: 181); while in her review of Butcher's retrospective at the Royal College of Art (RCA), Jenny Gilbert writes that 'as in any work by Butcher the emotional content is nil' (1997: 13). The question of limitation, whether actual or perceived, is discussed in the third section of the chapter, 'Building Dance'.

Since I am writing this as a movement performer/teacher rather than as a visual artist, musician or architect, the focus will remain on movement and the body, though, as will become clear in section three, this is not a straightforward task. In reviewing *Body as Site* David Hughes describes Butcher's collaborations as 'largely juxtapositional. Her movement material could exist on its sharply illuminated own' (1993: 42). I argue that in the *d's*, as in most of her work, this is not the case. The movement material is central, but contested by the other forces in operation within the performance arena, which at times dominate and always act on the movement content. The concept of contested space is in line with the subject matter of city living and within the everyday experience of any member of the audience. Over the years Butcher has experimented with and refined this contextual material, but to remove the dancers from their setting would be to make an entirely different dance.[4] Similarly in taking a detailed look at the movement of *3d* the influence of architecture resurfaces, so closely interwoven are the media. The simplified, distilled repetition and task-like elements she employs in her choreography are not an end in themselves, but an essential tool in retaining an opening for the body to be viewed as object, landscape, individual, part of a crowd, or field of energy.

The detailed attention to movement analysis in this section is not an attempt at definitive description, but a means of locating my interpretations in the multiple 'texts' of the work. Although, as Sarup suggests, a deconstructionist approach is one in which 'texts can only refer to other texts, generating an intersecting and indefinitely expandable web called intertextuality' (1988: 58), there are nevertheless limits on the content of these. The image of the web is apposite here, as a reminder of the delicacy required of readers as they track back and forth along its strands, without either destroying the structure at its centre or detaching to float off into the vague distance.

The fourth and final section of the chapter, 'Performing Poetry', presents an interpretation of *3d* that concentrates on showing how Butcher has opened up the space between categories, styles and disciplines, allowing dance to expand. She has chosen to limit and abstract her movement material in order to avoid narrative, developed relationships and expressed emotions. Yet the curious paradox remains that narrative, relationships and emotion are all evident in the performance, albeit in fragmentary form. Tensions and contradictions are rife, as the theme of perspective is explored visually, psychologically and metaphorically. The shapes of the human form against the vast structure diminish, or grow in stature, according to the sudden switches in style of movement and visual or aural content. It is a Beckettian world, in which the place appears simultaneously strange yet familiar: the dancers move in a way that is dislocated from reality but recognisably ordinary. According to the writer Charles Jencks, Le Corbusier had this same ability to temper the extremities of modernism with a subtle response to human emotional and spiritual need. Jencks's description of Le Corbusier's design of the church at Ronchamp in France (1950–55) could equally apply to Butcher's *3d*:

> an alternative world that is as tantalisingly rich and believable as the real one, having all the coherence one expects except conventional reference.
>
> (Jencks 1987: 153)

However Butcher created *3d* in 1990, and although interested in the ideas of Le Corbusier, her response to the stated subject of the piece, our relationship to the city, has a strongly contemporary flavour. The sociologist Anthony Giddens writes that in current society,

> the very tissue of spatial experience alters, conjoining proximity and distance in ways that have few close parallels in prior ages. There is a complex relation here between familiarity and estrangement.   (Giddens 1990: 140)

Butcher's use of fragmentation, layering, multiple viewpoints and repetition, creates rapidly changing textures alongside those of sound and design. The result is not chaos, but an order under threat of disintegration, saved at times by the powerful energy of the dancers who move in forceful unison, or, at other times, by the sudden simple clarity of form that communicates across distance, with complication temporarily swept away.

Over the years Butcher's dances have received mixed reviews, some full of appreciation, others expressing disappointment at her continuing interest in abstract rather than expressive content. The terminology commonly applied to

Rosemary Butcher's *3d* at the Tramway, Glasgow.   Photo: John Lyall

her dances – minimalist, cool, restrained, meditative – serves to undermine
much of the energy evident in the often fierce discourse that takes place across
disciplines in her performances. A multidisciplinary approach to interpretation
avoids an over-simplistic response to kinesics, since it takes on board the vital
interrelation between the dancers and other collaborators. Butcher cut the tie
with North American modern dance in the style of Martha Graham and Doris
Humphrey and she has not replaced this with some of the current postmodern
themes – the playfully intellectual world of Yolande Snaith for instance, or the
psychological depth and political challenge of DV8 Physical Theatre. In placing
the body in relationship to architecture she creates a distance combined with an
immediate relevance that opens up a world of subtle transformations. She creates a clarity of form associated with sculpture and releases condensed metaphorical resonance more common to poetry than to physical theatre.

Planning Dislocation

There are two main strands to this section, in which the concept of location is
considered both in terms of the placement of dance performance and the placing
of the dance amidst the pretexts shared by the choreographer and architects. The
first strand looks at how a body has to be 'framed within a performative situation
that establishes that it has to be taken as a sign' (Eco, referring to theatre, 1990:

110). In Butcher's case this framing is complicated through the use of non-dance venues which introduce new texts to the performance (associated with, for instance, the gallery, warehouse, church) and through the proxemics of audience and performers. Second, the dance is placed within the framework of ideas shared by the collaborators before and during its making. The concepts of ley lines and Le Corbusier's 'modular system' weave in and out of the performance.

Placement

There is little in the way of a history of choreographer/architect collaborations within which to set Butcher's work on the *d's*. There has, however, been a lively debate during the twentieth century about the placement of art and of dance. Duchamp's 'ready-mades', beginning with the *Bicycle Wheel* in 1913, began the placing of ordinary objects in an art gallery context. Art objects were placed in ordinary places. Museum walls were stripped (for example, the Toselli Gallery, Milan 1973, by Michael Asher). Mountains were wrapped in silk (Christo began his wrappings in 1958). Droves of artists left the galleries for found sites, while others used objects, as O'Doherty describes:

> As modernism gets older, context becomes content. In a peculiar reversal, the object introduced into the gallery frames the gallery and its laws.
>
> (cited in de Oliveira 1996: 13)

Each stage of these movements along a cultural and political edge called the status quo into question. Many of the ideas contested the place of art in society through the metaphor of the gallery as controller. Butcher does not show such overt political concerns. However, as she moves her performances into the galleries that visual artists have left, she reframes dance. Although this might initially have been a pragmatic move, Butcher has continued to show her work in galleries and other non-theatrical sites[5] – a choice that reveals one way in which she tackles the limitations of dance and provokes debate about its place, its relationship to visual art, and expectations as to how it should be viewed.

During the periods spent in America 1968–69 and 1970–72 Butcher had contact with many of the first wave of postmodern choreographers who, like the artists above, were questioning both the content and context of dance performance. Anna Halprin on the West Coast had long been using a variety of indoor and outdoor sites for performance, such as *Five Legged Stool* (1962), in which she 'used all the spaces in the theatre and sometimes moved outside the theatre as well' (Halprin 1995: 256). Butcher, like many of the other dancers (for example, Simone Forti, Yvonne Rainer, Trisha Brown and Meredith Monk) who came to work with Halprin, benefited from her encouragement to experiment in improvisation, across disciplines with other artists/musicians, and with placement.

Through Cunningham she would have been introduced to multifocal points in performance and to the attitude that assigned equal value to every area of the stage. Like visual artists, and frequently alongside them, choreographers of the Judson Church Theater, such as Trisha Brown, were keen to break with the constraints of modern dance and to extend the range of form and content. One aspect of this release was to realise the potential of a variety of sites for performance. As Trisha Brown, in typical humorous manner, put it: 'I have in the past felt sorry for ceilings and walls. It's perfectly good space, why doesn't anyone use it?' (cited in Banes 1987: 81).

The general climate and Rosemary Butcher's early choreographic experiences go only some way towards explaining her continuing preference for using non-dance venues for her performances. Asked recently at a post-production talk (RCA 1997) about her work with architects, Butcher stated that 'architecture has always been in the work'. Fleshing this out on a personal level, she described a long-term interest in architecture and a particular fascination with seeing how 'buildings change as you look at them, change as you move'. Conversely she is alert to the reflective quality of architecture on movement:

> It's a juxtaposition of moving people with the architecture around, which in fact makes the movement very alive and puts the dancers into a perspective.
> (Butcher, cited in Jordan 1992: 172)

The way Butcher works with dimension and perspective is multifaceted. She avoids the proscenium arch since it tends towards a flattened pictorial image, with a marked divide between audience and performers and certain theatrical assumptions. By contrast Butcher brings her audience close to the performance space, to witness the subtle relationship between movement and environment, that can, in an instant, twist the viewers' perspective. Like the best of architecture, many of her dances convey an understanding of the proximity of the ordinary and extraordinary, the semi-permanent and the fleeting, the functional and the expressive. The way in which this is present in the movement of *3d* is examined later in 'Building Dance'.

These concerns were clearly evident in some of Butcher's early works before she began to collaborate with architects. It is demonstrated by her use of found sites, such as *Passage North East* (1976), during which the dancers cross the Bristol Quay in a boat, and perform near the Arnolfini Gallery, in front of the dilapidated doors of a warehouse. In relooking at snippets of this work on video, Butcher noted with pleasure the juxtaposition of the dancers moving in white against the different textures of the building, and the desire she had to work with scale and perspective (Butcher, RCA 1997).

Given these architectural interests it is surprising that she has worked so rarely out of doors and recently not at all. Perhaps the reason for this is that, as she suggested in discussing the piece *The Site* (1983), she 'couldn't define the architecture outside enough' (RCA 1997). Just as the theatre venue was too limiting, so, ultimately, the outside sites were too open. The precision with which Butcher selects and focuses her movement is at risk of being diluted by extraneous stimulation from the outside setting. This in turn threatens the delicate balance she maintains between a created metaphoric world and its everyday counterpoint. The 'outside' in *The Site*, an archaeological dig, becomes the catalyst for work inside, inspiring her choreography and the sculpture for it by Heinz-Dieter Pietsch. Similarly Pietsch's jagged rusted metal supports for the fibre glass panels in *Imprints* (1983) are reminiscent of the form and texture of decaying city buildings.

For the artist Robert Morris,

> Ideally it is a space without architecture as background and reference, that would give us different terms to work with.   (cited in de Oliveira 1996: 23)

This might well apply to some of the work of the sculptor Richard Long, with whom Butcher has been associated; but is clearly not the case for her. Most of her pieces are linked to some form of human habitation, symbolised by the installations she favours, while some of them, including the *d's*, deliberately refer out to the further layer of the building beyond the installation. Stephanie Jordan's view that 'Landscape, often the country, is a constant preoccupation, linking her directly with an English pastoral tradition' (1992: 177), seems to overlook a much stronger and abiding fascination with architecture, whether it is buried, decaying, forming boundaries, buildings or layered through time

This interest is formalised in her work on the *d's* from 1989 to 1990. She took the city as her subject, the concept of ley lines and the architect Le Corbusier's work on the modular as her inspiration, and worked alongside architects Hadid and Lyall. The three pieces created over this period were vast in scale, presented in large inside spaces which gave her sufficient room to resume her work on perspective evident in the early outside pieces, while retaining much greater control. Before touring to various galleries *d1* was premiered in the Royal Festival Hall Ballroom. *d2* was performed in its final form at Christ Church in Spitalfields, London, and *3d* at the Tramway in Glasgow. The eclectic choice of a modern concert venue, baroque place of worship and late nineteenth-century tram manufacturers (now an arts centre) recreates across the project the historical layering of cities that is evident in each piece. By contrast many of the movement components remain constant across the three projects. Change is evident in the accumulation of new material and the restless reworking of the old. It is as if the dance is being built up into vertical space (the high walkways of *d2* and the scaffolding structure of *3d*) with the original lines of movement, like the architect's plan, still visible.

The artist, Michael Asher, in his description of the process of peeling paint from the Toselli Gallery, locates a formal, structural concern with the fabric of the building:

> Curiously enough, the white painted surface always covered over a much richer surface underneath . . . By sand-blasting the wall surfaces, I essentially brought the recollection of an outdoor material indoors.
>
> (cited in de Oliveira 1996: 125)

In making *3d*, Butcher uses the surface of the Tramway to set up a tension between outside and inside. A flyer for the piece states that the performance 'addresses current concerns surrounding structure and space, flexibility and delineation, boundaries and non-boundaries'. These concerns filter through every aspect of the construction and performance of *3d* and are dealt with in more detail below in 'The Framework', 'The Bricks', and 'Peeling Surfaces'.

Catalysts

At the time of making the *d's* Butcher had become interested in the idea of ley lines. Her exploration of this as a concept is most in evidence in *d1*. In *The Old Straight Track* (1925), the author Alfred Watkins created the terms 'ley system' and 'sighted tracks' to describe a phenomenon he had investigated, which would appear to reveal prehistoric tracks formed in straight lines across Britain. He suggests that the ley section was originally utilitarian, marking access to necessary materials for tools, over time. However, he argues that 'mystery and reverence for a superior knowledge grew around its making and its mark points' (1974: 215). Whether his theory is accepted or rejected, many artists have been drawn to the marking of lines on the land, both the leys of Britain and the Andean lines in Peru, Chile and Bolivia. It is not clear how Butcher interpreted the information she read on ley lines, but in interview she spoke of Zaha Hadid as being interested in two forms of physical space, 'energy that was physical and linear energy' (1995).

When *d1* was premiered at the Ballroom of the Royal Festival Hall (September 1989), there was a pause while the audience gathered informally around the edge of the space and looked at the series of straight white lines stuck to the Ballroom floor. Reminiscent of an enlarged version of an architect's design, they appropriately signal the start of the project. Yet as the space fills with sound and the rhythm of the dancers skipping in lines, groupings and pairs, with arms flinging ahead of them in the double arm swing characteristic of all the *d's*, it is clear that the lines are complete in themselves. They redefine the space between the pillars without closing it, drawing the eye back to the horizontal in sharp contrast with the dancers moving in strongly vertical vibrant formations. These simple lines, like the leys, mark a pathway between points accruing energy through the movement on their surface and lying as a layer between the present of performance and the past of the building. Since they offer boundary without enclosure, the site lines seem to extend from the performance space, to the edges of the Ballroom and out through the plate glass windows to the City of London beyond.

d1 is complete in itself (although flawed, in Butcher's view, through insufficient time for rehearsal) but acts simultaneously as a plan for the subsequent dances. It maps out many of the issues that will be reworked throughout the project, as the architectural designs become three-dimensional, rising up above the performers and altering the perspective.

As mentioned in my introduction, Butcher recollects that she was inspired by the work of the architect known as Le Corbusier (Charles-Edouard Jeanneret, 1887–1965), particularly in relation to the making of *3d*. During the Nazi occupation of France in the early forties, Le Corbusier set himself (and others) the task of devising a modular system of measuring, primarily for the design of architecture. He intended that this would address practical necessities of international communicability and construction, as well as having 'real aesthetic value' (Jordan 1972: 109). Based crudely on the human form rather than the arbitrary measurements of foot or metre, he created a precise system 'of differing but mathematically related dimensions, any one of which could be used in conjunction with any other one' (*ibid.*). In making *3d* Butcher was 'hugely influenced by that because of the way the proportions kept changing' (Butcher 1995). Without attempting to use the measurements in an exact sense, Butcher devised base units, in terms of movement and floor plan, that allowed her infinite variety within a harmonious whole.

Whereas in much of her previous work Butcher had given her dancers tasks and instructions to set boundaries on basically improvised performances, the idea of the modular scale demanded much greater precision in terms of the rhythm and the setting of the choreography. Le Corbusier's belief that form should follow function included a broad sense of the variety of functions required by people of their buildings. In the right hands, the seeming rigidity of the modular enabled great flexibility. He planned structures that 'would achieve the utmost freedom and flexibility in the interpenetration of inner and outer space' (Arnason 1979: 253). In *3d* it appears that, influenced by these views, Butcher finds a method of expanding an abiding interest in the distant and the familiar, stepping beyond the slightly claustrophobic feel of some of her earlier work. At times *3d* has a filmic quality, drawing the audience in on a dramatic or intimate moment, then with a swing of the focus driving them back out to view from a distance. The issue of perspective is activated on a physical, human and poetic level in relation to the subject matter of 'our relationship to the city' (*d1* programme 1989) through the use of constantly altering proportions.

Designing Uncertainty

The fact that artists share concepts prior to and during the making of the dance does not necessarily ensure a smooth passage in process or a unified result in performance. Issues of power and control between collaborators can themselves be viewed as 'texts' which emerge in the collaborative process and retain a presence in the dance. None of the artists seeks closure or singular meaning within *3d*. Their ability to work with uncertainty, I suggest, is linked with the holding open of the performance to multiple meanings. Attention to the intertextuality of the performance removes the pressure to seek one or two unified themes. Instead, the reader is free to allow the nuances and references generated by the dance to bounce off each other. This approach emphasises the active engagement of the viewer in the creative process and seems to me to be entirely appropriate to a multidisciplinary performance of layers and fragments. However, the absence of linear progression in performance makes demands on the viewer, as well as the artists, to tolerate a degree of uncertainty, which may be an uncomfortable experience.

If, as described in my introduction, Butcher perceives dance as limited, the close connection she makes with other art forms provides a means of breaking through this limitation. She is not isolated in this practice. Artists of all disciplines beg, borrow or steal from each other across media, driven on by the need to reinvigorate and refine their material. Le Corbusier drew on music as inspiration for the devising of the modular system. In 'Le Modular' he describes this in some detail:

> It was necessary to represent sound by elements which could be grasped, breaking up a continuous whole in accordance with a certain convention and making from it a series of progressions. These progressions would then constitute the rungs of a scale – an artificial scale – of sound.
>
> (Le Corbusier 1954: 15)

Butcher fed ideas from Le Corbusier's spatial scale into her choreography, and by collaborating with the musician Fulkerson, recycled them into the music. The interchange is not restricted to the arts, as shown by mathematical principles that support both the musical and architectural systems.[6]

To work with the ideas of another discipline is not the same as working with artists from it. I intend to draw attention to some of the specific difficulties cross-media relationships must negotiate, through a brief consideration of Butcher's working processes with, in particular, the architect John Lyall. Paradoxically these difficulties often have positive outcomes for the final performance. Since Butcher has sought consistently to work alongside artists of different media, it is possible that she perceives risk and uncertainty, with the ensuing provocative debates, as necessary elements in her process of creative development. When

Rosemary Butcher's *3d*.   Photo: John Lyall

Zaha Hadid left the project after her work for *d1*, Butcher approached another architect, John Lyall, whom she had known years before when they both worked independently at Riverside Studios in London. With the pressure of two further pre-advertised performances looming, and with work on the choreography under way, there was presumably the choice to take the simpler option of commissioning a set design. To do this would have been to leap over Butcher's preferred methods of co-working and in all probability would not have given her the outcome she wanted. By taking the risk to enter another collaboration Butcher acknowledges that the piece gained an 'integrated' environment, in which Lyall 'made the whole space alive' (1995).

In interview Butcher has spoken about the point of her collaborations as 'the energy, the time that is put into trying to come to grips with resolving the idea in a visual way' (1995). By sharing the creative process 'the person who is making the other element is actually working on the same sort of drive intellectually', although she isn't 'always linked with the ideas of that particular collaborator' and gets ideas from somewhere else. Throughout the process there is always the danger that 'you lose an element of control if you're not careful'. It would appear from these views that this form of cross-media work demands a broad range of opposing talents. The artists need to be open to influencing each other's work while not being totally reliant on the other, to be in charge of their work but not necessarily in control, and to be flexible yet able to argue a point of view. John Lyall deemed the collaboration with Butcher successful because they were, adult enough to actually offer up ideas and have them altered, adapted, or watered down or dispensed with, in favour of other things that come up in experimentation.   (Lyall 1995)

Butcher is unusual in acknowledging that this nitty-gritty aspect of co-work, in which ideas clash and are moulded by each other, can be more useful to her than the final artistic product.

Clashes arising from differences of aesthetic values, or from the difficulty of finding a common language with which to communicate across media, can threaten a project. This same friction in skilful hands can move the project on through the opportunity it provokes to clarify and distil the essence of an idea. When choreographer Ashley Page and designer Antony McDonald collaborated on *Fearful Symmetries* (1994), they clashed over costuming. Page favoured a stripped down costume to show the body, while McDonald refused to 'go on doing meaningless dance costumes' in the form of body stockings. In Page's view, the solution that emerged – close-cut, timeless looking costume – 'would not have been nearly so good' without the conflict (discussion chaired by Jordan, 1995). In the case of *3d* Butcher describes a similar discussion which arose over Lyall's wish to continue his use of slides developed for *d2* at Christ Church. He proposed projecting them onto swathes of material draped over the walls of the Tramway. This was unacceptable to Butcher, as it would have concealed the stripped brick work and softened the utilitarian cavernous quality of the building. Instead they worked closely together on lighting, which in three-dimensional form added a visual rhythm and many atmospheric qualities, leaving the shell of the building as plain counterpoint. Lyall describes in a letter they were not too 'precious' about their ideas:

> Through the process of working and experimenting we seem to come up with a result which neither of us would have expected.   (Lyall 1998)

Equally demanding are the clashes that emerge from the incompatibility of certain aspects of two media. Lyall became aware of this in *d2* when it was clear that the darker the space the better his slides would be seen, yet the dancers must have a certain degree of light to move safely. For dance, a fixed architectural structure within the space could be too rigid and dominant in form to accommodate the fast dissolving of images or themes so powerful in Butcher's choreography. Lighting was the area in which they worked most closely together, perhaps because it successfully mediated the extremes of the two disciplines. The colour, structures, focus and density of light were used to create external conditions that altered the audience's perception of both the movement and the bridge.

There are circumstantial as well as intentional forces operating on the formation of collaborative performances, as indeed on any artistic operation. Butcher is perhaps better equipped than most to deal with the uncertainty this can create, since she courts the unknown by engaging with other artists' creative processes close up to performance. It would be a mistake to assume that Butcher's ability to deal with setbacks, such as Hadid leaving unexpectedly or lack of funding, would be taken as an opportunity to compromise. The tolerating of uncertainty is matched by sharp attention to detail. When Fulkerson watched rehearsals at the beginning of the whole project, he picked up on the pulse that the dancers were repeating and used this as a basis for his music. Butcher recalls finding the first tape he sent too slow and the second slightly too fast. It was not right until the last day, when it was a matter of 'a millionth of a second between it being right' (Butcher 1995) or wrong.

Lyall's environment for *3d* consisted of a ramp alongside the brick wall of the Tramway which led onto a scaffolding bridge. This rose to eighteen feet and jutted out over the dance space, drawing attention to the height of the building. The bridge ended abruptly, mid-air and was given greater or less emphasis during performance through bright blue lighting from the underside. The permanent structure was contrasted with the fluidity of the lighting plan which included several distinct floor patterns at varying levels of brightness. At their sharpest, a rhythm was set up of white or coloured flashes on the surface of the dancers. The rich red and blue lights acted together as a vibrant contrast to the white stripes, and separately, as immediate evocation of atmospheres.

Busy theatre schedules and poor funding rarely allow choreographers to have more than a technical run within the performance area before the first night. Circumstantial uncertainty reaches unacceptable levels when, as in *3d*, the dancers had only two days to work on the structure, at times in half-light and with no safety net. Although Butcher had anticipated the bridge, the lack of time to develop the choreography using it operated to the detriment of the piece as a whole and has broader implications in limiting future similar experimentation. The choreographer Jonathan Burrows experienced similar frustration in his attempts to gain sufficient time to experiment on working collaboratively with lighting designers. He compares the situation here with 'other European countries where more production time is generally given to companies . . . it seems as though we neglect the very thing that can transform our work' (1994: 29). It is no surprise then, that in a subsequent collaboration with Butcher, Lyall came up with the infinitely more flexible idea of large oblong boards ('Tension and Compression' in *The Body as Site*). These could be bent by tightening the cords across them, or moved around the space by the dancers.

After a workshop with the American lighting designer Jennifer Tipton and choreographer Dana Reitz, Burrows wrote of the 'liberation' of being able to talk about dance, not in the borrowed language of theatre, in terms of location and atmosphere, but in the complementary language of structure, shape and texture.

(Burrows 1994: 29)

The close working across media can be interesting for the effect one discipline has on another but equally, as Burrows notes, can draw out qualities prominent in one medium and only inherent in the other. John Lyall alludes to this when describing his architectural process:

the architecture doesn't really happen until the building is finished and you can go back and actually look at how people are using it.   (Lyall 1995)

In designing new, clear, brightly coloured lifts for the Science Museum in London, Lyall describes an image he had in his mind 'of how dancers would use it, how the whole thing was a performance' and how subsequently he observed members of the public sitting watching it like an audience. Peter Cook, Bartlett Professor of Architecture at University College London, in conversation with the choreographers William Forsythe and Dana Caspersen, spoke of the façade of the building being the least interesting aspect, observing that 'the interior is like theatre, anything might happen' (Cook 1997).

Building Dance

Where the previous sections of this chapter focus upon external 'texts' and observe the path they trace into the dance, this section looks in detail at the movement and shows how the dancers both absorb and transform movement ideas. The choice made in this section to describe the dance through the use of some of the terminology of architecture acts as an acknowledgement of the subjectivity evident in the selection of descriptive terms and as a reminder of the focus of the chapter. Similarly the choice of what to describe is selective, providing the reader with detailed observations of movement to be read alongside the broad structural outline in Table 1. The latter acts as a model of the structure of the dance in which the detail can be located.

Just as Lyall considers the architectural task incomplete until he sees people move in the building, so Butcher, I believe, experiences the reverse: the dance is incomplete until the spatial context is set. Image, drama and meaning emerge from the relationship between the moving body and its surrounds. In writing about the movement component of the dance, it becomes clear that it is not possible to divorce the context from the content, so deeply embedded are Butcher's visual concerns of structure, space and texture. This view would seem to be borne out by her teaching, in which the instructions for improvisation relate to shaping the body in the space.[7] On an individual level this operates as a layering of movement over time, with the dancer's repeated movement phrase contrasted with variations. Two or more dancers may find themselves creating a 'frame' for each other's movement in a kaleidoscopic shift that alternately flips one to the foreground and the other to the back. Or, when the dancers work in unison, the 'volume' of the piece is greatly increased. In this respect, Butcher can be said to be working with her dancers in much the same way as I have described the cross-media interaction. The following description of the movement component of *3d* aims to explore how the tightly honed dance material is built up, dissolved and rebuilt with a fluidity that is able to encompass the functional, dramatic, communicative and metaphoric capacities of the body.

The Framework

The dance lasts approximately one hour and twenty minutes, and is divided into six sections signalled by distinct changes in music, movement, lighting, costume and number of dancers involved (see Table 1).[8] Each section has its own individual quality, but is linked with other sections through repetitions of the components and through an overall style. A clue to understanding the complexity of the structure lies perhaps in Butcher's view of architecture quoted earlier: that it is always changing according to how you look and how you move. With some movement phrases settled, a similar approach can be taken to the dance in which the elements are re-viewed, realigned, turned sideways, decreased, run backwards, driven high up onto the bridge, run in parallel, split apart, lined up, dissolved, turned inside out, and so on. This list refers to spatial aspects, but time-based structure is equally important. Although the piece draws heavily on the use of broken and unbroken lines, the structure is far from linear, it relies on multifocal patterning in the space and accumulation of layers over time.

Although, as mentioned in the introduction, *3d* has some of the attributes of poetry and sculpture, dance is fleeting and does not allow for lingering perusal. The spaciousness associated with much of Butcher's earlier work was attained partly through severely moderating the pace and allowing for many still poses. In the faster paced choreography and larger scale of *3d* the space to keep re-viewing the dance is still present. This is achieved at the start of the performance in the exposure of the building blocks that make up the dance, and through the seemingly contradictory process of distancing her audience in order to make them familiar with a world she creates.

The Bricks

The opening of *3d* is like staring in through a crack in a door.[9] All that is visible is a white stripe of light on the floor accompanied by the sound of repeating sequences of electronic music. Fragments of a dancer, her white canvas shoes, forearms and her face, can be seen in motion criss-crossing over the strip of light. The dance is opened up as two, then three shafts of light form a grid on the floor. There are momentary glimpses of other dancers caught in the light then hidden in deep shadow. A fresh line of melody rides over the top of the original music as four dancers weave through the space, each keeping the rhythmic pulse in the swing of their arms and their stepping.

From the start the audience is alerted to the way in which the elements interrelate, both within and across disciplines, building up layers, fragmenting, disturbing a pattern, highlighting or concealing each other. The dancers move in a relaxedly purposeful way. But what their purpose is remains concealed. Since the movement does not obviously relate to familiar gestures or to Western theatrical dance styles, the viewer is jogged out of a settled perception. Kevin Lynch applied Roland Barthes' idea of an 'image repertoire' to urban geography. He suggests that 'every urbanist . . . carries an image of "where I belong" in the mind's eye'. He found that

> his subjects compared new places to this mental snapshot and, the less the two corresponded, the more indifferent the subjects felt about their new surroundings. (cited in Sennett 1994: 365)

In *3d* the door may open on an unfamiliar place, but Butcher breaks through this resistance to make the unknown familiar.

The choreography of *3d* emphasises the lines of the bones of the body over the musculature through a predominant use of the angular, joint-based movement. The dancers' spines are mainly held in vertical with the horizontal and vertical axes of movement emphasised rather than the actions of rounding or twisting. The angularity is countered through the use of a relaxed, loose-limbed technique which allows the limbs to respond to the pull of gravity and momentum. This anti-illusionist aesthetic, which emphasises the underlying skeletal structure of the body, is pursued further in the exposure of the dance structure, and in the reduction of the quantity and complexity of movements to a bare minimum. Of these the most frequently used is the double-arm swing skip that was seen in both *d1* and *d2*. It is worth pausing to consider it in a little more depth, since it appears to operate like one part of Le Corbusier's modular scale, a recurring point against which everything else can be measured.

In this movement both arms are flung forward, bent at the elbow and allowed to swing back behind the body. The swinging arms keep the pulse while the dancer can travel at a skip, walk, gallop or even stand still, fitting the steps to the rhythm of the arms. As both arms are flung forward simultaneously, the movement bears little direct relation to Western historical dance forms (with Morris dancing being one of the exceptions), nor to the usual diagonal swing of the body in pedestrian motion. The overall shape of the body in performing this movement is of a rectangle, reinforced by the rectangular patterns traced by the dance on the floor. The regimentation that this suggests is dissolved by the skipping rhythm which, with its bounce to a breath pulse combined with the looseness of the swung arms, has a childlike vitality. Over the period of the dance the audience becomes very familiar with this unfamiliar movement. Like the poles of the scaffolding or the repeated system of the music it is exposed as a base unit of the dance.

Cornices

The task-like uniformity that enters in with such a high degree of repetition of individual units is subverted through the use of three distinct approaches. In the first, despite the structure of the dance calling for the units described above to be perfectly timed, there is an individuality associated with each dancer's execution of the movement based on body type/training and attitude. No attempt has been made to eradicate these differences which, although muted, allow the audience to develop a certain intimate awareness of the dancer's style and distinctive attributes. Secondly each unit is varied in a number of ways. For instance, the double-arm swing skip outlined above is performed at various speeds, or sometimes both arms are flung up and over the head, or one leg is swung forward extended in line with the arms. Finally there are many moments and extended sequences which bring in new material that does not reappear or obviously relate to the established sequences.

Mortar

The regularity of the pulse rhythm in *3d*, reinforced by Fulkerson's music, marks this dance out from Butcher's earlier work. As mentioned, Fulkerson took the timing of the music from the dance rehearsals he watched, 'deconstructing the pulse' (Butcher 1995) in an energetic single-minded interrogation of the variants within chosen melodic and rhythmic sequences. The pulse established in the first section is the element shared between dance and music, opening up a fluid yet forceful relationship between the two media. At times the music dissolves into long sustained sung notes, or the rhythm stumbles into disintegration, or disappears altogether (for the whole of section 4). Frequently the rhythm of the music and dance diverge, which like sudden dissonance in a context of harmony, can create an edgy, disturbing atmosphere.

In many of Butcher's earlier dances there is a naturalistic feel to the rhythm, since it is determined by task-based improvisation unaccompanied by sound (in, for instance, *Spaces Four*), or with sound that adds atmosphere and might indicate phases of the dance, but does not control the dynamic (for example, *The Site* or *Imprints*). For *3d*, improvisation was used in rehearsal to create the choreography, but the performance was fully set within the parameters of the music. With less left to chance, Butcher was able to manipulate her material more tightly, including greater use of unison work to build up and then disperse the energy in the space. Boundaries are created in surges of energy when all elements converge in a repeating rhythm, or when the dancers move into formation heading in a single direction. Yet no sooner are these clear patterns formed than they are broken up; the moment of unity passes as one component clatters against another, or the dancers peel off in individual directions.

With so much reiteration, the sense of the pulse lingers even when absent from the movement or the music. It underlies the whole piece, whether proclaimed in a forceful shout by the company of dancers moving in fast formation, and driven by the heavy, almost manic beat of the music, or as a whisper filtering through the silent stylised gestures of a duet. Held together by this beat, Butcher is able to explore the texture and angling of the dance, filling and emptying the space, sending the dancers in a variety of directions, weaving elaborate patterns on the floor and up onto the bridge in the space above.

Performing Poetry

Sarup describes Derrida's concept of '*sous rature*' or 'under erasure' in the following way: 'since the word is inaccurate, or rather inadequate, it is crossed out. Since it is necessary it remains legible' (1988: 35). In this final section the movement described in detail earlier is shown to have a similarly inadequate yet necessary function. One movement is wiped out with the appearance of another, but each repetition of the same sequence alters in meaning according to both the immediate context and what remains in the memory from before. The audience members are drawn in to make their own connections and in doing so become the other essential collaborators in the performance. If the viewer has seen either of the connecting dances *d1* and *d2*, then further possibilities of 'reading' the dance are opened up, as familiar movements are transposed across time and distance. However, each of the *d's* was made to be complete in itself and, I suggest, they become all the richer for active viewing from any of many angles rather than from a single, specialist approach. The 'reading' of the performance *3d* offered below draws on the threads of the previous sections and seeks to reweave them back into the dance.

The City

The programme notes for *d1* indicate a context within which to view the performance, as an examination of 'the relationship between ourselves and the created environment of the city, its space, its light and its vertical power' (1989). The intention is elaborated upon in the programme for *3d*. Brief quotes from

Rosemary Butcher's *3d*.   Photo: John Lyall

philosophers and architects are juxtaposed to highlight the conflict in attitude towards the relative merits of unified city planning over the random accumulation of buildings over time. By extension it is suggested that random accumulation is an example of 'chance rather than the will of men using reason' while unified planning shows 'The triumph of reason over madness' (Descartes and Benjamin, cited in programme, 1990).

Once the performance begins any idea that it might plunge into one of these conflicts is dispelled as it glides over the surface, reflecting fragments of debate alongside lived experience. The prominence of the overall patterning of the piece at first seems to keep the audience at a distance, not allowing them to be drawn into a single story or dialectic. Acclimatising factors are established, yet even in these early stages nothing is quite comfortable. The swing of the arms might be loose and buoyant but the music stutters and strains at its format, threatening to disintegrate. Whether across disciplines or amongst the dancers, unity is shown as fleeting. Consistent symmetry is defiantly denied as Butcher seems caught instead by the many lines of energy that overlie and disturb each other in a continual process of fragmentation. It is not that the forces of madness are shown to triumph over reason, but that the tension between the two gives an urgent edge to the precision and repeating patterns of the dance. Purity of form is under threat, yet by a strange quirk, the movement can be seen to both stave off and feed on the energy of encroaching chaos.

Roger Copeland describes a similar attitude towards the city in the work of Merce Cunningham who, instead of 'lamenting fragmentation and disunity . . . encourages us to savour the peculiarly urban experience of "non-relatedness"' (1994: 195). But while Cunningham chooses to build this into the fabric of his dance through a variety of chance procedures, the pleasure in 'fragmentation and dis-unity' evident in *3d* has no base in 'non-relatedness'. The feeling of variety and chance occurrence do not derive from random process, but from Butcher's careful orchestration of the elements. She plays with the proportion of one in relation to another in a method that is drawn from Le Corbusier's modular system, but is applied differently to suit her distinctive medium of movement in relationship to design and music.

In Section 1, the lines of music suddenly diverge in rhythms counter to the movement, while the stripes of white light across the floor disrupt the dancers' rhythm as they cross in and out of darkness and light. Within each medium the building blocks criss-cross each other in a form of ruthless exposure. The performance space is de-centred through the use of multifocal points and the uneasy interweaving of components. This, combined with an avoidance of consistent narrative or single climax, allows viewers of the dance to spread their gaze across the whole 'city' landscape, or to home in on an intimate section of the movement. As mentioned earlier, Giddens notes a complex relationship in our society between 'familiarity and estrangement'. He writes that it is a mistake to perceive 'impersonal clusters of city-centre buildings' as the 'epitome of the landscape of modernity', since 'equally characteristic is the recreation of places of relative smallness and informality' (1990: 142). In *3d* Butcher works with this complexity to create in microcosm the frequent and abrupt contrasts so familiar in city living

The Street and the Square

Section 1 ends abruptly, as if a pause button had been pressed, leaving the dancers motionless with their arms held up, mid-swing. This heightens the contrast with the subsequent section, since the image of a busy space alive with energetic sound still hovers, as the steady beat of a metronome is heard and a single dancer (Michael Popper) double-arm swings alone in easy insouciance. Unruffled by the gradual addition of percussive sounds or the syncopation of the rhythm, he is joined by a second dancer (Gill Clarke) who is equally at ease. In an extended duet they swerve away from each other on their individual paths only to be drawn back together in perfect unison. The timing of their movements as they lunge forward in a half curtsey with arms flung to the side is impeccable. Their kinetic awareness of each other is so intense that it appears as if the two bodies are driven by a single impulse.

Butcher provides no reasons for this pairing. She does not weight them down with the baggage of narrative or character development, maintaining instead a lightness of touch that focuses attention on the simple pleasure of watching the clear shapes of the movements, performed in time, with a matter-of-fact, light-hearted quality that is untarnished by sentimentality. The dancers dip down as their arms spring wide out to the side and they hang momentarily in the air, connected across time and space. Whether this is by chance or intention does not seem to matter. The sharp contrasts in energy operate across the dance in a wave-like motion that places the hubbub of the city street with its fast, purposeful commuter energy next to the refreshing calm of the open square.

The use of contrast elicits other responses. The tightly controlled movement juxtaposed with the openness of content simultaneously channels the viewer's response and leaves it wide open. Butcher thereby gives imaginative and intellectual stimulation without closure, allowing each viewer the space to enter into the collaborative process through his/her own reading of the dance. Over the course of the dance the wave-like formation becomes more extreme in a cumulative process in which the theatre space becomes extraordinarily alive, as shifts in density take place, drawing the viewer deeper into Butcher's created world.

High Levels

After the sharp focus of Popper and Clarke's duet the dance returns to the complexity of Section 1 with three dancers, mainly using the double-arm swing gallop, creating an ever-altering variety of floor patterns and formations. In addition, the scaffolding, which has up until this point been an unemphasised presence in the space, is used for the first time, as Popper moves slowly up and down the ramp before joining the other dancers.

A dramatic contrast in atmosphere at the beginning of Section 4 signals the start of the second part of the dance. The driving rhythm of the music, the bounce and fling of the movement, and austere grey of the scaffolding, are swept aside, to be replaced by the appearance of the bridge, lit blue, riding out over the silent, still space. In the sudden absence of clamorous sound and vibrant patterns of red and white light, there is for a moment a vast dark quiet place without proportion.[10] Cutting across this temporarily unmeasureable space hangs the glowing line of blue light. Dressed in white, the dancers emerge slowly from the darkness, and introduce new movement material of high held arm gestures in walking. Clare Baker moves up on the bridge, which seems at first to float, until the light increases beneath it to reveal the scaffold supports and the familiar red and white bars on the floor that fleck Fin Walker as she walks across them. Apparently unaware of each other, Baker and Walker slip in and out of unison. The intense energy of the previous sections still resonates in the space, but is gradually replaced by a quality of reflection and a sense of subtle communication across vertical and horizontal distance.

The viewers are metaphorically dropped into a more meditative and serious space, where the rules of time dictated by the steady pulse of the first three sections are no longer present. The new perspective added to the piece, that of volume extending up and away from the floor, could be read as an allusion to other more shadowy dimensions, or, as easily, to daily life in a city that demands and can sustain many different levels of living. The silence of this section, combined with the calm, poised movement of Walker and Baker, allows the viewer time to absorb the dual aspect of the power of high buildings both to inspire with their upward energy and diminish the individual through their sheer massive presence.

It is clear that Butcher needed 'a living space' not a scenic backdrop in order to realise her vision for *3d*, since, whether intentionally or not, the modular scale seems to operate across disciplines as well as within each medium. When the place empties of sound a greater emphasis is placed on the movement between dancers, while stillness drives attention on to the architectural structure. The manipulation of sound and design components, combined with the placement of the movement, alters the viewer's perspective of the dancers' relationship to their surrounds. However, the dancers' use of formation, dynamic and shape is just as forceful in determining shifts of proportion and scale within this relationship. The changes in density created by applying a version of the modular scale to all the components allow Butcher and her co-workers the flexibility to trigger different levels of perception in the viewer, too often dulled to monotone by day-to-day living.

This shift in levels need not be a retreat from the daily grind, but can be found through even a momentary relinquishing in favour of the less familiar view of routine life as patterns forming three-dimensionally across space and time. Section 5 opens with the five dancers emerging from the dark edges of space, to the sound of high voices singing open vowel sounds. Two dancers carry another over their shoulders like a heavy sack. The light forms white stripes on the floor across which the dancers travel from light to shadow, each absorbed in his/her own slow paced sequence of actions. The atmosphere is reminiscent of the setting up of a market early in the morning, before speed is necessary, with the sun filtering through the buildings to form a grid on the ground.

Broken Bridge

The reading of Section 5 as the setting up of a market and passing of a day is plausible, but unusually linear for Butcher's work. She encourages multiple viewpoints through re-angling sections of the movement so that it is seen and re-seen, and through spreading the viewers' gaze across several points of activity of equal emphasis. Lyall reinforces this method of working through his use of depth, allowing one structure to be seen on top of another. The use of scaffolding generates images of building sites in which the scaffolding is the functional but temporary cladding for a permanent but temporarily dysfunctional building. In *3d* the position is partially reversed, since the scaffolding structure stretches away from the functioning, intact brick walls of the Tramway into empty space. Connected with a ramp, it forms a broken bridge. The design breaks with the expected both in theatrical terms of creating an illusion that hides the external structure, and in terms of construction by failing to fulfil the requirements of bridges or of scaffolding. As it arches over the dance space, at times lit bright blue, the bridge acts as spark for the imagination, forming a potent symbol that is literally open-ended.

Communication across distance is a recurring theme in *3d*. A poignant example arises in Section 6 with two dancers visible high up in the space: Clare Baker on a metal platform that is part of the Tramway building and Michael Popper at the end of the eighteen-foot high bridge. They move in place with slow arm gestures, interrupted by sudden jerking movements of the elbow bending in a sharp angle as the hand reaches down the spine. The audience must gaze high up to see them and their positions are obviously precarious. Vulnerability is only one rather obvious aspect, since they both move with a certainty and composure that destroys a simple sentimental interpretation. The open-ended bridge, the blueness, the breathiness in the sound of the music, the chasm between the dancers and the coinciding then diverging movement act together to create a multisensory stimulus to the imagination. Like the condensed imagery of poetry, the moment can sustain many meanings to do with the issue of separation, ranging from the imposition of a physical gap between people to the metaphysical distance between life and death. The gap between the dancers is allowed to resonate with dramatic intensity, but without specific meaning. The ensuing uncertainty is the creative space available for each viewer to fill or leave empty as the individual chooses.

Peeling Surfaces

Emphasis on lines and broken lines means that the dancers track and retrace their steps over the space. Like the example of ley lines referred to earlier, the meaning of the dance is to be found in the layering that takes place over time and across media. If, as described under 'Bricks', each component is stripped back to the raw essentials within the microcosmic world, new building begins layer on layer. Most cities are not 'designed and built in the single extended moment' (Benjamin, cited in programme, 1990), but amass buildings over centuries in a tangled response to the dictates of fashion and practical necessity. The old and new exist side by side or, as in the case of the Tramway, coexist in a process of adaptation to change. Built in 1890 for manufacturing trams, the building has been recycled several times; first of all as a repair depot when the manufacturing business was moved to Manchester in the 1930s, and then as a museum of transport which closed in 1988. Peter Brook was one of the driving forces behind reopening it as a theatre, originally to stage his production of the *Mahabharata*. Butcher allows the history of the building to filter into the performance, since she insists that the fabric of the walls should be visible, and she makes opportune use of the metal platform jutting out from one side of the building. Within the terms of her own created world of *3d*, Butcher reveals a time-based as well as spatial response to the concept of three dimensions.

With Butcher's expressed interest in ley lines contributing to the emergence of the *d's*, it is hardly surprising to find that the relationship between past and present discussed above is a theme that is integral to the choreography of the whole project. It is most explicit in *d2*, which begins with the whole of the choreography of *d1*. In more subtle form, the 'bricks' of the movement in *3d* are shown to be highly adaptable. They are refashioned in different combinations with each other and are reframed through juxtaposition with new movement material. Towards the end of the final section, Popper can be seen moving up on the bridge with three dancers below in double arm swing formation and two others walking and turning with a single arm outstretched. Each performs in the present while pulling at threads from the past. So the high held arm moves to the music from Section 1, but flags memories of the silence of Section 4. Popper's ever-confident, even defiant, double-arm swing skip up the slope of the bridge has a different quality from the same movement performed in the warmth of the red light or the coolness of the blue below.

Doorways

Towards the end of Section 5 the light dims to blue, the sound decreases, and four dancers walk slowly in line between two others, who stand still opposite each other. For a moment the image of a doorway is conjured up, then dissolved as the 'gate-post' dancers turn from their position to join on the end of the processing line. With such economy Butcher stimulates connections with the closing up of a market square (the opening of this image starts the section), the ending of a day, or simply the lowering of energy and slowing of rhythmic pattern. The closing of one image is the opening of the next, as she allows the dancers to travel between levels, across space and through time.

The same illustration exemplifies the way in which people both inhabit and create their environment. The city, like the body itself, has a basic structure that is made and remade to fulfil the wide range of requirements demanded of it. The dance has an undulating, rather than climactic structure, and it is thus entirely appropriate that the end is more like a sudden pause mid-action than a gradual completion. It is as if it has ended with the door held open on a place that could again burst into action.

The fragments of images, or momentarily complete forms stimulate the viewers, but keep them at a distance by preventing blinkered pursuit. Through the dramatic changes of dynamic, with pauses placed against rushes of energy, the viewer is drawn in and out of the rhythms of the city. As the title indicates, we are asked to look beyond flat surfaces to the complex places that are continually opened up. The sense of process being a part of product is brought into the performance not as improvisation, but through Butcher's choreography. She has the ability, like an architect, to create structured spaces within which her audience can take an imaginative walk. Their entry is the completion of her piece. Since her medium is movement, these spaces are shown in constant motion, equally defined by dynamic, density of action and gestural allusions as by the more architectural aspects of shape, line and light.

The contradictory elements of Butcher's performances mentioned at the start of this chapter do not act to snuff each other out, but are evidence of the tremendous demands she makes on dance. Perhaps it is as true today as twenty years ago that she does 'not want to be in a situation with answers' (Butcher 1977). This would account for a style of choreography that seems to be always in the process of self-reflexive interrogation. However, the questioning of the limits of dance through intense dialogues with other art forms is not an end in itself, but is absorbed into her chosen subject matter. The dancers in *3d* reflect back to the audience a fractured view of city living , but one that is enriched rather than diminished by the presence of uncertainty and a sense of dislocation. The life, the energy and the poetry of the piece emerge from a constantly shifting perspective, presented by the dancers and by their relationship to sound and spatial context. By turns the dance is disturbing or peaceful, familiar or strange, chaotic or ordered, forceful or calm, in Butcher's ruthlessly sensitive response to the challenges posed by city living.

Notes

1. The term used by Butcher when interviewed 1995.
2. In discussion with Butcher at her retrospective held at the RCA 1997, she connected the *d's* with *Flying Lines* (1985) and not with the current direction of her work.
3. 'As an art form dance is very limited' . . . 'The language of dance is restricted, not being able to expand ideas in the way other arts can.' (From talk on collaboration at RCA 18 February 1997.)
4. Even altering the venue while retaining the created design can make a dramatic difference to the dance. For instance, when *Body as Site* was performed in Guildford Cathedral (1995) each of the four installations and dances reverberated with the new context. The vast size of the building, the quality of the materials (large marble flagstones, pillars, and so on), and the religious symbolism all played a part in changing some aspects of the dances when compared with their performance in the smaller, contained and more ascetic spaces of the RCA

(1997).

5. Butcher described her use of the Serpentine Gallery in London for the showing of *Pause and Loss* as an easy way of finding a venue. (Talk on collaboration, RCA 1997.)

6. The borrowing across art forms extends into the language used in the analysis and appreciation of art products. One example is Jencks's description of Le Corbusier's Unite: 'Intense rhythms flow over the surface. Light and dark rectangles alternate at a certain tempo and then are inverted and played at twice the speed. This is the most musical of Le Corbusier's buildings' (1987: 144). How this enters into the process of cross-art collaborations, if at all, is too large a subject to embark upon in this chapter.

7. In a choreographic workshop given to MA students at Surrey University 1995 to demonstrate how she begins to work with her dancers on a new piece, Butcher started by asking each student to work on the base levels of movement, the 'substrata'. Once a repeatable system was chosen, two more layers or 'strata' were to be found relating to the first so that the dancer could drop from one level to another quite suddenly. While the students worked she had already noted how the moving bodies paired to best complement each other. Each pair moved through its own sequences; they made no direct contact, but framed and reframed each other in a sculptural relationship. The next stage, Butcher commented, would be to work within a physical framework.

8. This analysis is made from a video of the performance by students of Glasgow Art College. Occasional pauses and selective videoing make it impossible to be completely accurate about the timing and some of the overall patterning of the dance. The dance was premiered on 14 September 1990 at the Tramway Theatre Glasgow. The dancers in the piece were: Clare Baker, Maxine Braham, Gill Clarke, Dennis Greenwood, Michael Popper and Fin Walker. Rosemary Butcher was the choreographer, John Lyall, architect/designer and Jim Fulkerson musician.

9. An image, incidentally, that receives much more direct treatment in *Unbroken View* (1995). In one section of this piece the dancers move in front of a filmed doorway projected onto the wall behind them.

10. Similar perhaps to the sensations experienced in flotation tanks.

References

Arnason, H.H. (1979), *A History of Modern Art*, London, Thames & Hudson.

Aston, E. & G. Savona (1991), *Theatre as Sign-System*, London, Routledge.

Banes, S. (1987), *Terpsichore in Sneakers, Post-Modern Dance*, New England, Wesleyan University Press.

Burrows, J. (1994), 'Leading Lights', *Dance Now*, Vol. 3, No.1: 28–9.

Butcher, R. (1977), 'Fragments of a Diary', *New Dance*, 1, January: 19–20.

Copeland, R. (1994), 'Beyond Expressionism: Merce Cunningham's Critique of "the Natural"', in J. Adshead-Lansdale & J. Layson (eds), *Dance History: an Introduction*, London, Routledge: 182–97.

Dempster, E. (1995), 'Women Writing the Body: Let's Watch a Little How She Dances', in E.W. Goellner & J.S. Murphy (eds), *Bodies of the Text*, New Brunswick, NJ, Rutgers University Press: 21–38.

Eco, U. (1990), *The Limits of Interpretation*, Bloomington: Indiana University Press.

Giddens, A. (1990), *The Consequences of Modernity*, London, Polity.

Gilbert, J. (1997), 'Do Dancers Dream of Electric Frogs?' *Independent on Sunday*, 9 March: 13.

Halprin, A. (1995), *Moving Toward Life: Five Decades of Transformational Dance*, Hanover: Wesleyan University Press.

Hughes, D. (1993), 'Review of Rosemary Butcher, The Body as Site', *Hybrid*, Issue 2, April/May: 42–3.

Jencks, C. (1987), *Le Corbusier and the Tragic View of Architecture*, London, Penguin.

Le Corbusier (1954), *The Modular*, London, Faber.

Jordan, R. F. (1972), *Le Corbusier*, London, Aldine Press.

Jordan, S. (1992), *Striding Out: Aspects of Contemporary and New Dance in Britain*, London, Dance Books.

Meisner, N. (1997), 'Rosemary Butcher', *Dance Now*, Vol. 6, No. 2: 22–6.

Oliveira, N. de, N. Oxley & M. Petry (1996), *Installation Art*, London, Thames & Hudson.

Sarup, M. (1988), *An Introductory Guide to Poststructuralism and Postmodernism*, London, Harvester Wheatsheaf.

Sennett, R. (1994*), Flesh and Stone: the Body and the City in Western Civilisation*, London: Faber.

Watkins, A. (2nd edn, 1974), *The Old Straight Track*, Great Britain, Sphere.

Letters, Interviews and Public Talks

Butcher R. (1995), Personal Interview with L. Worth, May and August.

———— (1997), Talks during *Rosemary Butcher in Retrospect* at Royal College of Art, Gulbenkian Galleries, Kensington Gore, London SW7 2EU, February.

Caspersen D. and Forsythe, W. (1997), *Choreographers, in conversation with Peter Cook*, Bartlett Professor of Architecture, Royal Geographic Society, London, 7 March. Organised and recorded by Artangel.

Jordan, S. (Chair) (1995), *Ashley Page and Antony McDonald discussion on collaboration between Designers and Choreographers*, Ballroom Blitz, Royal Festival Hall, London, August.

Lyall, J. (1995) Personal Interview with L. Worth, February.

———— (1998), Letter to the author, 5 February.

Students of Glasgow Art College, (1990), *Video of 3d performance at The Tramway*, Glasgow, September.

PART 1	Section 1	Section 2	Section 3
Time	00.00–14.54	14.54–21.11	21.11–29.06
No. of dancers	5	2	4
Design	Costume 2 x M, 3 x B.* Strips of light open up the space. 3 stripes of light remain on floor as light increases. Flashes of red paint on floor. Structure is visible.	Costume 2 x M. Starts with dim lighting. 3 stripes on floor and faint red as in Sec. 1. Changes to 2 stripes, then 1, both with red flash.	Costume 2 x M, 2 x B. Low light with red flash faint on floor. 1 stripe > 2 > 3 stripes. Structure visible with dancer on it.
Sound	Music of synthesiser. Use of repetitive melody and rhythm with a steady pulse. Melody begins to vary and speed increases to a manic pace with deep heavy beat. Heavy beat dropped at end of section.	Metronome sound as base unit with many percussive additions, including bells, tinkling sound and drum beats. Lively, almost playful sound.	Synthesiser. Lively repetitive melody and rhythm. Seems to disintegrate at times. Stumbles, then picks up pulse again.
Movement characteristics	**Primary movements:** double arm swing skip, double arm circle, single arm dive. All performed in skipping and walking with some individual variations. **Dynamic:** lively, energetic skip to pulse of breath rhythm. Increases in speed. **Space:** dancers' bodies held upright, with some forward bending. Extensive use of criss-crossing the space, mainly in straight lines of varying length and zigzags. Use of bunching, pairing, lining up, backward and forward movement. **Structure:** Opens with one dancer, gradually increasing to five. Introduces many of the movement components of whole dance. Ends with four formation arm dives.	**Primary movements:** Popper in solo using double arm swing in skip and walk. Duet with Clarke, introduce new mvt. of double arm fling wide. Much mvt. in unison. Contact introduced in simple fall and catch. **Dynamic:** solo steady pace. Duet lively with slow moments. Relaxed, loose in limbs. **Space:** body level as in Sec. 1 with added fall back. Use of large oval floor pattern and lines. Often dancers close, but they do separate. **Structure:** solo, slight pause, duet.	**Primary movements:** Double arm swing in skip, walk and gallop. Popper set apart from others through being on structure. He repeats restricted structure mvt. on floor in place. **Dynamic:** Lively skipping. Popper on ramp slow – walk pace. **Space:** Bodies in upright. Use of bridge. Wide variation of formations, pairing-up, separate paths and four formations. **Structure:** first full introduction to a dancer moving on bridge. 1 + 3 formation until Popper comes down. Elaborate patterning of bodies in space.
Qualities	Calm and restrained with a light joyousness in skip. Meeting and parting of dancers matter of fact. Restraint somewhat released as speed grows.	Bright, lively. New element of contact added, gentle and understated.	Clarity in movement resources and floor pattern, throws viewer attention onto ever altering formations. Contrast between limitation and variety.

Table 1: Choreographic Outline of Rosemary Butcher's *3d*

	PART 2 Section 4	Section 5	Section 6
Time	29.06–36.27	36.27–55.57	55.57–79.31
No. of dancers	3	6	6
Design	Costume 3 x W. Bridge under lit blue appears while space empty. Ramp lit to look like a sloping white line, rising to meet bridge. 3 stripes on floor.	Costume 6 x W. 3 stripes of light on floor. Blue bridge appears above with blue light reflected on floor. White light fades away until space all lit by blue from bridge.	Costume 2 x W, 4 x M. Bridge lit blue. Light on floor from blue to blue and red flashes. Brightens with white light and stripes. Alternates between colour and white stripes.
Sound	Silence	Opens with very high and very low sounds, followed by long extended notes of chorus of female voices. Rhythm changes to fast syncopation and then suddenly to slower extended voice sounds.	Slow, melodious, breathy sound. Distorted bell then sound of bell tolling. Beat from earlier melody and then melody from Sec.1 returns. Speed increases. Pulse-like repetitive rhythm/melody returns.
Movement characteristics	**Primary movements:** New mvt. of single arm gestures while walking. Extensive use of single raised arm in walking. Mixture of mvt. performed in unison and separately. **Dynamic:** slow, walking pace with moments of stillness. Relaxed and smooth. **Space:** Baker moves on bridge with Walker directly beneath. Walk up and down slope and large circles on ground. **Structure:** new part to dance delineated by abrupt changes in pace, costume, sound, mvt, lighting of bridge. Opens with 1 dancer up, 1 down, then 1 dancer up and down while 2 walk in large circle on ground.	**Primary movements:** New mvt. of dancer carrying a dancer over shoulder as 5 enter from edges of space. Mixture of new (lifts, hand support, and carrying) with material from previous sections esp. Sec. 4 and Sec. 2. As light changes to blue, dancers form poses including 'gateway'. 3 dancers pass through this to end. **Dynamic:** slow < lively > slow, mixture of both and a slow ending. **Space:** bodies mainly upright. Dancer travels up and down bridge. Emphasis on entering space from outside, less use of formations. **Structure:** created by dynamic and contrast in old and new mvt. material.	**Primary movements:** Extended duet between Popper on high end of bridge and Baker on high metal wall platform introduces new mvt. of slow arm gestures with jerks. As they descend 3 dancers travel up and down slope, slowly with pauses. Mixture of new and familiar mvt. in varied combinations. **Dynamic:** slow, controlled gestural, speeds up, becoming a mix of fast and slow. Ends with bouncing whole group formation. **Space:** much use of bridge and platform with gap between. Floor patterns and formations highly complex and rapidly altering. **Structure:** accumulation of old elements, constantly reworked and added to.
Qualities	Sparse and peaceful. Sense of subtle communication across vertical and horizontal distance.	Less abstract with intro. of voices in sound and dancers carrying each other. Sense of layering of new with old and the passing of a day in a market square.	Starts with dramatic tension of high level duet across gap. Rich interweaving of old and new with simultaneous performance of contrasting dynamics. Ends mid formation.

*KEY. **Costume**, M = white top, black trousers; B = all black; W = all white.

9

A 'Streetwise, Urban Chic'

Popular Culture and Intertextuality in the Work of Lea Anderson

Sherril Dodds

A key characteristic of postmodern society, it is often said, is the effacement of the boundaries between high art and popular culture (Jameson 1988; Wilson 1990). It is a society in which the hegemony of high art has clearly been called into question as cultural forms are no longer privileged, with the result that an academic study of 'street dance', for instance, is as valid as a research project on the Ballets Russes. Whereas modernism is said to be hostile towards mass culture, postmodernism is able to deal with the interplay of popular images that constantly refer to and overlap with each other (McRobbie 1986). Although modernism, with its dissonant images and emphasis on the agency of the individual, was originally considered to be a type of 'oppositional art', it has since lost this subversive element (Jameson 1991). Modernist works are described as contemporary classics; they are commercially successful and integrated into the education system.

Postmodernism is believed to have emerged with the institutionalisation of modernism and the development of a consumer society and media culture. Jameson posits that 'its formal features in many ways express the deeper logic of that particular social system' (1988: 28), and accordingly postmodern art may be said to reflect the fragmentation, commodification and prominence of popular culture that constitute contemporary life. While modernism is concerned with elitism, depth and authorship, postmodernism embraces pluralism, surface and pastiche. It aligns itself with popular culture in being transient and playful. Art, as Baudrillard (1990) notes, is no longer private and unique.

One reason for English choreographer Lea Anderson's degree of popularity is considered to be her recycling of texts and images from popular culture. Whether it is in commercialising her work through television, as in the 'Tights, Camera, Action' series (1993, 1994), or by creating a vernacular dance where codes and signs are to be readily consumed by a media-literate audience, Anderson is keen to exploit the popular form. Lea Anderson is one of Britain's most prolific choreographers, regularly producing work for her two companies, The Cholmondeleys (with whom she is a dancer) and The Featherstonehaughs. She has received numerous awards[1] – both an indication of her critical acclaim and providing a means of funding the companies. Anderson's work was initially characterised by a distinctive use of elaborate hand gestures and by sharp wit, which many critics described as zany, quirky and off-beat (Mackrell 1986; Jordan 1988; Macaulay 1989). Through time, however, much of the analysis of her choreography has shifted emphasis as critics have begun to recognise the subtle complexities of her work. Scott describes it as having a 'streetwise, urban chic' (1993: 14), and references to fashion-consciousness and popular appeal resonate across much of the writing that attempts to pinpoint her success. This success may be seen not only in artistic recognition, but in terms of breaking through audience barriers, appealing to a wider network of people than the traditional dance audience (Newman 1987; Burnside 1990).

For this reason, Anderson's work provides a rich area for the study of intertextuality. Her homage to popular culture, as demonstrated through the multiple references to fashion, subcultures and vernacular genres, is an ideal source for intertextual play. This chapter therefore sets out to examine Anderson's use of texts and images from popular culture and some of the implications of this practice. Three strands of ideas, connected to the concept of intertextuality, run throughout the chapter. The first strand analyses Anderson's appropriation of existing texts into her own work and, in turn, how this intertextual device demonstrates a number of key postmodern characteristics. The second point of focus deals with the way in which her explicit borrowings of other texts creates a particular identity for her work and strongly typifies the way in which popular culture operates. The final thread addresses the potential use of intertextuality as a political strategy. It is important that these three strands of ideas are not seen to be distinct, but as overlapping and intersecting discourses, woven together both in theory and practice. Before examining Anderson's work in more detail, however, it is perhaps useful to consider the concept of popular culture and its relevance to intertextuality.

Popular Culture: Identity, Pleasure and Meaning

The development of a contemporary popular culture has been traced back to the nineteenth century when the urban population grew and industrialisation placed new emphasis on speed and time (Chambers 1986). The telephone and train redirected cultural life through the rapid exchange of information and the capacity to travel longer distances, while a new sense of time was constructed through collective labour, factory systems and mechanisation. This set a clear divide between work and leisure alongside a general sense of cultural disorder that accompanied the urban population explosion of the early twentieth century.

Before the advent of the machine, or more specifically the 'standard inter-changeable part', only the wealthy could afford to be stylish, since goods were hand-made. Ornament was considered a social marker. With the Industrial Revo-lution, however, money and leisure time increased and as mass production came into force quantity became a necessity for the economic viability of the ma-chines. Due to the rapid turnover of commodities, fashion styles accelerated and there emerged a popular culture based on value for money, accessibility, novelty and impact.

For several decades popular culture remained distinct from high art, and to an extent it still does. The skill and creativity involved in television commercials and video games, for example, are generally considered to be in a different league from opera and classical music. It is only recently that popular forms and media culture have been recognised as legitimate areas of study by academic institutions. Yet in some ways, the Pop Art of the 1950s had already redefined the boundaries between high art and the popular culture of media and advertising (Chambers 1986). Pop Art turned the objects of everyday life into aesthetic experiences and in so doing made an ironic comment on the values of high art, a comment not available to the 'ordinary' spectator. A cultivated knowledge of the history of art is not required in order to appreciate the popular images and icons of Pop Art such as Marilyn Monroe, Campbell's soup cans and cartoons, but it is if the irony is to be perceived. Hence the relevance of intertextuality.

Popular culture, in being less concerned with functionality than with mean-ing, identity and pleasure, is an ideal concept with which to exemplify intertex-tuality, and the phenomenon of the commodity demonstrates this well. Com-modities are both material and non-material, ranging from a brand of beer to a celebrity's name. A commodity has two functions, and although in some in-stances they may overlap, they operate in distinct ways. The first is a material function, which tends to be associated more with physical needs and satisfac-tion, while the second is cultural and is concerned with meanings and values.

Fiske argues that popular culture is not simply the buying and selling of commodities but 'an active process of generating and circulating meanings and pleasures within a social system' (1991: 23). He posits that one of the most distinctive features of popular culture is that it exists as a type of textual poverty. Whereas high art is something to be preserved, popular culture is based on novelty, impact and transience. It functions in terms of meanings, pleasures and identities that may be constructed only intertextually. Fiske (1991) insists that the consumers of popular culture are not an indiscriminate mass who blindly consume ready-made culture. It is the consumers who activate the cultural meanings and values of commodities in order to construct self-identities and social relations, and these supposed 'masses' do not operate as a single force. Popular genres constantly shift across social categories. Individuals may belong to different groups at different times and may pass from one to the other quite easily. As heterogeneous groups make up society, meanings are polysemic. Depending on the reader, a single commodity may provoke meanings that both perpetuate and resist the dominant ideology, hence one of the pleasures of popular culture, as of intertextuality as a mode of analysis, lies in the construction of alternative or oppositional meanings. The pleasures, meanings and identities that circulate through popular forms are clearly evident in the work of Anderson, who draws overtly on the rich bricolage of everyday life, the result of which is that she achieves a level of popular appeal.

Clubs, Gigs and Cabaret Culture

Anderson's ability to attract a following beyond the traditional dance audience came into practice with the formation of The Cholmondeleys in 1984. Rather than performing in established dance venues and showcases, Anderson initially opted to show her work in clubs, pubs and cabaret venues, often alongside rock bands, comedy acts and films. The Cholmondeleys performed their early works, between 1984 and 1986, in fashionable venues such as the Wag Club and the Fridge in London, or else in non-traditional performance sites such as the Woolwich pedestrian tunnel, public parks and galleries.

This was a shrewd move on Anderson's part as it gave her work a degree of accessibility on a number of levels. First, performing everywhere from pubs to parks automatically allowed her to attract a wider audience. As the dance world is relatively small in relation to the rock or cabaret scene, Anderson created more opportunities for her work to be seen. Second, its accessibility was enhanced in that such venues have a less formal layout than traditional dance spaces. Whereas the latter organises the audience, whose sole presence is to watch the show, into ordered rows, the former allows people to sit or stand in a relaxed sprawl with the option of drinking and socialising during the performance.

Even more significantly, these audiences were positioned to use intertextual strategies appropriate to her work, since its format bears more similarities to gig and cabaret culture than to traditional theatre dance. Her early work consisted of sharp, short pieces, often the length of a 'single'. By creating short works Anderson is perhaps satisfying the spectator's desire for what has been characterised as the 'three-minute culture', born of media saturation and the rapid exchange of information. Society is said to be immersed in superficial cultures, and is unable to deal with cultural forms of any length or depth. Thus Anderson's collection of one-off pieces reflects these fragmented narratives of postmodernism. Even though her current works take the form of full-length performances, they are generally made up of many short segments, maintaining the gig format.

Performances by The Featherstonehaughs (The Cholmondeleys' 'brother' group) have consciously been constructed on a similar basis. *The Bends* (1994) was initially presented at a London rock music venue, the Brixton Academy, and was followed by an all-night rave; while during 'numbers' in *The Featherstone-haughs Go Las Vegas* (1995), the dancers casually wandered on and off stage drinking bottles of beer. Similarly, a number of earlier works were closer to cabaret than pure dance events. *The Show* (1990) and *The Big Feature* (1991) included songs, monologues, jokes and sketches. These intertextual references to youth culture events such as rock gigs and cabaret provide a key to identifying Anderson's style. There is also perhaps an element of resistance to theatrical convention in Anderson's decision to reject the formality of high art perform-ances. The audience clearly takes pleasure in slugging a beer at the gig venues and chatting during the outdoor events.

Anderson's choice of music for her dance is highly eclectic. Although she has used two regular composers for much of her work, she has also employed a variety of popular forms: rock and pop, blues, film soundtracks and easy listening music from the 1950s. Her use of these popular forms is in keeping with the gig-like informality and structure of her performances and keeps open a wide range of intertextual possibilities. The Cholmondeleys danced to Nina Simone in *Baby, Baby, Baby* (1986), The Featherstonehaughs used the Jimi Hendrix Experi-ence, Neil Young and Janis Joplin in *The Big Feature*, and *The Featherstone-haughs Go Las Vegas* features the Elvis Presley classic 'Teddy Bear', thus fusing art dance with popular music in a manner typical of postmodernism.

Although Anderson uses some of her musical accompaniment directly from popular culture, for much of her work she has commissioned two composers: Drostan Madden and Steve Blake. Blake's music is jazz-based and uses mainly saxophone and percussion, although the insistent beat and penchant for volume reflects pop or rock music. Discussing Blake's jazz score for *Flesh and Blood* (1989), Macaulay finds that its 'irony, fragmented recycled melody and imper-sonal urgency catch Anderson's tone perfectly' (1989: 25). Madden uses 'col-lected sounds' that he samples and reassembles in a type of electronic collage. This offers a number of intertexts through these aural fragments. The soundtrack for *The Featherstonehaughs Go Las Vegas* evokes a radio dial being moved up and down the airwaves of American broadcast radio. Aside from the crackling and buzzing between stations, snippets of 'popular favourites' may be heard: 'Dancing Queen' by Abba, the country ballads of Tammy Wynette and Patsy Cline, and the unmistakable breathy vocals of Marilyn Monroe. Again, it is these references to specific texts that closely align Anderson's work to a popular vernacular. To recognise these 'classic' tracks is to have some affinity with the codes and signs associated with the music.

To some extent, Anderson's intertextual references to music from different genres and decades within the space of a single performance reflects a key postmodern characteristic: 'the end of history'. Indeed, it has been noted that popular music in general reflects a variety of postmodern features (McRobbie

1986; Connor 1989). Connor (1989) suggests that popular music appears to have no history in that it is a 'flat present' of eclectic styles, which constantly interchange in the form of comebacks, cover versions and remakes, recycling music to challenge 'authentic originality'. The producers of pop music no longer even need the ability to play instruments when a plethora of musical sounds may be reproduced, through electronic equipment and 'samples' may be taken from existing music. The 'sampling' process is based on the fragmentation and reassemblage of 'borrowed sounds', or 'texts', causing a redistribution of power and negating authorship. The production of pop music has therefore become a fast, uncontrollable process that is highly intertextual. McRobbie (1986) asserts that black, urban music has used this means to create a cultural identity for a subordinate group; its use of plagiarism, pastiche and façade creates a black 'otherness'. The multiplicity of styles that exist in popular music, which may be recycled and reappropriated, allow for the construction of vernacular, ethnic identities. It is these postmodern notions of identity and difference that give popular music a potentially political perspective.

To return, however, to the concept of the end of history which is not only pertinent to popular music, but to postmodern society in general. The idea reflects how contemporary life is constructed through diverse and anachronistic texts, a notion which also accounts for the fragmented images similarly revealed in Anderson's work.

The End of History

The particular condition of contemporary society which Jameson (1991) has referred to as the age of late capitalism, has been designated by a number of other titles that attempt to sum up its unique state. One of the most widely used descriptions, the society of the spectacle, highlights the prevalence of the image in contemporary society over spoken and written language. The two-dimensional representations of television, advertising, magazines, cinema, and cyberspace saturate daily life like a type of collage, constructing an artificial reality or represented world (Chambers 1986). Baudrillard (1993) posits that as the technological era allows for rapid reproduction, the multiplication of images is potentially infinite; if the media images that litter everyday life have no finality, this suggests they have become out of control. He describes the image as a sign, or simulation, that exists at a point between the real and the imaginary. In its unlimited pervasiveness there is a danger that its pretence of reality becomes more real than the real.

The pervasiveness of the image has considerable implications in relation to the concept of time. It is suggested that time has become an incoherent experience (Baudrillard 1993; Jameson 1991), since the past is always out of reach and all that remains is 'texts'. History is therefore formed out of old written and verbal texts and popular images or stereotypes. The result is a present that takes a fragmented and heterogeneous form, an 'anachronistic now'.

> Historicity is, in fact, neither a representation of the past nor a representation of the future (although its various forms use such representations): it can first and foremost be defined as a perception of the present as history.
>
> (Jameson 1991: 284)

Anderson's television work, *Cross Channel* (1992), reflects this well. The piece follows a trip from Dover to Calais and does not appear to be linked to a particular period. Although the ferry, the train and the station are clearly contemporary locations, the piece nevertheless has a dated feel. One of the most pertinent examples of this is the beach scene that recurs throughout the work. The very theme of a trip to the beach has a nostalgic air. In a society of increased leisure time where people have the capacity to travel greater distances, beach holidays and exotic locations are not unusual. Yet the piece seems to romanticise the notion of a traditional 'seaside break' by focusing on every aspect of the journey, and the dancers are stylised in dress, wearing old-fashioned bathing suits. The women's are based on a 1950s look with halter-necks and low-cut leg lines, while the men are dressed in 1920s bathing costumes with swimming caps. There is no modern leisure equipment and the activities in which they indulge are based on simple pasttimes. The men are seen gingerly attempting to paddle and then floating on large rubber tyres, while the women sunbathe and read fashion magazines.

To consider only the women for a moment, the reader would perhaps locate this period as the 1950s. They lounge on their sun beds with large black and white parasols, and white wooden beach huts can be seen in the background. The prevalence of black and white, also seen in their swim wear, alludes to the fashion shoots of Richard Avedon, or Herb Ritts, who photographed glamorous women of that era in moments of leisure. Yet as Baudrillard (1993) has implied, this glossy popular image is the stereotype into which history has disappeared. The perception of the past may have little to do with the actual reality of the era. Regardless of the fact that a modern P&O Ferry passes across the background and the women have contemporary hair styles, the reader retains the sense of 'pastness' through these recognisable stereotypes. This striking juxtaposition is part of the pardoxical style of Anderson's work.

The anachronistic nature of *Cross Channel* perhaps reflects our eclectic and fragmented present. The constant juxtaposition of eras is typical of the multiple texts and images that construct contemporary life. One sequence in particular neatly sums up this sense of temporal fragmentation. The men and women are situated in a bar, the women wear their 1950s bathing suits, along with feather boas which, in contrast, have associations of an earlier era, the 1920s. The men

The Cholmondeleys in *Flesh and Blood*.   Photo: Chris Nash

wear colourful Bermuda shirts, which have a late 1960s feel; yet they drink their glasses of beer in a single mouthful, provoking associations of 1980s 'lager louts' with their tasteless holiday wear and crude behaviour. It is equally difficult to locate the bar within a particular era. The sign outside is made of neon strip lighting, which gives it a contemporary look, but inside the image is more dated. The waiters, dressed in white shirts with black bow ties, stand soberly drying glasses with tea towels. It could even be suggested that these texts, Bermuda shirts, the sophisticated women, the foreign location and the rotating fans, create a look of certain 1970s films, such as the Roger Moore era of the James Bond series, which popularised exotic locations. It is perhaps futile to try and place the film within a past era and more appropriate to accept that this excerpt represents the heterogeneous and anachronistic images of contemporary life. Another textual perspective may argue that, as the reader is able to locate components from very specific historical eras, rather than demonstrating the 'end of history', a very clear, although in this instance fragmented, sense of chronology emerges. The radical juxtaposition of historical texts that charac-terises Anderson's manipulation of images is also apparent in her choice of costumes. Paying no heed to logic or convention she puts together startling and incongruous elements.

Satin Gowns and Doc Marten Boots

In much the same way that Anderson's choice of venue and music gives her dance pieces a sense of popular yet ironic identity, her use of costume has a strong fashion element:

Perhaps the secret of Anderson's success is to style dance much in the way of a fashion shoot that would not look out of place in *The Face*. She has worked on this from the start. From Chris Nash's funky publicity stills to costume designer Sandy Powell's latex gowns and sub-Gaultier kilts. (Scott 1993: 14)

Indeed her two companies have appeared in a number of glossy magazines from *Time Out* to *GQ*. As with popular music, the fashion industry operates in a manner that could be said to reflect the postmodern condition and Anderson's placing together of eclectic and contrasting styles is perhaps typical of a postmodern aesthetic.

Connor (1989) and Wilson (1990) trace a modernist era of fashion back to the 1920s in which women's clothes were designed with a focus on purity and function: smooth, simple designs, neutral colours, a rising hem line and a liberation from the corset and unnecessary ornamentation. Wilson posits that women's fashion of this era was intended to represent 'postwar newness' and the functional machine. In contrast, Connor (1989) and Wilson (1990) refer to postmodernist fashion as a return to ornament and decoration and cite the 1960s as a key time for this transition with its concern for novelty and heterogeneous styles. The space age dress reflected the popular science fiction novels of the era, while the psychedelic patterns were influenced by Op Art. Hebdige (1979) notes the postmodern use of parody and irony in fashion such as the mods of the 1960s who adapted the Savile Row lounge suit, and the bricolage and anti-unity of the punks of the 1970s, who recycled metropolitan life in the form of safety pins, zips and PVC.

Like music, fashion is able to create identity, difference and 'otherness' and to offer conflicting styles within one event. Connor describes this as 'an implicit politics of style, using fashion to quote, invert and distort dominant meanings' (1989: 191). Bearing these notions in mind, it is significant that Anderson places great importance on style and image, creating a strong visual identity to her work. It is also reflective of the anti-hierarchical stance of postmodernism in which the 'look' of the work is given the same priority as the movement.

The costume designer with whom Anderson regularly works is Sandy Powell, who has designed for the art films of Derek Jarman and Sally Potter, as well as for the Hollywood movie *Interview with the Vampire* (1994), and the experimental performance artist Lindsay Kemp. Many of the costumes for Anderson's dance are styled on past eras, which ties in with the postmodern notions of nostalgia and pastiche identified earlier. Wilson notes this is not so much to do with creating an accurate historical representation of the past, but more to do with the style of 'pastness' that is symptomatic of our present: 'fashion has relied heavily on "retro chic" in recent years' (1990: 224).

The Cholmondeleys often wear long, glamorous gowns that are from no recognisable era, but their opulence and extravagance suggest that they are not a

part of contemporary society. In *Precious* (1993) the women look like 'the sump-
tuous sensual red vamp of the Hollywood icon' (Bain 1993: 24) and in *Perfect
Moment* (1992) they wear 'Hartnell satin gown look-alikes, familiar from covers
of magazines such as *Vogue*' (Briginshaw 1995: 39). In *Flesh and Blood* a similar
sense of a past is evoked, but without a definitive historical accuracy:

> [with their] long, simple dresses, made of a fabric that has the dull glow of
> pewter or tarnished silver. [The] women . . . appear to have stepped out of
> Byzantine icons and fourteenth century Italian altar panels.
>
> (Constanti 1990: 363)

It is also notable in *Flesh and Blood* that the women have short, contemporary hairstyles and wear heavy make-up; yet this sense of fragmentation from
such a mixture of texts is typical of the bricolage of postmodern fashion. This
may also be an ironic comment on the part of Anderson. The bold, modern
hairstyles provide a stark contrast to the highly feminised gowns of previous
eras.

Some costumes make intertextual reference to popular genres such as the
pink, fluffy baby doll lingerie and the sophisticated silk pyjamas in *Walky Talky*
(1992) that are typical of Hollywood films, while other costumes consist of
everyday streetwear, suggesting the vernacular of youth culture. In *Precious* both
companies race around in the opening 'Black' section in Doc Marten boots, the
trendy urban footwear appropriated from working men's boots. In all their
pieces The Featherstonehaughs wear their familiar two-piece suits. Although
they are occasionally modified to complement a particular theme, such as the
silver lamé 'numbers' in *The Featherstonehaughs Go Las Vegas*, the use of suits
links the performers to an everyday look rather than an art dance context. This
appears to be a conscious decision, avoiding the 'men in tights' stigma that
surrounds the male dancer in favour of a streetwise sensibility.

This precision in design and costume serves two functions. One is tied up
with meaning. The spectator is able to construct levels of understanding as s/he
locates various intertextual references. For example, the pink twin sets, pearls
and dark glasses that The Cholmondeleys wear in *Car* (1995) immediately conjure up images of Jackie Kennedy, leading to links with the assassination of John
F. Kennedy, which took place in a car. On one level, the 'intertext of dress' may
be used as a means of interpretation. The second function is tied up with
pleasure and identity. The constant references to chic glamour wear and contemporary fashion trends place the two companies within a context of stylishness
and cutting-edge image, equally evident in the 'clubbers' and 'arty types' who
visibly make up much of Anderson's audience.

It is notable that although Anderson's performers may wear different coloured outfits, they are always dressed in otherwise identical styles, like clones. It

is also pertinent that their clothes are never simply everyday wear, but highly stylised and tailored. It could even be suggested that Anderson relishes the sense of disguise that comes with 'dressing up'. The two companies have masqueraded in a wide selection of outfits, and dark glasses and wigs are regular features of her choreography. These ideas tie in with another central characteristic of the postmodern condition: 'the death of the subject'. This so-called 'end of indivi-duality' is clearly a useful concept with which to examine the clone-like appea-rance of Anderson's performers.

The Death of the Subject

It could be argued that the concept of the individual has been called into question by the plethora of images that invade the subject's public and private space. Whereas modernism posits a unique self which has a private identity and personal style, postmodernism is said to mark the end of individualism (Jameson 1991). This partly derives from the way daily life is bombarded with media images of life styles, appearances, and values. Television, cinema and advertising constantly display, define and redefine such phenomena and the result is not a free-thinking individual as in Cartesian philosophy, but a politi-cally constructed subject. For instance, were it not for the ubiquitous images of supermodels, diet magazines and cosmetics advertisements, it is unlikely that the contemporary consumer would be quite so concerned with personal appea-rance. The postmodern belief, illustrated by this example, is of a subject who is not a 'natural, free-thinking self' but a social and cultural construct. It could even be argued that the notion of individualism is an ideological construct intended simply to give the subject a 'sense' of uniqueness.

Jameson (1988) comments on this theory from two positions. He suggests that up to a certain point in history the individual subject existed as part of the dominant bourgeois class, but ceased to exist with what he describes as the 'demographic explosion': that is, the reduction of the 'individual' to a series of statistics. The second position that he takes is more radical:

> Not only is the bourgeois individual subject a thing of the past, it is also a myth . . . This construct is merely a philosophical and cultural mystification which sought to persuade people that they 'had' individual subjects and possessed this unique personal identity.   (Jameson 1988: 17)

This concept, which is often described as the 'death of the subject', is relevant to Anderson's work in a number of ways. For instance, she introduces each of the short films in the 'Tights, Camera, Action' (1993) series in radically contrasting guises. She presents *Flesh and Blood* while reclining on a chaise longue like a Hollywood starlet, dressed in a pink negligée with marabou trim, and introduces *Perfect Moment* as an 'S&M dominatrix' complete with black rubber dress and 'fetishist' platform shoes. The most fascinating aspect is that she speaks and behaves in the same straightforward manner without demonstrating any of the characteristics of her 'look'. She presents herself as a blank canvas onto which an image may be placed. There is no suggestion of a permanent and personal style, but a superficial 'look' that has been borrowed temporarily and reproduced directly from images of popular culture.

Within the work itself this is seen in the presentation of the dancers, who switch easily from one unrelated image to the next. At one moment in *Cross Channel* The Cholmondeleys wear demure 1950s dresses and primly clutch their handbags; at another they become 1960s women in party attire who 'knock back' drinks and twist the night away. There is no suggestion of individual depth or character psychology, but rather a series of interchangeable, mass-produced images that are placed on the dancers for no apparent reason other than to display a particular 'look'.

The death of the subject is not only reflected in costume and design, but also in the unison movement prevalent in much of Anderson's work. *Perfect Moment* is loosely based on a social event, and at one point the performers stand in a straight line, facing the audience and perform a movement sequence focused on cosmetic preparation. Their spatial arrangement draws comparison with an assembly line and its mechanised repetitive actions. Each predetermined subject goes through identical activities, which are not the product of some unique self but are a series of acquired patterns of behaviour.

It is interesting that the unison formation is a hallmark of Anderson's choreography, whereas solos and individual motifs are rare:

> What these women do is personal, sometimes private – except that it isn't. You see them do it side by side in twos, threes or fours; you see them do it together like clockwork. (Macaulay 1989: 25)

Although on one level Anderson's work may be said to reflect the end of individualism, many commentators, in contrast, consider a distinctive feature of the two companies to be the sense of individuality of the dancers (Jordan 1988; Robertson 1993). The Cholmondeleys and The Featherstonehaughs display a vast range of build and height (from five foot to six foot five inches). Individuality is further highlighted by the variety of hairstyles, which have ranged from shaved heads with tufty fringes to henna-dyed, shoulder-length hair. This, however, perhaps reverts back to traditional notions of individuality, which could arguably be denounced as a superficial myth. The range of physical characteristics that set each dancer as being quite distinct from the next perhaps comments more on Anderson's anti-elitist stance than on notions of inherent individualism. Whereas a ballet company uses dancers of a prescribed height, weight and look to create an apparently identical set of performers, Anderson has attempted to create a less elitist body of performers by including body images unconventional in dance. Yet the post-structuralist thinker would insist that although each dancer appears distinct s/he nevertheless remains a constructed subject. There is no natural self, and the subject acquires movement behaviour in the same way that the subject's appearance is constructed through the numerous images that saturate daily life. Whether it is due to studying ballet as a child or from wearing stiletto shoes, the subject does not possess a 'natural' style of movement but a highly constructed body. Although each dancer may appear distinct on a superficial level, by using identical, unison formations and prescribed movement patterns Anderson is challenging notions of individualism. Part of this complexity clearly derives from the intertextual confusion that arises out of Anderson's appropriation and fragmentation of heterogeneous images. Yet even further debate arises from the notion that if the subject is completely constructed, then this does not allow for the possibility of agency and therefore change. There is clearly not the space within the context of this chapter to resolve these ideas fully, so it is perhaps best for the moment to leave behind this contentious area as part of the postmodern paradox and move on to the ideas and images that Anderson draws upon as the subject for her choreography.

Image Fragments

The themes Anderson uses in her work are located in popular culture and the lived experience, which perhaps accounts for the accessible nature of her work. Burnside suggests,

> This type of work with its deadpan humour and strong sociocultural content has an implicit relationship with the audience. It relies on the audience's recognition of those aspects of society upon which it comments.
>
> (Burnside 1990: 15)

The thematic content of Anderson's work is often rooted in popular culture and vernacular texts and can range from playful parody to social critique. For instance, *The Clichés and the Holidays* (1986) draws upon 'airport art' through parodies of bullfights and flamenco, and 'Car Wars', the opening section of *Car*, plays with images of the ubiquitous 'superhero'. Meanwhile some subject matter takes a more serious theme such as 'Bomb Around the Clock' from *The Big Feature*, a comment on the ills of war, and *Health and Efficiency* (1986), which calls attention to the pressure of the beauty industry on women. Yet regardless of whether the subject matter is treated by light-hearted play or social commentary, it is necessary for the audience to recognise the images from their sociocultural background in order to appreciate the jokes or criticisms that Anderson makes. It

The Featherstonehaughs Go Las Vegas.   Photo: Chris Nash

is probably for this reason that Anderson prefers not to use abstract, formalist movement, but instead draws upon texts from popular culture and everyday life. The images are fleeting and often open-ended in their meaning; yet these recognisable human shapes provide a means to understanding and interpreting the work.

One hallmark of Anderson's choreography is her use of gesture, which may be closely identified with human behaviour (Mackrell 1986; Macaulay 1989). It is notable that her appropriation of everyday movements does not result in simple dance patterns; rather the mass of fragmented texts are intricately woven together to create a complex web of movement. Anderson uses choreographic devices such as repetition, rhythm and dynamic phrasing to structure pedestrian movements into a form that bears closer resemblance to dance. Nevertheless, it is possible to recognise some of the sources of the gestural content.

In the television piece *Perfect Moment*, and its stage version, *Birthday* (1992), this use of gesture is apparent in the bathroom scene, when the performers, dressed in white towelling dressing gowns, execute a movement sequence based on preparations for an evening out. The excerpt begins as pairs of dancers tease and manipulate each other's hair and stare into imaginary mirrors, like hairdressers attending to a client. A series of gestures ensues, resembling the precise steps of facial cleansing: eyebrow and lip lines are traced, a dabbing motion occurs and then the cheekbones are smoothly rubbed in a continual calm, flowing pattern. The partners then begin to massage each other's feet, measure each other's arms and at the same time check the other person's watch and pulse. The images do not always strictly allude to the cosmetic preparation for an evening out, but there is a general sense of 'check-up' and inspection. Yet although these movements derive from a recognisable source, they are performed with a cool detachment, devoid of expression, which gives the sequence an air of uncertainty and double-edged sensibility. This leaves the reader to question whether it is a subversive act or a postmodern play.

At times the source of Anderson's movement is highly apparent and whole sections employ recognisable images; the 'kissing sequence' from *Perfect Moment* is based on various ways of kissing, and a section in *Cross Channel* uses images of sunbathing. *Precious*, however, is a work that takes a more abstract theme based on the ancient art of alchemy, which was believed to transmute base metals into gold. To display this in such obvious movement terms as in the previous examples is clearly not possible; yet although the dance is more abstract, Anderson still draws upon movement that is recognisable as fleeting images and dynamic qualities from the everyday. Rather than using highly abstract and codified techniques, she draws upon the pedestrian activities and shapes that come out of daily life. In the opening section, entitled *Black*, the dancers run, jump, stride and overbalance in a style akin to the everyday but with a bounding energy that gives it a high dynamic thrust. This sense of energy notably reflects the type of unleashed dynamic expressed by rock performers and audiences alike.

It is perhaps not only the content of the movement, but the way in which The Cholmondeleys and The Featherstonehaughs have come to perform that allows Anderson to challenge straightforward notions of style:

> There is an absence of virtuosity and stylish façade, and a preference for movement that looks raw and natural.   (Nugent 1992: 9)

That is not to suggest that Anderson's movement is easy to perform; on the contrary it employs complex rhythms and patterns. Yet the pedestrian quality to the movement draws on apparently accessible texts. Performers in both companies employ a matter-of-fact, no-nonsense expression in their work. Not only does this give the work a streetwise accessibility, it also reflects the sense of emotional detachment and cool attitude typical of a postmodern consciousness.

At times the deadpan looks and 'punkish demeanour' (Nugent 1987: 29) have a confrontational quality. The movement may be comical and various emotions may resonate across the music, but the dancers remain detached. They stare at the audience in an almost challenging fashion, which Jordan describes as a 'knowing and subversive intention' (1988: 27). Their cool detachment is perhaps a forthright invitation for the audience to deconstruct the multi-coded references manifest in Anderson's work. It is notable that although many of the movement images that Anderson employs are clearly recognisable from everyday life, they are not structured in a linear fashion, but in a fragmented and aleatory form. The way in which she assembles eclectic images side by side is typical of the postmodern concept of 'depthlessness', and a deeper probing of the term can reveal how Anderson's work is both literally and metaphorically 'without depth'.

Depthlessness

The multiplicity of images that construct the fragmented present is said to result in a type of flattening or sense of depthlessness. Chambers argues that the very nature of image reproduction manifests a depthlessness in its artificiality and seriality:

> The reproduced object hides nothing. It has no secrets, no ulterior meaning. Its 'flatness' is its profoundest statement, reminding us that which is obvious matters, that surfaces matter, that the surface is matter. (Chambers 1986: 10)

In its postmodern sense the concept of depthlessness refers to the effect of multiple surfaces placed side by side rather than to a lack of complexity or profundity. In a review of *Flesh and Blood*, Hughes (1990) discusses the problematics of this term in relation to Anderson's use of gesture. One textual perspective refers to a belief that 'depth' is an artistic attribute revealing profound meaning and therefore value, whereas surface and superficiality are considered worthless and shallow. As Hughes notes,

> Culturally there is a need to seek out 'depth' for the aesthetic and semantic authority which derives from it. In this work there is no 'depth' of that kind, but it is neither superficial nor shallow, it simply deals in surfaces.
>
> (Hughes 1990: 44)

This idea resonates throughout Anderson's work, where incongruous images and associations exist side by side, and where 'texts' compete within the intertextual space.

For example, the short 'wetsuit section' from *Perfect Moment* provides a plethora of incongruous images and associations. The section, set on a bed of sand with the performers dressed in wetsuits, begins with a series of unison duets. The opening image depicts one partner kneeling with the other partner's head resting on her/his lap. The kneeling partner stares upwards, as if to heaven, while the lying partner remains outstretched and still, as if ill or even dead. This image is typical of much religious iconography in which figures pray

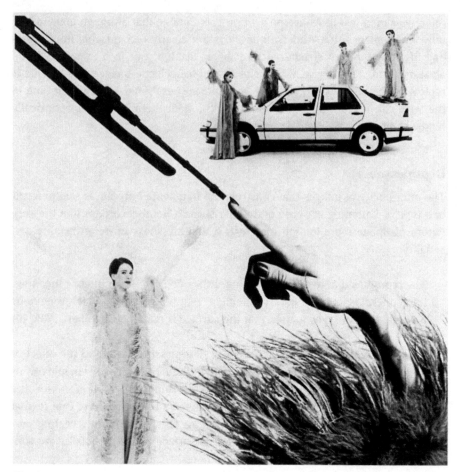

The Cholmondeleys in *Car*.   Photo: Chris Nash

over or care for the sick. As the kneeling partner gently touches the shoulders, chest and forehead of the performer who is lying down, images of caring or nursing are brought to the fore. At moments there are signs of giving, yearning and reaching as the dancers glance upwards or hold out an open hand, while at other moments there are signs of resistance, seen in the stiff legs and flexed feet or the stilted steps forward. Connotations of vulnerability are demonstrated in a number of 'foetal' positions and a hand-patting motif, similar to a child's game, occurs between partners. In some instances the performers appear awkward together and attempt to manipulate each other's stiff bodies as if in an uneasy social dance, and at other points there is a sense of caring as they relax in an embrace or support someone collapsing. At one point the performers recline in a stylised 'Hollywood' pose; moments later images of death appear as bodies appear to hang from their clasped wrists, and arms are placed across chests as if boxed into a coffin. In one instance the dancers are assured adults, deftly catching their partners' wrists as they throw their arms up in the air, and moments later they are vulnerable and childlike as they hold hands behind a leader. Incongruous images sit side by side. Anderson's work does not offer a single fixed meaning but in its very form is multilayered and open-ended. The contradictory fragments provide another set of texts that contribute to the para-doxical effect of Anderson's work.

It has been suggested that, just as society is dominated by the image, the world itself has become flat as everything is commodified into a two-dimen-sional representation. Jameson (1991) uses the example of Marilyn Monroe as a human figure who has been transformed into her own image, which he sees as a dangerous phenomenon: all that exists is representation. In some ways it could be suggested that the choreographic designs of Lea Anderson lend themselves well to this literal description of a flat world of images. Whereas some dance practitioners are concerned with motion and travelling through space, Anderson displays a predilection for static shape, the space around the body and tableau scenes. Anderson has clearly been influenced by the two-dimensional form of painting, which stems from her art school background and a fascination with cinema. Many of her choreographic ideas are derived from images that she collects in notebooks:

> Lea's material is 'found' movement, contributed by her dancers, observed on the street or frozen in photographs. She accumulates scrapbooks of images and ideas – postcards, movie stills, newspaper cuttings.   (Parry 1992: 60)

Anderson's working process often requires her dancers to imitate these images, hence the two-dimensional look to much of her work. She says of *Flesh and Blood*,

> I'd taken lots of images from late Renaissance nativity paintings and the dancers just made a series of different shapes – we called them badges.
> (Lewis 1992: 13)

This is another way in which images or 'texts' slip into her work. In some instances Anderson actually removes a dimension so that the movement is performed while lying on the floor, which becomes like a canvas for the dance, and then filmed from above. *Sardinas* (1990) is filmed from an 'overhead shot' while the dancers wriggle and roll across the floor. Not only does this provide some extremely unusual forms of movement and illusory tricks, but the dance has literally been made flat.

> Choosing to have [*Sardinas*] filmed from above, Anderson flipped the dan-cers through 180 degrees, turning the white studio floor into the picture

plane and, having dispensed with gravity, persuaded them to loll, fall and snuggle across the floor in diamanté black, like tea dancing couples in a Nasa exercise.   (Scott 1993: 14)

Throughout the chapter much has been made of Anderson's use of wit and postmodern play, and thus it is perhaps tempting to see no further than the humour and fail to engage with the more discursive elements of her work. Yet it is often through the humour that she makes pertinent social commentary.

The Playful and Political Potential of the Image

Although it is presented in many forms, and functions for a number of reasons, the presence of humour as a choreographic device creates a sense of informality in which the audience may feel relaxed and share a joke. It is significant that this sense of play is one of the formal features of postmodernism. Whereas modernism is often referred to as the 'age of anxiety' (Jameson 1991), postmodernism is often described as playful, pleasurable and jokey with its use of parody, irony and ambiguity (McRobbie 1986). This is also subversive of high art seriousness. One device that Anderson uses is parody, a type of humour in which the idiosyncrasies and stylistic eccentricities of a particular genre are highlighted in order to ridicule. For parody to work effectively, the audience must be aware of the original in order to recognise the way in which it is being ridiculed.

One example of Anderson's use of parody is in 'Legs, Legs, Legs' from *The Big Feature*, a spoof on Irish dancing. The title hits a playful note, as traditional Irish dancing does not use the arms. It is almost as if the title is mockingly reiterating the point. The piece begins with the dancer earnestly following the rules of Irish dance. He hops and skips on the spot, with his arms by his side and his back held upright, occasionally shooting a leg out in front. The music, although played with jazz instruments, is reminiscent of an Irish jig. Occasionally the dancer becomes carried away and his arms spring up in a rebellious moment, or a wave ripples through his torso. In one instance he gallops across the room with his arms fixed firmly by his side, making this moment of freedom appear awkward and all the more comical.

On some occasions Anderson uses humour to highlight or subvert dominant beliefs and values. 'Bar Stool Blues' from *The Big Feature* draws upon the notion of machismo. The piece is set to the blues song of the same title by Neil Young, which highlights the cliché of the male who drinks his sorrows away. The dance moves through various intertextual references to the intoxicated male who takes it upon himself to air his frustrations with his fists. The two performers execute a stylised boxing routine performed as a unison sequence. The patterns of punching and ducking are a male ritual that is echoed through a range of intertexts from popular culture, from cowboy films to the boxing ring. There is almost a relaxed, habitual edge to the movement, reiterated in the lilting melody, as if to highlight how predictable and rehearsed this type of behaviour is in male culture. The various clichés that ensue are comical, as the reader almost expects to see them. They are straight out of a macho, Hollywood film: the bloody nose that the participant roughly wipes, the exhausted loser's exaggerated staggering and shielding of his head, and his final collapse to the floor when he is knocked out. Anderson is both emphasising the degree of machismo that pervades society while ridiculing the theatricalised posing that it involves.

In some instances her humour almost catches the reader's own prejudices at work. In *Immaculate Conception* (1993), The Featherstonehaughs perform a routine, each holding a 'baby' wrapped in a blanket. Obviously the title of the piece immediately gives a comical edge to this section, but much of the humour derives from the 'maternal' behaviour, which is not generally associated with men. The dancers pick up their babies with undivided attention and care, rock them, nurse them, coo over them and adoringly show them to the audience. This behaviour, which tends to be characterised as feminine, clearly exposes our deep-rooted prejudices because such a role-reversal appears so humorous.

Another feature of textual play is found in the use of language. To begin with, the very names The Cholmondeleys and The Featherstonehaughs are unsettling as they are pronounced quite differently from the way they are written (the phonetic sounds are 'chumlees' and 'fanshaws'). This notion of ambiguity and knowing 'that things are not what they seem' (Jordan 1988: 27) is resonant in postmodernism. Also this play of names ties in with the element of popular culture that uses codes, signs and subcultural identities. To know how to pronounce their names is to have some affinity with the group, and part of this pleasure is the ability to recognise and read their signs; more ardent followers of the two companies fashionably refer to them as 'The Chums' and 'The Fans'. It is also interesting that Cholmondeley and Featherstonehaugh are traditional upper-class English names. Anderson is perhaps redistributing power by placing them within the realms of an alternative clique, outside the upper classes. This notion of a distinct language mirrors the popular forms of 'street speak' that use private languages to create identity and difference. This type of playfulness, which is typical of intertextuality, creates both immediate access to the work, but also constructs notions of identity and difference on which subcultures are based.

It is clear that Anderson is not concerned with the angst and alienation that preoccupied the modernists, but instead draws upon the popular texts and images that pervade our society. Not only has she created a vernacular dance of fashionable appeal based on pleasure, meaning and identity, but her distinct manipulation of such signs perhaps supports the idea of a redistribution of power:

The vivid languages of the cinema, television, pop music and magazines are

228   *Sherril Dodds*

translated into personalised styles, manners, tastes and pleasures: under given conditions, in particular situations, we take reality to pieces in order to put it back together with a further gain in meaning. The signs are inhabited, appropriated, domesticated.   (Chambers 1986: 185)

To draw the chapter to a close, it is again worth examining whether the employment of intertextuality as an artistic device offers some element of sub-versive or oppositional potential, or whether it is a type of 'blank pastiche'. This hinges on the question of whether Anderson's appropriation of existing texts and images is simply a type of 'empty quotation', or whether her reassemblage of texts creates alternative meanings or redistributes power in some way. Much debate surrounds this issue, and many of the theorists cited in this chapter take strongly opposing views. Jameson (1991) sounds a pessimistic note by descri-bing pastiche as the recycling of dead and empty styles. In contrast, McRobbie (1986) sees the reproduction and reassemblage of images as an opportunity to create 'fictional identities'. She asserts that the replication and manipulation of texts and images creates an 'otherness' in which minority cultures may be heard.

There are clearly occasions when Anderson manipulates images in order to deconstruct dominant values. Towards the end of *Perfect Moment* all the women wear full-length ball gowns and long, white gloves. This image of a feminine stereotype, however, is subverted as the women have dark underarm hair, many of them sport cropped or short boyish hairstyles and they confront the camera with deadpan stares. The glamorous image is further deconstructed when the dancers move away; the Featherstonehaugh men appear from under their dresses in vulnerable, foetal positions, which in turn challenges a male stere-otype. The women subvert feminine connotations by appearing dominant in their upright stature, and confrontational in their cold, blank looks; women are traditionally required to smile and appear content. On one level the appearance of the foetal figure from beneath their skirts symbolically alludes to women's traditional role as child-bearers; yet they calmly walk away from the men as if negating any maternal images.

Chambers (1986) and Fiske (1991) suggest that to deconstruct and subvert images it is necessary to operate within them, which is perhaps what Anderson is attempting to do in her choice of the feminine ball gowns. As Chambers states,

We need to disrupt the presumed coherence of ideology, texts and images – the world of representations in which we come to recognise our social and sexual 'selves' – and rediscover the detail of the bits that go into their making. That means living inside the signs. It means engaging in the contra-dictory pleasures of fashion, style, television soap, video games . . .

(Chambers 1986: 212)

Hebdige (1979) suggests that subcultural styles are immediately subversive in that they are a form of 'refusal'. He notes that everyday objects, images and events take on an alternative symbolic value when they are appropriated into subcultures and so dissolve the dominant values that they represent. It could be argued that the intertextual images Anderson takes from popular culture, such as the feminine glamour wear and the Hollywood scenarios, are a part of The Cholmondeleys/Featherstonehaughs subculture and constitute their 'fictional identities' (McRobbie 1986). Hebdige (1979) asserts that even a smile or a sneer is an act of defiance, and likewise the detached looks that accompany much of their performance may have a subversive value: although The Cholmondeleys are placed within an image of 1950s femininity in *Cross Channel*, their matter-of-fact performance quality is perhaps an act of resistance.

In typical postmodern fashion, Anderson has created a type of vernacular dance with its own identity and language. Some commentators, however, have used this as a criticism. In the same way that popular culture is based on novelty, impact and transience, critics question the 'sell-by-date' of Anderson's work. Nugent says of The Cholmondeleys and The Featherstonehaughs,

> Neither group has had an easy ride marrying audience appeal with funders' approval. Both are viewed, in some circles, as cultish 'fly by nighters' whose lives are bound to be short-lived.   (Nugent 1992: 9)

It is perhaps the subcultural element of Anderson's work that has caused criticism. Those outside her cult following are possibly unable to fill the intertextual gaps that give pleasure, identity and meaning to her work. They may, however, even recognise the subversive potential in her work, as seen through notions of resistance and otherness, which may prove somewhat threatening to the established order of everyday life. Irrespective of whether Anderson's work plays simply on gimmickry or has a subversive undercurrent, it undoubtedly provides a rich illustration of the intertexts of contemporary life.

Notes

1. In 1987 and 1988 The Cholmondeleys received Digital Dance Awards in addition to a GLC award in 1988. The Featherstonehaughs received the 1990 Time Out/01 for London Dance and Performance Award, and in the same year Anderson won the Bonnie Bird British Choreographers Award and the Rencontres Chorégraphiques Internationales de Bagnolet competition.

References

Bain A. (1993) 'Golden Moments of Rich Alchemy', *Scotland on Sunday*, 21 March: 24.

Baudrillard, J. (1990), *Revenge of the Crystal: Selected Writings on the Modern Object and its Destiny 1968–1983*, London, Pluto Press.
———— (1993), 'The Evil Demon of Images and the Precession of Simulacra', in T. Docherty (ed.), *Postmodernism: A Reader*, Hemel Hempstead: Harvester Wheatsheaf.
Briginshaw, V. (1995), 'Getting the Glamour on Our Own Terms', *Dance Theatre Journal*, 12, 3, Winter: 36–9.
Burnside, F. (1990), 'British Spring Load', *Dance Theatre Journal*, 8, 1, Summer: 15.
Chambers, I. (1986), *Popular Culture: the Metropolitan Experience*, London, Methuen.
Connor, S. (1989), *Postmodernist Culture*, Oxford, Blackwell.
Constanti, S. (1990), 'First and Last', *Dancing Times* LXXX, 952, January: 363–4.
Dodds, S. (1995–96), 'Lea Anderson and the Age of Spectacle', *Dance Theatre Journal* 12, 3, Winter: 31–3.
Fiske, J. (1991), *Understanding Popular Culture*, London, Routledge.
Hebdige, D. (1979), *Subculture: the Meaning of Style*, London, Methuen.
Hughes, D. (1990), 'Cholmondeleys', *Dance Theatre Journal* 8, 1, Summer: 39, 44.
Jameson, F. (1988), 'Postmodernism and Consumer Society', in E. A. Kaplan (ed.), *Postmodernism and its Discontents*, London, Verso.
———— (1991), *Postmodernism, or the Cultural Logic of Late Capitalism*, London, Verso.
Jordan, S. (1988), 'The Cholmondeleys Spring '88', *Dance Theatre Journal*, 6, 2, Autumn: 26–7.
Macaulay, A. (1989) 'Dance Umbrella', *Financial Times*, 21 November: 25.
Mackrell, J. (1986), 'Cholmondeleyism', *Dance Theatre Jounral*, 4, 2, Summer: 14–5.
———— (1992), 'The Pause that Refreshes', *Independent*, 30 January: 13.
McRobbie, A. (1986), 'Postmodernism and Popular Culture', in L. Appignanesi (ed.), *Postmodernism: ICA Documents 4*, London, ICA.
Newman, B. (1987), 'Lea Anderson of The Cholmondeleys', *Dancing Times* LXXVIII, 926, November: 130–2.
Nugent, A. (1987), 'Springing to Life (2)', *Dance and Dancers* 448, June: 29.
———— (1992), 'Looking Good and Feeling Great', *The Stage*, 13 February: 9.
Parry, J. (1992), 'Playing Kissy-kissy', *Observer*, 2 February: 6.
Robertson, A. (1993), 'Colour Made so Precious', *Daily Mail*, 2 April.
Scott, S. (1993), 'All the Right Moves', *Sunday Times* 14 March: 14.
Wilson, E. (1990), 'These New Components of the Spectacle: Fashion and Postmodernism', in R. Boyne (ed.), *Postmodernism and Society*, London, Macmillan.

10

Zebra Talk: the Absurd World of Philippe Decouflé

Intertextuality, Popular Culture and the 'Art' of Dance

Litza Bixler

Surfing the Intertext: an Introduction

Two faceless creatures fall forward and embrace like long-lost friends, push each other away and awkwardly locomote across the televisual space, two thin azure bodies with white stripes, precariously poised over large webbed feet. They could be escapees from the set of *The X-Files*, or fragments from a child's disturbed dreams; and it is difficult to believe that they are human, that underneath the costumes are skilled bodies which eat and sleep. This is an image from a work by Philippe Decouflé, the Parisian choreographer who produces surreal concoctions of images influenced by modernist movements such as the Bauhaus, Russian constructivism, surrealism and futurism (Anon. 1992: 20). Combined with references to pop culture, and the circus, the resultant aesthetic leaves no historical stone unturned.

Philippe Decouflé was born in 1961 and went to circus school at the age of 15 to become a clown. There he studied mime (with Marcel Marceau), acrobatics and movement. His experience at the Centre de Danse d'Angers left a lasting impression, and he cites the choreographer/director Alwin Nikolais as a strong influence on his work: 'Alwin Nikolais taught me the importance of light and costumes, he gave me the confidence to mix all these things together' (Decouflé, cited in Fretard 1993: 27).

He, like other French new dance choreographers, also alludes to Merce Cunningham as an important figure in his development: 'Merce Cunningham taught me the most about dance . . . I learned to master problems of distance and geometry, the basic rules of optics and movement' (*ibid.*).

Despite Cunningham's influence, Decouflé's work is a good example of the recent shift in French New Dance away from Cunningham-inspired abstractionism and towards more theatrical and fragmented narratives which do not necessarily separate dance from theatre or 'high art' from popular culture (Adolphe 1990). He has performed with Karole Armitage and Régine Chopinot, sharing with them an affinity for popular culture and a quirky Cunningham-influenced style of movement. Like Michael Clark, he possesses a camp sensibility, a penchant for cross-dressing, and a desire to subvert the codes of high art in favour of a more popular appeal.

He formed the Compagnie DCA in 1983, and created five pieces for the company before reaching international fame with his extravagant televised spectacle for the 1992 Winter Olympics. No stranger to television, Decouflé had already won an international dance video award in 1988 (IMZ Festival, Vienna) for his work (1987), choreographed and directed three short films, as well as two British pop videos (New Order, *True Faith*, 1987; Fine Young Cannibals, *She Drives Me Crazy*, 1988) before directing the opening ceremonies for the Olympics.

Standing as an intertext between avant-garde modernism and popular culture, between the world of the elite dance venue and the pop video, Decouflé giggles in the wings as he invites us into his bizarre world of misfits, a world in which the clowns, magicians, jugglers and athletes in *Triton* (1991) and *Technicolor* (1998), or the elves, comic-book wrestlers, and cyborgs in *True Faith* (1987), become 'iconographical units' from within Western culture, which may mean many different things depending on their context and the relative perspective of the reader. Intertextuality thus functions as a frame of reference which contests 'modernist assumptions about closure, distance, artistic autonomy, and the apolitical nature of representation' (Hutcheon 1989: 99) by recognising that the seemingly 'natural' structures of language and narrative are culturally produced and open to deconstruction.

As such, Decouflé's work is littered with 'intertextual frames' or 'stereotyped situations derived from preceding textual traditions' (Eco 1988: 448), like the classic fight between good guy and bad guy found in the wrestling scenarios from *True Faith* (1987) and *She Drives Me Crazy* (1988). He then invites the reader to attach variable meanings to popular archetypes such as the 'wrestler', the 'magician', and the 'clown', as he manipulates them in a variety of ritualised spaces such as the circus or wrestling ring. Similarly, as acknowledged by Adshead-Lansdale in her introduction (p. 15), these notoriously noisy archetypes continually break out in flurries of self-referential chit-chat, and escape linearity by existing in a present that is constructed from recycled bits of information. Thus rather than introduce new images to an audience, as in modernism, Decouflé speaks to an audience through their own culturally produced images, and 'from within the values and history of that [audience]' (Hutcheon 1989: 12).

Decouflé also exaggerates these images or presents them out of context, as parodies of the past rather than mere nostalgic references. Consequently, he constructs and reconstructs images through a 'play of entirely contemporary references to the *idea* of past' rather than through references to a tangible past which 'can be read, understood and transcended' (Kaye 1994: 20). Thus while the Bauhaus choreographer Oskar Schlemmer explored the mechanical and 'object' qualities of his dancers in relation to form (space and light), Decouflé's figures are placed within an erratic space and manipulated by an outside force. For example, in the New Order video *True Faith* (1987),[1] three figures dressed in costumes reminiscent of Oskar Schlemmer's *Triadic Ballet* (1922) (Goldberg 1988: 111) are seemingly 'forced' to fall backwards when another figure tightens the televisual visor in front of his eyes, thus giving the impression that the figures are 'inside' the screen he manipulates. The Bauhaus-inspired figures[2] could be perceived as nostalgic references to German abstractionism (chosen because of their inherently 'beautiful' or 'interesting' aesthetic attributes); yet instead they become parodies of that past. Hence the perfect modernist space periodically tilts, causing the figures to fall unpredictably so that their mechanical dance becomes grotesque and chaotic rather than ordered and elegant. In this instance, Decouflé is not necessarily concerned with spatial properties for their own sake, nor with reducing his performers to pure architectural forms, as was Schlemmer (Goldberg 1988), but with deconstructing space and enlarging or exaggerating form in order to challenge conceptual conventions which, like the rules of gravity, are viewed as infallible. Hence Decouflé quotes from modernism in order to examine, challenge and confront it, thus introducing a postmodernist's penchant for undermining certainty.

Whether modernist or postmodernist, perhaps the text itself has not changed, but the way it is read has:

> A text is not a line of words releasing a single 'theological' meaning (the 'message' of the Author-God) but a multi-dimensional space in which a variety of writings, none of them original, blend and clash.
>
> (Barthes 1988: 170)

Therefore, as Adshead-Lansdale makes explicit in her introduction to intertextual theory, meaning is produced through the process of *reading*, rather than writing; and the reader can potentially participate in the act of creation. Thus 'a text's unity lies not in its origin but in its destination' (Barthes 1988: 171). Decouflé seems aware of his own authorial fallibility and creates work that is open to suggestion, 'as if it might embrace any and all of the characteristics a reader, observer or performer may care to assign to it' (Kaye 1994: 40).

A deconstructive approach to analysis is particularly appropriate for Decouflé's work, since he is concerned not with a narrative that 'naturally' produces a dominant singular meaning, but with one that allows the construction of multiple (and even competing) meanings and associations. In this instance, he is no longer concerned with the telling of *a* or *the* story, but with the telling of many stories. These 'stories' are then interwoven with strands from Decouflé's own eclectic background to form an absurd and chaotic world of animated creatures and grotesque hybrids – a strange world of alien beings moving in alien ways, who exist only in the artificial present of the television screen.

Essentially, my primary agenda in this chapter is to use intertextuality as a tool to compare and contrast a cross-section of Decouflé's work and thereby 'uncover behind superficial contrasts of subject and treatment, a hard core of basic and often recondite motifs' (Reader 1990: 177). These motifs, or common elements, create stylistic unity and place his work within his own canonised frame and within the frame of French new dance. However, to construct De-couflé as *auteur* goes against the grain of the 'death of the author', and is a somewhat naive and contestable approach of which the choreographer himself might disapprove. Nevertheless, despite the inherent ambiguity often associated with intertextual readings,[3] Decouflé's stamp is undeniably recognisable in all of his work, and whilst many of the images he uses are lifted from other sources, the manner in which he juxtaposes these images and the ways in which he arranges elements of the *mise en scène* are unique to him. Thus whilst I am not proposing that Decouflé has discovered something entirely new (in the modern-ist tradition), he is producing work that is distinctive in character and worth examining.

Although Decouflé has produced work for the stage, it is his film and video work that is most readily available. Therefore, I concentrate my analysis on works to which I have had video access: the two pop videos he directed for New Order (1987) and Fine Young Cannibals (1988), as well as the film *Codex* (1987). In addition, reviews and pictures of his stage works *Triton* (1990) and *Techni-color* (1988) offer some idea as to how this work fits in with his video and film projects. Where appropriate, I include relevant observations about this work.

Decouflé in Context: French Dance, Postmodernism, Popular Culture

To contextualise an artist is to open up additional avenues of understanding. Thus whilst contextual information is rarely articulated in appreciation, it is an essential aspect of analysis, in that it provides several pathways through a rather dense forest of signs and images. It is with this perspective in mind that I offer a brief summary of the development of French new dance.

French contemporary dance is generally considered to have developed in the late 1960s, although it did not start receiving a large amount of public and government support until the early 1980s (Bonis 1988). Strongly influenced by the American 'postmoderns', as well as by Cunningham and Nikolais, French contemporary dance was arguably an example of modernist 'pure' dance, in that abstract movement or motion (not emotion or narrative) was felt to be the most important aspect. Additionally, like other modernist avant-garde movements, it 'defined itself through the exclusion of mass culture and was driven by its fear of contamination by ... consumer culture' and other art forms (Hutcheon 1989: 28).

However, by the beginning of the 1980s, French dance, 'undoubtedly swept along with the international tide across the arts away from abstraction' (Jordan 1989: 22), began to develop in a more theatrical vein. This new style seemed to 'abandon abstraction in order to rediscover more traditional forms of figuration and narrative' (Louppe 1989a: 34). However, the 'rebirth' of narrative into French new dance was not a cloning process, in that narrative is not dealt with in a *traditionally* theatrical way. On the contrary, it is often disrupted through the illogical interplay between other art forms or historical movements and aspects of contemporary culture. It is subsequently within this context that both French *new* dance and Philippe Decouflé's work developed, and as a result French new dance is often referred to as 'postmodern' rather than modern.[4]

In the light of this history, it might be appropriate to view Decouflé's work within the theoretical context of postmodernism. However, such telling characteristics as fragmentation, absurd parody, the breakdown between high and low art, and the synthesis of various art forms, can also be traced back to earlier European modernist movements such as surrealism, the Bauhaus, and absurdism. What links Decouflé to postmodernism is his use of elements from these past movements, in combination with aspects of *contemporary* culture. Thus, unlike the futurists, dadaists, and surrealists, who saw the past as an example of all that was negative in the arts (Goldberg 1988), for Decouflé, there is no single past to be reviled or future to be celebrated, but a multiplicity of pasts and futures, rather like a kaleidoscope of continuously shifting stories.

Postmodernism, as its very name suggests, confronts and contests any modernist discarding or recuperating of the past in the name of the future:

> It suggests no search for transcendent timeless meaning, but rather a re-evaluation of and a dialogue with the past in the light of the present. It does not deny the *existence* of the past; it does question whether we can ever *know* that past other than through its textualized remains.
>
> (Hutcheon 1988: 19–20, emphasis in original)

Given the preponderance of contrasting theories, however, postmodernism and particularly postmodern *dance* have remained ill-defined and problematic. Thus, rather than delving into the intricacies of postmodern theory and how this theory is applied to dance, this chapter briefly outlines characteristics that are generally accepted as aspects of *a* rather than *the* postmodern aesthetic, since 'every critic "constructs" postmodernism in his or her own way ... [and] all are "finally fictions" ' (Hutcheon 1989: 11).

This chapter also focuses on characteristics located within the French postmodern dance tradition, for example:

(1) a fascination with quoting from past styles and traditions;
(2) a merging of artistic styles;
(3) irony/pastiche/parody;
(4) the blurring of boundaries between popular culture/mass media and high art;
(5) intertextual collage;
(6) criticism of technological innovation

French postmodern dance, as distinct from other Western manifestations, also embraces various aspects of French 'folk' and popular culture, including the circus, cinema, café culture, comic books, and haute couture fashion, to name but a few (Louppe 1989b; Dannatt 1991). The above features are also applicable to the work of Philippe Decouflé and are apparent in the works I have chosen to discuss. Therefore, I will make reference to them in the following sections of this chapter.

Decouflé and Popular Culture

Postmodernism and intertextuality, it might be argued, share the capacity to give rise to methodologies which depend on the highly educated reader for comprehension. As a result, artists who embrace these methods of production could be accused of cultural elitism, in that only 'those who recognise the sources of parodic appropriation can understand the theory that motivates it' (Hutcheon 1989: 3). For example, by using avant-garde modernism as source material – which 'was oppositional and marginal within a middle-class . . . philistine or gilded age culture' (Jameson 1992: 140) – Decouflé alienates an audience that does not possess the knowledge necessary to derive 'meaning' from the work. Paradoxically, on the other hand, one could argue that as inhabitants of a postmodern age, we have become accustomed to dealing with the complex and fragmented images associated with late twentieth-century media culture. Perhaps the circuses of old have been replaced by these 'media circuses' in which movie stars, talk-show hosts, and newscasters function as ring leaders.

In response to accusations of elitism, Decouflé is quick to point out that his 'basic culture comes from cartoon strips, rock music, and night club dancing' (Anon., 1994: 15). In addition, clowning and other wordless circus acts such as juggling, acrobatics and trapeze are consistent features of his work (*Triton* and *Technicolor*) and are forms of theatre which were often far more popular and influential than classical tragedy and comedy (Esslin 1991). Perhaps then, it is appropriate that Decouflé, who was originally trained in the circus and admits to a fondness for advertising (Kelly 1991) should take French new dance forward from the circuses of the past to those of the future. Indeed, by drawing on these traditions of antiquity, as well as contemporary comic traditions (such as comic

Philippe Decouflé's *Codex*.   Photo: Marc Enguerand

books and postmodern parody), Decouflé produces work which is both avant-garde *and* populist (*ibid.*), and is also extremely marketable. Thus by offering us a world of French pop and folk culture, pre-packaged and ready to be launched onto a global economy, he 'transforms dance, making it a malleable medium with a pop sensibility and circus-like flair for fun' (*ibid.*: 87).

Additionally, like Britain's Michael Clark, who performs in kilts and Doc Martens (symbols of 'Scottishness' and English punk rebellion), or French personality Jean-Paul Gaultier, Decouflé constructs an aura of 'Frenchness' around his work and persona to create a decidedly 'French choreographic product. In its tone and fabrication' (Louppe 1989b: 9) it is extremely recognisable to French audiences and when seen by foreign audiences is regarded as 'extremely French' (Dannatt 1991: 17). Consequently, Decouflé is both producer *and* product. He produces pop videos, sellable commodities and advertisements for other products (pop groups) just as he produces himself, the quintessential French choreographer, enough of a product in his own right to warrant the coining of a new word, 'decouflesque' defined as 'anything with a touch of the choreographer's stylish froth' (Mitchell 1994: 50).

Yet, the very idea of choreographer or dance as 'product' is contentious. Thus whilst '[French] dance has rifled design magazines, [and] collaborated with fashion shows, rock clips, or television publicity' (Louppe 1989b: 8), there are those who feel that the arts should offer resistance in a world where advertising and the media are so prevalent. Whereas Decouflé willingly locates himself within the realm of consumerist, popular and hence accessible culture through his work in advertising and pop promotion, his attitude has sparked criticism among the French choreographic avant-garde, a group of Cunningham protegés who bemoan the loss of purity in dance and criticise Decouflé (among others) for his high place in 'low' culture, and for the 'showiness' of his work.

> As a consequence of his fantastic success with the Olympic games he [Decouflé] is now in 'show business' and no longer in dance; people app-reciated his last piece, but did not regard it as a choreography, just as a show . . . the choreographers do not look at him as one of them anymore.
>
> (Beranger 1995: 1)

Decouflé's relationship to popular culture and the media also contests modernist assumptions about artistic originality and capitalist notions of owner-ship and property (Hutcheon 1989). In the postmodern arena of self-conscious, self-quoting, televised, repeatable and reproducible imagery, nothing seems new or original. Decouflé's work cannot remain independent of the media, and by placing his work on the open market, it has been appropriated by the same media Decouflé himself quotes from. A recent advertisement in Britain for 'Just Fruits' (1995) mimics the costumes and movement from Decouflé's New Order video *True Faith* and consequently challenges the belief that an idea can be traceable to a single person.

Disruption and Distortion: (De)constructed Spaces

Despite the poststructuralist tendency to question the relevance of the artist's biography to the analysis of a work, different artists choose different images to express similar themes. Consequently, the formal qualities of an artistic work, rather than the themes, often become the deciding factors that separate one choreographer's work from another.

One consistent feature of Decouflé's work is his use of contained or 'rit-ualised' spaces which are framed by a series of rules or parameters. For example, *Triton* is set inside a circus ring, *True Faith* takes place both inside a television monitor and inside a boxing/wrestling ring, the third section of *Codex* takes place on a game-board, and *Technicolor* in a gym. In each instance, Decouflé has chosen a space that has been marked off beforehand as a consecrated spot, a temporary world designed for specific activities, inside which an absolute and peculiar order reigns (Schechner 1976). These activities are played out within this specified space, yet in most situations they are either dysfunctional or they are replaced by activities that do not belong. In *True Faith* (1987), a one-legged man wrapped in wire with a television monitor attached to his head attempts to build a structure from various shapes (sphere, cube, triangle) and fails. Regardless of the variations attempted, he never succeeds; thus the experiment goes awry, a solution is never found, and science is refuted. Similarly, in *Triton*,

> a clumsy magician and his prettily-posing female assistant make total shambles of a few tricks . . . He becomes engrossed in tracing shapes on a pane of glass but the brisk, and recurring stage crew cart away his props.
>
> (Brennan 1990: 18)

The magician's act fails because his magic is exposed by the presence of the stage crew and the reality they represent. The performance is thus 'meta-theatrical' in that the artifice is revealed. In another instance, a tailor works next to the orchestra pit to complete the costumes for the finale, and the audience witnesses the act of creation. Thus Decouflé presents us with a 'world of illusion, only it is subject to interruption, to things going wrong, and we can see when there are strings attached' (Brennan 1990: 18). By revealing artifice, Decouflé also presents us with an intertextual ball of string, with the disrupted stage space at one end and the multiple meanings it references at the other. Therefore, the audience loses faith in the rules of the performance space, whilst also losing faith in much more than this – they lose faith in rationality, reason, and the sensible and explicable nature of the world.

In *Codex* the game-board space is disrupted by the human figure that traverses its squares. There are no game pieces, and there are no players; instead the figure wanders from square to square without rule or reason in an illogical journey. Therefore, the space is disrupted by the absence of rules and by the presence of a figure out of context. Without winner or loser, the 'order' of the game is refuted and contextual meaning denied. In *True Faith* the figures in the boxing/wrestling ring fight to the death. The rules of this game are also absent or broken, since the fight continues to its inevitable conclusion without interruption by a referee. Additionally, the punching bag has a human head, is subject to injury, and dies at the end as a result of incessant punching. Here, the rules of preparation are suspended since the punching bag should only *represent* a human opponent, rather than become one.

The figures in the video are also located inside a television monitor attached to the one-legged man's head. The man has control over the figures and governs their position in space by tilting the monitor. The contained space of the television screen is violated by the man's ability to control elements within the space as if they were real (rather than televised images). Furthermore, like the magic act disrupted by the stage hands, many of the inhabitants of Decouflé's spaces are controlled by others or outside forces. In *Technicolor*, a performer is suspended from a pulley and controlled by another performer who teeters on the edge of a large platform. Every movement one performer makes causes the other performer on the pulley to ascend or descend through the space (Jordan 1989). In *Triton* (1990) a man and women are tied to either end of a suspended rope so that the movement of one automatically affects that of the other, and a quarrel ensues as each tries to regain control of his or her movements (Brennan 1990). In the end, Decouflé disrupts preconceived notions of space, time and gravity, and consequently challenges those aspects of material reality usually taken for granted. Moreover, by reversing the hierarchical relationship that normally exists between humans and their environment, Decouflé's 'characters' are stripped of their 'tool-wielding' and 'environment-yielding' powers, and the 'space' is able to exact a form of revenge.

Decouflé also uses the medium of film/television quite deliberately to disrupt or suspend 'realistic' notions of space. For example, the framed space can be utilised to eliminate or exaggerate depth of field so that it ceases to resemble a real space. This occurs in the film *Codex* during a scene in which a man in rubber hip-waders sings whilst rain falls on his head and two other men perform a duet in the background. The action is framed so that the face of the singing man appears in extreme close-up (in profile) whilst a dancer lies flat in the background. The flatness induced by the lighting accentuates the extreme difference in size between the singing man's face and the dancer's body so that it appears as if a giant disembodied head floats near the scene. Additionally, at this point, the rain that appears to fall in the foreground touches neither the singing man's face nor the dancer, and it appears to exist in a separate plane without affecting the surrounding planes.

In another section, the dancers occupy several planes at once, but the monochromatic colour scheme flattens out the space. Since no effort is made to rectify this by lighting or other means, rather than moving towards and away from the camera, the dancers appear to grow and shrink in size. At other times, the viewer becomes acutely aware of the depth of field when a dancer runs towards the camera, altering the percentage of the body visible in frame. Hence through framing, the camera can direct the gaze of the viewer, and parts of the body or the *mise en scène* can be isolated or fragmented.

In *Codex*, this type of framing seems to dehumanise the characters by denying the viewer an image of the whole. For example, during the first section, the camera often cuts to a close-up of the dancer's torso or hand, and in the second section, isolated shots of the singing man's rubber trousers or mouth frequently fill the screen. These fragments become something 'other', having lost their relationship to the rest of the body. In another instance, the camera tightly frames the torso of a figure whilst revealing a full second or third figure in the background. It also frames part of a figure so that it becomes a shape in the frame that emphasises negative space. On other occasions, the scene is shot from above so that only the tops of the figures are seen, and only part of the figure (its flippers) protrudes into the space. This implies that the space extends beyond the frame, where the camera functions as a window onto an entire world, although the viewer might only be experiencing a small section of it.

These framing devices de-emphasise character and narrative by avoiding shots which frame the human figure from the knees up, or medium close-ups which frame it from the chest up. Thus whilst framings have no absolute or general meaning, within the context of *Codex* they work to reduce familiarity and identification with the characters and to disrupt the traditional film narrative (Bordwell & Thompson 1993).

(De)constructed Narratives

Decouflé also manipulates narratives by using discontinuous editing to fracture any organised temporal-spatial coherence so that 'events are juxtaposed for their disturbing effect' (Bordwell & Thompson 1993: 465). Like surrealist cinema, which was 'based on the belief in the omnipotence of dreams, and in the undirected play of thought' (*ibid.*), Decouflé peppers his work with non-sequiturs, subverts the laws of time and space, and places events in illogical sequences. As a result, his work is both beyond reason, and beyond aesthetic or moral codes, consisting as it does of 'bizarre and evocative imagery . . . [which] teases us to find a narrative logic that is simply absent' (*ibid.*). For example, in *Codex* non-sequiturs, such as the singing man in the rain, defy logical coherence by refusing to provide a causal reference for the rain; the scene is indoors, there is no sky, there are no clouds, and there is no hole in the roof with a view of the sky. Most importantly, there is no clear relationship between any of the sections or among any of the characters. Even during a contact duet, where the move-ment suggests a relationship, the two men never look at each other, never embrace, and never push one another away. Their physical connection results in little more than a series of shapes, and the effect is one of abstract alienation. Similarly, there is no established relationship between the singing man and the two men. The singing man is often shown looking into the distance, but never appears to look directly at the men. Eye-line matches and point-of-view shots (both of which establish relationships between characters) are never used, so that rather than looking at something off-screen (which could be the two men), the singing man looks directly at the camera.

In Decouflé's work, 'causality is as evasive as in a dream' (Anon. 1995: 2) and, as with dreams, we can either accept these images without understanding why they occur, or we can read them as sub-conscious Freudian symbols. In this case, the water might be seen as a symbol of sexuality, the singing man's rubber hip-waders as a symbol of sexual protection, and the mixed-gender clothing as a symbol of sexual confusion. This view takes into consideration the historical and cultural position of the audience as a self-reflexive, post-Freudian, pop-psycho-logical machine. Surreal imagery can also evoke historicised concepts of 'surrealism' as an offshoot of Freudian psychology. In this instance, Freud functions as an intertext between the work and surrealism in that the ability to read certain images as surreal is dependent upon the viewer's own particular comprehension of this term. Furthermore, to arrive at such a reading would imply an understanding of how the Freudian subconscious can reveal hidden meanings and desires through our dreams. This concept is decidedly appropriate considering that Decouflé himself 'talks of getting his ideas while asleep' (Iyer 1992: 48).

(De)constructed Bodies

Another stylistic feature of Decouflé's work is his use of the grotesque. The grotesque is the expression of an estranged or alienated world, where the familiar is seen from a perspective that suddenly renders it strange (Thomson 1972). This strange world is either comic or terrifying or both; and it is the unresolved conflict between the ludicrous and the monstrous, the desire to laugh and the desire to cry out in fear, that is its primary characteristic. Defined by conflict and disharmony, images or characters are presented as a mixture of the heterogeneous, as conflations of disparates, or as physically abnormal combinations of plant, animal, human and object. It is this 'interweaving of totally disparate elements' (*ibid.*: 15) that produces strange and often unsettling emotional conflicts. Similarly, Decouflé's work is filled with intertextual bodies which reference 'grotesques' of this century such as side-show freaks and cripples.[5] Frankensteinian monsters drag their stitched-up, birth-defected bodies through a bleak landscape of televisual snow. Rather than revealing the elegant, machine-like precision of perfectly tuned dancing bodies, Decouflé shows us bodies which have been deformed, either by nature or by 'man'. Like the disrupted theatrical devices of the space, these bodies have also 'gone wrong'.

Influenced perhaps, by French theorists such as Roland Barthes and Michel Foucault, who opened up a discourse about the *mutable* body in which meaning is culturally produced and not inherent within the biological form (Louppe 1989b), Decouflé presents the body as an intertext, as an object which contains and reflects meaning like a still yet deep pool of water. He then stimulates a vortex within this placid abyss, by intentionally manipulating the available meanings of the body as he alters, distorts, and constrains its various parts through costume and props. In both *Triton* and the Fine Young Cannibals' video *She Drives Me Crazy* body parts (breasts, bottoms, hips, legs) are enlarged, exaggerated, or multiplied. In *Triton* 'torches shine from boobs, legs are lengthened by stilts' (Bonsu 1990: 21), and bodies are used as weight-lifting bars or attached to inanimate objects such as tea cups. In *True Faith* bodies are altered and dehumanised by costumes that enlarge the legs, stomach, and arms. The central figure's legs are combined with wire and fabric into one leg so that, like a pogo stick, he hops from place to place.

Likewise, in *Codex* the characters are presented as human, as object, and as an aggregation of the two. The zebra-striped, body-encasing costumes in the first section distort the hands, head and feet of the figures. They appear as part fish or frog, part human and part other-worldly creature. Consequently, identification with them is difficult, and their strangeness is magnified. The resultant abnormality of these creatures becomes comic, and the comedy is exaggerated by the use of television, since the 'reality' of live performance (the breathing of the dancers, the occasional glimpse of a human face or eye) is suspended by the artificiality of the medium. For example, at one point, the camera emphasises the 'frogness' of the creatures by shooting from directly above. Their crouched bodies lose their humanness since the long shot emphasises their flippered feet and bulging bellies. At another point, two figures hold a shape together and, as a result of the lighting and the psychological distance created by the television screen, seem to merge into one twisted three-legged being. The distance between viewer and image is extended so that the figures become less like humans and more like objects. As the viewer now identifies less with the 'objects', the tendency to laugh at the difference is heightened and the situation becomes comic. However, should this difference become so far removed that one is no longer able to link the subject to reality (it becomes so distorted that it is completely unrecognisable), laughter might turn to fear or disgust.

Codex never reaches this stage, as the figures still appear human. They walk, run and move in a way that is clearly representative of a particular style of dance (a Cunningham/ballet-derived vocabulary). The fact that these movements are performed in flippers rather than bare feet, ballet slippers, or pedestrian shoes, points to their more absurd and comic character. The flippers, like the clown's oversized, bulbous-toed shoes, represent a chaotic and disproportionate element of the costume – funny, grotesque and sometimes ridiculous, but hardly frightening.

Still, the piece does retain a disturbing edge, as illustrated by these fish-like creatures who hobble around on flipper-fused limbs which are decidedly inappropriate for dry land, like the beached fish that wiggles and flaps in desperation, each gasping breath bringing it closer to death. These creatures can perhaps survive only so long out of place and context. Witnessing their futile attempts at locomotion is humorous, perhaps even ridiculous, but also a little sad. Similarly, when the singing man in *Codex* limps through the space with a large board attached to one foot, he is also handicapped. He shakes his head in frustration as he attempts to manoeuvre through the space, then drops to the ground to bang his fists on the floor, angry perhaps at his physical futility. Again, there is something absurdly funny about a board being attached to this man, but it is easier to laugh at something when it seems to be a fool's own doing (why doesn't he remove the board?) than at something out of a person's control (the true handicap). Yet dwarfs, hunchbacks and people with other physical defects

Philippe Decouflé's *Triton*.   Photo: Brigitte Enguerand

have inspired laughter just as much as the mentally defective fool, again illustrating the paradoxical nature of the grotesque: that which should inspire revul-
sion or empathy often has the opposite effect, and that which is meant to inspire
laughter (the clown) can often elicit fear (Willeford 1969).

When we are presented with these grotesqueries, the absurd humour of their
situation is occasionally eclipsed by the darker forces at work behind their
condition. For example, in *True Faith*, a female figure who is part human and
part punching-bag stares blankly at the television screen. Face blackened, and
hair singed, with her head protruding from a jungle-green 'bag', she is both
army commando and turtle. Is it armour, a shell, or a bullet proof vest, the
viewer wonders? In any case, the soft human flesh underneath seems in need of
protection from an increasingly violent and hostile world – a world of hegemonic
machines in which the human head, the centre of *human* thought, is replaced by
the techno-thought of the television monitor, a monitor that recreates the human
face inside a two-dimensional space, a face whose features are smoothed and
flattened by a piece of thin glass which is capable of exerting enough material
and symbolic force to draw its human occupant to its knees.

The effect of these grotesque, mutated bodies is apocalyptic, reminiscent of
the *Blade Runner* or the *Mad Max* films. Post-nuclear, post-bionic man, post-
virtual reality, these are the bodies of the twenty-first century. 'Gender-less' or
'gender-more' (as in the case of the three-breasted woman in *Triton*), they are

part circus sideshow and part premonition: a warning perhaps, that the relationships between humans and machines can only result in unnatural 'creations' – in Geiger-like aliens, Frankensteinian monsters and Terminators, creatures who have no place in this world, except as destroyers.

Thus the cyborg comes streaking out of the science fiction thriller and into our postmodern imagination, made real enough by digital special effects to reveal the horror of the impossible made possible. Decouflé's post-nuclear mutants and twenty-first century cyborgs – bound and dominated by technology, dissected by wires, enveloped by headsets and television monitors, and fused with machines, metal limbs and objects – serve as reminders of the destructive potential of industrialisation and 'techno-evolution'. Decouflé therefore calls 'into question the messianic faith of modernism, the faith that technical innovation and purity of form can assure social order' (Hutcheon 1989: 12).

Parody and Clowning: Humour in Decouflé's Work

'Precisely in such explosive times as the ones we're living through, comedy, irony and even the grotesque come more and more to the fore' (Anon. 1994: 15). Alternatively, Decouflé's mechanisation and deformation of the body can be seen as parody or satire rather than as a serious and dramatic damnation of technological progress. In the legacy of the Dadaists and the Theatre of the Absurd (Fretard 1993), Decouflé 'ridicules everything that smacks of solemnity or ethical precepts' (Goldberg 1988: 102) and denies morality and humanism by reducing history to parody, and his performers to nonsensical abstractions. 'Rather than assert coherent, critical or celebratory expression of a fundamental reality, [Decouflé tends] towards irony, parody, and playfulness' (Seale, in Briginshaw 1991: 44). Decouflé's work, then, is a combination of parody (ironic quotation, pastiche, appropriation) and absurdity. With a cast of clowns, misfits, fools and madmen, 'it repeatedly demonstrates the deep poetic power of wordless and purposeless action' (Esslin 1991: 335).

Like clowns, the grotesque figures in *Codex* succeed in reducing order to chaos by ridiculing the idea that victory over chaos is possible through the observance of rules of conduct. Since they are not entirely human, they can exist outside these rules, outside order, and outside belief. Furthermore, as they are 'deficient in the normal understanding and in the normal appreciation of order, [they] re-admit the magical power of chaos' (Willeford 1969: 114). This likens Decouflé's world to the fantasy world of cartoons, where the laws of reality are temporarily abolished: inanimate objects can move and talk, animals become partly human, and the laws of time, space, and gravity are suspended.

This is particularly evident in parts one and two of *Codex*. Here, Decouflé often turns the camera upside down so that the dancers seem to be suspended in space or standing on the ceiling. Alternatively, he shoots upside-down figures upside-down, so that the space is reversed whilst the figures appear not to be. He also manipulates time by speeding up, slowing down, or reversing the film, creating an artificial time not possible in real life. This affects the way the viewer perceives the movement, and distances the subjects from reality. For example, when the figures in part one start running inhumanly fast within the frame, the effect is of charged atoms cutting across the space and bouncing off unseen barriers. Eventually they are moving so fast that it is impossible to confirm that they are tangible objects as they metamorphose into streaks of colour. The central figures then move so slowly that they appear in 'normal' speed.

However, postmodern parody is not necessarily, in the words of Briginshaw (1991: 44) 'lighter and more relaxed', but is often presented with a touch of cynicism. Decouflé, in particular, delivers his with a razor's edge. *True Faith* begins with two figures who repeatedly slap each other's faces to the beat of the music. Rather than presenting a slapstick aesthetic in which one or both of the figures react to the slap in mock pain and confusion, or by returning the slap *after* responding physically (falling over) or verbally ('Now why did you have to go and do that?'), the figures deny us the reactions of the traditional clown and instead slap one another mechanically without missing a beat. Eventually, the slapping becomes aggressive. The elf creature punches his opponent in the stomach and initiates a stylised rendition of a wrestling match. Initially, the brightly coloured 'clowns' grimace at the camera in a parody of masculine aggression; yet the match inevitably turns violent, until all the participants (including the 'punching bag') lie dead. The one-legged 'mutant' then hobbles on hand and foot through the corpses to exit the screen. The result is an inverted or subverted version of the classic slapstick situation. Whereas traditional clowns make it their business to escape injury, these clowns are all too human, and suffer death.

Ultimately, the inhabitants of this world are emotionless automata who deny the passionate aspect of violence, and their situation thus highlights the way the media can sanitise it. In show wrestling, for example, violence takes on a surreal, cartoon-like quality as, like clowns, the subjects of the violence never seem to suffer injury or death. In police dramas and action thrillers, the hand that pulls the trigger is usually some distance away from the death, thus the visceral and perhaps emotive act of violence is denied. Western culture has moved away from the realities of death, both in the entertainment industry and in 'real life'. American capital punishment now involves lethal injection rather than electric chairs or hangings; clean, quiet and unobtrusive, like supermarket displays, it is a way of neatly packaging the death process by cutting out the 'nasty bits' and trimming the fat, until all that is left are rows of unidentifiable meat products wrapped in shiny plastic.

There is, then, something incredibly frightening about the worlds Decouflé creates. Comic, surreal, brighter and larger than life, in technicolour brilliance they shine like beacons in the dark. Yet their duplicitous humour conceals the cacophonic nightmare of contemporary culture. Thus, however 'warm, playful, and celebratory' (Briginshaw 1991: 45) postmodern performance is meant to be, it will always have a darker edge to it, since the death of God, the author, and history has surreptitiously robbed us of our innocence and intellectual virginity. We have been raped by our own discourses and, in the light of deconstructionism, question whether we can ever look at the world as 'pure' again, where grass means grass and sky means sky and your version of a story is the same as mine. Instead, it seems we have arrived at an impasse in which the existential refusal of God has resulted in a refusal of meaning (Barthes 1988).

The Absurdity of Existence: Meaning Lost and Found

> *Codex* offset the earnestness of most of the entries with its romanticism of the absurd. It is a beautifully graphic poem, filled with non-sequiturs: Dancers with flippers nonchalantly hobble around. The face of a man singing in the rain blocks our view of a male duet.   (Towers 1989: 57)

This review highlights another way of approaching Decouflé's work, which is as an example of absurd theatre. The videos *True Faith* and *She Drives Me Crazy*, as well as *Codex*, are indeed absurd, in that they are all composed of nonsensical images which do not necessarily exist in the 'real' world. Like the absurd silent comedy, Decouflé's work

> has the dreamlike strangeness of a world seen from outside with the uncomprehending eyes of one cut off from reality. It has the quality of nightmare and displays a world in constant, and wholly purposeless, movement.   (Esslin 1991: 335)

The idea that the action is purposeless seems also to imply that it is meaningless, and this to a certain extent denies the task of analysis. When approaching Decouflé's work, my initial impulse was to ask 'why?' and to try to find the links, however immaterial, between image and action, space and design. If the work is examined as a piece of absurd theatre, links between events, and understanding of cause and effect are of no consequence, for the emphasis can be put on siutation. Why do the figures in *Codex* appear as half-human and half-frog or fish? Why does it rain only on the singing man? Why in *True Faith* does the punching-bag come to life and speak to us in sign language? Unlike surrealism, which looks to the dreaming subconscious for answers, the answer here is simply 'because'. The resultant absence of correspondence between 'the mind's need for unity and the chaos of the world the mind experiences' (Hinchcliffe

1969: 36) forces the viewer to abandon the construction of a linear narrative in favour of a fragmented collection of elements.

These elements can be taken on their own, or juxtaposed with others, and it is this *juxtaposition* of elements that creates absurdity:

> Absurdity springs from a comparison ... between a bare fact and a certain reality, between an action and the world that transcends it. The absurd is essentially a divorce.   (Camus 1955: 33)

Thus the absurdity of something lies in its context: by taking familiar objects out of context and robbing them of their quotidian uses, they are also robbed of their familiarity. Diving flippers on dancers rather than divers, made of cloth rather than rubber and decorated with zebra strips and fringe, become absurd. So in the case of both the absurd and the postmodern, meaning is not necessarily sewn into the form, but is constructed from the outside through the assimilation of overlapping contextual threads, which become the intertexts of analysis. The viewer is then challenged to make sense out of non-sense by constructing a personalised reading of the 'text' based on her/his own particular knowledge and experience. In this way, the absurd is assigned meaning through references and traces rather than solid material descriptions.

> The text to be read and the *mise-en-scène* to be deciphered are no longer the guardians of a single meaning that has to be found, interpreted and transmitted ... They have become this 'obscure object of desire' which the rhythm of theatrical enunciation [enunciators: performers, music, costumes etc.] constitutes according to a 'multiplicity of points of view'.   (Pavis 1986: 18–9)

On the other hand, the emphasis on the absurd arguably disregards meaning and renders something pointless and purposeless. As in the case of Esslin's Theatre of the Absurd, this pointlessness is derived from a renewed post-war interest in Nietzschean existentialism:

> For those to whom the world has lost its central explanation and meaning, it is no longer possible to accept art forms still based on the continuation of standards and concepts that have lost their validity; that is, the possibility of knowing the laws of conduct and ultimate values, as deductible from a firm foundation of revealed certainty about the purpose of man in the universe.
>   (Esslin 1991: 400)

In Decouflé's case, the absurdity of the human condition is reflected in a theatre devoid of meaning. However, the contextual placement of Decouflé's work links it with both post-war existentialism/absurdism (there is no meaning to life, God is dead) *and* poststructuralism (meaning is ambiguous, God is a construct) (Snyder 1988). Therefore, it might have absurd elements that intentionally evade interpretation; yet these elements also resonate with a variety of historically and socially constructed meanings. One element of the *mise-en-scène* can then generate a host of associative meanings.

For example, hip waders have a domesticated use: they keep water *out* of fishermen's trousers. In *Codex*, however, because of the rain that falls on the singing man, the hip waders are filled *with* water, and keep the water *in*. The purpose and meaning of 'hip wader' becomes absurd in this context. Likewise, flippers, which aid the diver/swimmer in the water, are absurd when used on land as they prevent the bipedal human from executing everyday patterns of movement such as running or walking.

Unlike existentialism, intertextual analysis seeks to construct meanings (rather than to question their existence), and places Decouflé's work beyond the historical demarcations of absurd theatre. On the contrary, the proliferation of intertexts within a specific work or body of work, actually *creates* meaning, or rather meaning(s). The reader, critic or theorist then decides at which point he/she would like to enter the text, and which 'facts' she or he would like to focus on to support his or her interpretation. Consequently, intertextuality becomes a quest not only for meaning, but for a personalised way of seeing. It is a middle ground between truth and deception, between fact and fiction, between intellectual life and philosophical suicide and, unlike the absurd, it does not negate meaning, but simply accepts its ambiguity. To assign meanings (however multifarious) to the absurd, is to impugn its absurdity. Thus, rather than viewing the world as meaningless because it is senseless, the post-structuralist *modus operandi* is to make sense of a world which is ultimately nonsensical.

> The world in itself is not reasonable, that is all that can be said. But what is absurd is the confrontation of the irrational and the wild longing for clarity whose call echoes in the human heart.   (Camus 1955: 26)

Perhaps post-structuralism, and its manifestation in intertextual discourses, is yet another way of satisfying this longing. In the end, if one accepts that meaning can be *de*constructed, then one also accepts its *con*struction, and as such it cannot be lost – just reformed.

The final section of *Codex* challenges the notion of a futile existence by leaving the text open. For example, a man wanders pointlessly on a chessboard and, like the biblical figure Job, is hindered by several external forces (the board attached to his leg, the water in his trousers, the collar around his neck). He appears frustrated by his circumstances (shakes his head, drums his fists on the floor), yet he has an unwavering faith in the 'game'. Even when a figure in white (angel or devil in disguise) attempts to alter his position, he continues on the same path. Some would say that to continue in the face of such opposition is noble; others would say that Job's faith is blind, as he suffered as a result of it. Perhaps Decouflé allies himself with the former position where God, like life, provides constraints, and it is up to the individual to carry on despite them.

> A childhood friend of mine had cancer and ended up losing a leg. He was 18. To walk, he would jump along on his good leg. I danced a duo with him. This desire to work with constraints comes from life, from chance.
>
> (Decouflé, cited in Fretard 1993: 27)

Either way, like the mythical Sisyphus, the central protagonist is condemned to a life of vain and hopeless labour, in which the final prize at the end of the quest – the grail or the object of desire – does not exist. However, the piece denies closure by refusing to finish on this note, which would be a truly absurd conclusion: a scenario in which the man would continue his sojourn, without pause, until the lights dim and the audience leaves the space, or the television cuts out. Instead, it is the figure himself who blocks our view of the scene by placing the board attached to his foot directly in front of the camera. Lightning strikes, and thunder cracks, as the viewer is left to imagine his or her own possible ending. Decouflé then makes use of a popular cinematic convention: the cliff-hanger. Does the man continue faithfully, like Job, in the face of opposition? Or, do a series of new events cause him to break this pattern? Tune in next week!

Such a convention prevents the piece from functioning as a parable or myth (like the tales of Job or Sisyphus), because it does not offer the reader a moralistic conclusion or solution. Instead, it remains unfinished, as if each story continues to loop back upon itself over and over again, even when the window through which we see Decouflé's world has closed.

> Therefore, through the residual traces of dreams, nightmares, and myths, Decouflé leaves his world open yet full of hidden passageways and locked doors – a codex which is readable yet full of secret codes and ancient messages. And rather like a sort of patchwork . . . there is no centre, only cases, singularities, and shooting stars.   (Vernay 1993: 6).

So what do you do when you find yourself in this world of swimming zebras, grotesque cyborgs and demented clowns? Stand on your head and start singing.

Notes

1. The video consists of various clips of the band interspersed with choreographed segments by Decouflé. The piece begins with a one-legged figure looking into a television monitor attached to his head. As a result, the rest of the video appears to occur in the monitor. There are several 'mock' wrestling sequences intercut with images of a 'human' boxing bag illustrating the lyrics of the song in sign language. The video takes place in a boxing/wrestling ring, on scaffolding, and on an urban street.
2. See Adshead-Lansdale's discussion of intertextual ambiguity in her section on interpreting dance (pp. 19–20).
3. See the issue on French Dance in *Dance Theatre Journal* (Summer 1989) for further information regarding the history and development of French New Dance.
4. It is not my intention to offend or appear 'politically incorrect'. I have chosen such terminology because I feel it represents an intertext in itself in that such words are 'loaded' with past and present meanings (whether negative or positive). In my opinion, to use more contemporary nomenclature would not conjure up the desired historicised images which are necessary to make the analogy work.
5. In this section of the Fine Young Cannibals' video *She Drives Me Crazy* a figure whose head is replaced by a television monitor appears on the screen with its arms outstretched and roses in hand, like a jilted lover offering his apologies. He then slowly drops to one knee and pleads with the viewer.

References

Adolphe, J.M. (1990), 'French dance of the 80s: what's at stake in a new art?' *Ballett International*, No 1, January, 69–72: 182.
Anon. (1992), 'Past Masters of the Imagination', *The European*, 13–19 February: 20.
Anon. (1994), 'Philippe Decouflé's Latest Spectacle Conquers the French Stage', *Ballett International*, No. 4, April: 15.
Anon. (1995), DCA Compagnie: Information pack. Paris: DCA Compagnie
Barthes, R. (1988), 'The Death of the Author', in D. Lodge (ed.), *Modern Criticism and Theory*, London, Longman.
Beranger, E. (1995), Interview with author (unpublished), March.
Bonis, B. (1988), 'The Shaping of French Dance: a Phenomenon and its History', *Ballett International*, No 8/9, August/September: 29–34.
Bonsu, R. (1990), 'Circus Setting for Dance and Humour', *The Scotsman*, 28 May: 21.
Bordwell, D. & K. Thompson (4th edn, 1993), *Film Art: An Introduction*, New York, McGraw-Hill.
Brennan, M. (1990), *Triton* (review), *Glasgow Herald*. 25 May: 18.
Briginshaw, V. (ed.) (1991), *Postmodernism and Dance (Discussion Papers)*, Chichester, West Sussex Institute of Higher Education.
Camus, A. (1955), *The Myth of Sysiphus*, London, Hamish Hamilton.
Dannatt, A. (1991), 'Triton: Théatre de la Ville, Paris', *The Times*, 11 January: 17.
Eco, U. (1988), 'Cult Movies and Intertextual Collage', in D. Lodge (ed.) *Modern Criticism and Theory*, London, Longman.
Esslin, M. (3rd edn, 1991), *The Theatre of the Absurd*, London, Penguin.

Fretard, D. (1993), Interview with Philippe Decouflé, *Le Monde*, 4 November: 27.

Goldberg, R.L. (2nd edn, 1988), *Performance Art: From Futurism to the Present*, New York, Harry Abrams.

Hinchcliffe, A.P. (1969), *The Absurd*, London, J.W. Arrowsmith.

Hutcheon, L. (1988), *The Poetics of Postmodernism*, London, Routledge.

———— (1989), *The Politics of Postmodernism*, London, Routledge.

Iyer, P. (1992), 'At the Starting Gate', *Time Magazine*, 17 February: 48.

Jameson, F. (1992), 'Periodising the Sixties', in P. Waugh (ed.) *Postmodernism: A Reader*, London, Edward Arnold: 125–52.

Jordan, S. (1989), 'A Taste of Paris', *Dance and Dancers*, No. 472, July: 21–4.

Kaye, N. (1994), *Postmodernism and Performance*, London, Macmillan.

Kelly, D. (1991), DCA Compagnie review, *Dance Magazine*, April: 87.

Louppe, L. (1989a), 'French Dance: The New Narrative, its Literary and Cinematic Roots', *Dance Theatre Journal*, 7:1, Summer: 34–6.

———— (1989b), 'The Origins and Development of French Dance', *Dance Theatre Journal*, 7:1, Summer: 2–9.

Mitchell, E. (1994), 'Decouflé Whips Up a Soufflé', *Time Magazine*, 144:14 October: 50.

Pavis, P. (1986), 'The Classical Heritage of Modern Drama: The Case of Postmodern Theatre', *Modern Drama*, March: 18–9.

Reader, K.A. (1990), 'Literature/Cinema/Television: Intertextuality in Jean Renoir's Le Testament du Docteur Cordelier', in M. Worton J. Still (eds.), *Intertextuality: Theories and Practices*, Manchester, Manchester University Press.

Schechner, R. (ed.) (1976), *Ritual, Play, and Performance*, New York, Hawthorn.

Seale, G. (1991), 'Apocalypse Now or Back to the Future?', in V. Briginshaw (ed.) *Postmodernism and Dance (discussion papers)*, Chichester, West Sussex Institute of Higher Education.

Snyder, J. (1988), 'Introduction', in G. Vattimo, *The End of Modernity*, New York, Hopkins.

Towers, D. (1989), 'Grand Prix de Video Danse', *Dance Magazine*, 63:3, March: 56–8.

Thomson, P. (1972), *The Grotesque*, London, Methuen.

Vernay, M.C. (1993), 'Decouflé Springs Eternal', *Liberation*, 12 November: 6.

Willeford, W. (1969), *The Fool and his Sceptre*, London, Constable.

Index

Lightning Source UK Ltd.
Milton Keynes UK
UKOW031218170113

205001UK00001B/27/P

9 781852 730642